The Second American Revolution

THE SECOND AMERICAN REVOLUTION

John W. Whitehead
Illustrated by Wayne Stayskal

David C. Cook Publishing Co.
ELGIN, ILLINOIS—WESTON, ONTARIO

The original of the painting on the cover, *The Spirit of '76,* hangs in the Selectmen's Room, Abbot Hall, Marblehead, Massachusetts.

THE SECOND AMERICAN REVOLUTION
© 1982 John W. Whitehead
Illustrations © Wayne Stayskal

David C. Cook Publishing Co., Elgin, IL 60120
In association with Nims Communications
Book design by The Cioni Artworks/Ray Cioni
Printed in the United States of America

Library of Congress Cataloging in Publication Data

Whitehead, John W., 1946-
    The second American revolution.

    Includes bibliographical references.
    1. Religious liberty—United States. 2. Church and state—United States. I. Title.
KF4783.W44   342.73'0852   82-1389
ISBN 0-89191-575-9   347.302852   AACR2

To Carol

Table of Contents

ACKNOWLEDGMENTS

I would first like to express my gratitude to Franky Schaeffer V Productions, Inc., most particularly Franky Schaeffer and Jim Buchfuehrer, who worked with me during the writing of this book. Their company financed and arranged for the research and contributed greatly to the development of this book and the film of the same title.

Various persons contributed to the work necessary for the publication of this book in its present form. Dr. Francis A. Schaeffer, Dr. Harold O. J. Brown (Trinity Divinity School), Professor Herbert W. Titus (O. W. Coburn School of Law), Professor Daniel Benson (Texas Tech University School of Law), Dr. R. J. Rushdoony, Dr. Jeremy C. Jackson, and Udo Middelmann served as editorial consultants and researchers. Their time and efforts are greatly appreciated, as is the fine editorial work of Janet Hoover Thoma and the illustrations and design of Wayne Stayskal and Ray Cioni.

The typing and proofreading of the original manuscript have been done by my beloved wife, Carolyn, whose thinking and questioning greatly furthered this work. Moreover, she, along with my children, Jayson, Jonathan, Elisabeth, and Joel, were very patient during the tense periods involved in putting this project together.

Finally, I would like to thank Franky Schaeffer for his original conception of this project. His creativity, insight, and encouragement made this book possible.

JOHN W. WHITEHEAD
Manassas, Virginia

FOREWORD

In this book John Whitehead courageously takes on the present systems of American law and government and challenges them to fulfill our founding fathers' commitment to religious liberty.

John attacks and exposes an issue that has been festering, hidden beneath the surface and ignored by too many Christians, for far too long. The issue is that of church and state: Christian and religious freedom versus a secularist, humanistic elite, which increasingly controls our society. The government, the courts, the media, the law are all dominated to one degree or another by this elite. They have largely secularized our society by force, particularly using the courts.

In this comprehensive book John gives us a firm understanding of the Judeo-Christian tradition and base this country once had. He explains why and how we have departed from it, and then traces what the courts have done and the role they have played. No Christian can fully understand or change the age in which we live without such knowledge of our country's history and present situation. John Whitehead's book stands as a crucial statement on this subject. Because of its lucid and well-written nature, as well as its profound depth, it will appeal to layman, lawyer, minister, judge: all, alike.

If there is still an entity known as ''the Christian church'' by the end of this century, operating with any semblance of liberty within our society here in the United States, it will probably have John Whitehead and his book to thank. For this book lays the foundation and framework for fighting the tyrannical, secularist, humanistic power, which has separated our country from its Judeo-Christian base and now dominates this nation and its courts.

This is certainly the most important book that I have read in a long, long time. It is well-documented, and one of the most completely researched popular sources that has been written on the subject to date.

I cannot recommend this book too highly. I wish to take this opportunity to say how glad I am for John Whitehead and his writing. He has provided us all with a weapon of strength and power.

FRANCIS A. SCHAEFFER
L'Abri, Switzerland 1982

ABOUT THIS BOOK

During the last decade two men have been expressing similar thoughts about the courts, government, and our society—an attorney and author, John Whitehead, and an editorial cartoonist, Wayne Stayskal. These men have never met or collaborated. But once John Whitehead's book was written, it seemed natural to include Wayne Stayskal's editorial cartoons, which have appeared in the *Chicago Tribune* and have been widely syndicated throughout the United States.

The cartoons are not necessarily juxtaposed with corresponding issues in the text. Only the drawings at the opening of each chapter were created specifically for this book. As an editorial cartoon stands as an individual entity on the editorial page of a newspaper or in a magazine, the cartoons speak for themselves—about the essence of this book.

Editorial cartoons are as old as Uncle Sam himself, whose familiar figure was created by the famous cartoonist Thomas Nast. With a few well-drawn strokes and about sixteen square inches of space, the cartoonist refines the scope of an issue until only the ridiculous essence remains. Editorial cartoonists destroyed Tammany Hall (the only criticism that ever bothered Boss Tweed was, "those cartoons!") and highlighted the absurdities of Watergate. Even President Ford, as he gazed at a gallery of U.S. political cartoons, conceded, "The pen is mightier than the politician." This book is dedicated to that concept: "The pen (and the greater Truth behind it) is mightier. . . ."

Chapter One

The
Dilemma

"Hail, Caesar! We who are about to die salute you!" The gladiators of first-century Rome raised their right hands straight out, signifying full allegiance.

Thousands of others assembled in the crowded Roman Coliseum cheered, voicing their total commitment to the man-god Caesar, and a fifty-piece band struck up a rousing march.

This same fervent salute was repeated much later in history by thousands of goose-stepping soldiers in severe black uniforms: "Heil, Hitler!"

But the salutation "Hail" comes to us in yet another dramatic way. In Nazareth of Galilee at the same time gladiators pledged their allegiance to Caesar, the angel Gabriel appeared to the Virgin Mary, declaring: "Hail, thou that art highly favoured, the Lord is with thee; blessed art thou among women." Both this salutation and the salute in the Roman Coliseum were religious. But they recognized total commitment to two different kings and two diverse kingdoms.

The era of Christ's birth was alive with the expectation of a world savior. At the appearance of a strange star in the year 17 B.C., Augustus Caesar inaugurated a twelve-day advent celebration. The Roman college of priests, headed by Augustus, gave the masses absolution from past sins. The coinage hailed Augustus as "Son of God."[1] The state was claiming to bring salvation as well as prosperity.

Not too many years after Augustus Caesar was proclaimed "Son of God," a disciple of Jesus Christ declared a challenge to the religious and civil leaders of Judea: "Neither is there salvation in any other: for there is none other name under heaven given among men, whereby we must be saved" than Jesus Christ (Acts 4:12).

When a state claims divine honors, there will always be warfare between Christ and Caesar, for two rival gods claim the same jurisdiction over man. It is a conflict between two kingdoms, between two kings, each of whom claim ultimate and divine powers.

Unfortunately we are involved in that same head-to-head confrontation in the United States today. The state—the federal bureaucracy and the courts—have become the modern divinity. It is now generally recognized that Communism, despite its commitment to atheism, is a religion. This makes its bitter conflict with the church inevitable. What is less clearly perceived in "Christian" America is that our government has also become a religion and is already involved in a bitter conflict with the religion of Christ. Obviously, Christianity and the new state religion of America cannot peacefully coexist.

Of course, if the United States president were to demand to be hailed as "divine Caesar" and the state created an open religious cult like Roman state paganism, Americans in their vast majority would rebel. But as long as these claims come in quietly and without fanfare by a shift in the basis of law and government, Christians remain tranquil. Meanwhile the pagan state continues to enlarge and consolidate its gains. If this continues for much longer, we will wake up when it is too late.

"Christians are like a frog sitting in a pot of warm water, which is gradually being heated to a boil. The frog is slowly being boiled to death, but Christians don't even perceive what is happening," Dr. James Kennedy, pastor of the Coral Ridge Presbyterian Church in Fort Lauderdale, told members of the National Association of Evangelicals and the National Religious Broadcasters at their combined annual convention in 1980.

"Christian freedoms are in great jeopardy, and we sit like a frog in water silently waiting for it to happen."

Pastors, laymen, concerned Christian leaders throughout America are beginning to realize that secular humanists have declared a war on Christianity in this country—and are making great strides toward victory.

If this is indeed true, what has happened to the United States? How did we move from a country that was founded "under God" to a nation that has lost its religious heritage? And how did we move from a federalist government where the Supreme Court was to interpret the Constitution to a

"I've discovered he's insensitive, unscrupulous, and devoid of moral character. . . . We were lucky to get him!"

country where the Supreme Court has begun to make law?

We as Christians share a major responsibility for what has happened, since a significant factor has been the dwindling influence of Christianity, which has allowed humanistic thought to rise and dominate. The pronounced effect this has had on our world is illustrated by the evident moral decadence of the West. British theologian H. G. Wood candidly notes in *Christianity and Civilisation:* "Somehow the whole bottom has fallen out of our civilisation, and a change come over the world, which if unchecked will transform it for generations. It is the death, or deathlike swoon, of Christianity."[2]

"Only by terrific moral recovery are we going to keep the world from becoming a dark age,"[3] the Quaker philosopher Elton Trueblood remarked in an interview in the *Los Angeles Times* in 1978. Likewise, Harvard law professor Harold Berman is concerned that the "whole culture seems to be facing the possibility of a kind of nervous breakdown."[4]

A key to understanding the declining influence of Christianity is to recognize that a shift has occurred in the way our thoughts move. Instead of Christian ideas being expressed in the general culture, a secular pagan ideology now dominates the various cultural and professional outlets: literature, education, law, the media. Harvard law professor Harold Berman describes the signs of this disease:

> One major symptom of this threatened breakdown is the massive loss in the confidence in law—not only on the part of law-consumers but also on the part of lawmakers and distributors.[5]

Too often the word *law* is understood only in the context of civil and criminal conduct. However, law, like religion, is a fundamental reality, which is related to the entire structure of a society. Law, in essence, is a basic social phenomenon, which holds society together.

Good law is limiting. It prevents the exercise of arbitrary power by the state and its agencies. If, however, the foundation undergirding law in a Christian society shifts from a Christian to a humanistic base, then a "nervous breakdown" occurs. Anarchy may result, and, if it does, history teaches that an imposed order will be inevitable.

What Is Law?

In 1907 Supreme Court Chief Justice Charles Evans Hughes remarked that "the Constitution is what the judges say it is."[6] Thus, in Hughes's view, law is arbitrary and is shaped by what a majority of nine Supreme Court justices say it is. Such an attitude is not that far removed from the 1936 decree of the Third Reich Commissar of Justice: "A decision of the Fuhrer in the express form of a law or decree may not be scrutinized by a judge. In addition, the judge is bound by any other decisions of the Fuhrer, provided that they are clearly intended to declare law."[7]

Here, too, law is bound up in what man says it is. In one case it is a judge, and, in the other, it is a fuhrer. In both statements, the only limitation on law is the belief system of the person making the pronouncements.

Justice Hughes's statement was representative of a clear break with the American legal past. His view of law deviates from the American concept of constitutionalism—limited government under the rule of law.

This concept was laid down in the colonial documents, including both the Declaration of Independence and the United States Constitution. By its adoption of the English common law (which applied accepted biblical principles in judicial decisions), the Constitution was acknowledging that a system of absolutes exists upon which government and law can be founded. Moreover, under constitutionalism the people are governed by a written document embodying these principles and, therefore, not by the arbitrary opinions to be found in the expressions of men.

For the framers of the Constitution rule of law was the essence of constitutional government. "The government of the United States," said Supreme Court Chief Justice John Marshall in 1803, "has been emphatically termed a government of laws and not men."[8] This meant that even the state, its agencies, and its officials were under the law, not above it.

The presupposition of constitutionalism was implicitly refuted by Justice Felix Frankfurter when, in speaking of the Supreme Court justices, he said that "it is they who speak and not the Constitution."[9] Also the Supreme Court itself held in a 1958 decision: "Article VI of the Constitution makes the Constitution the 'supreme Law of the Land.' . . . It is emphatically the province and duty of the judicial department to say what the law is. . . . It follows that the interpretation of the [Constitution] enunciated by this Court . . . is the supreme law of the land . . . "[10] These statements are affirmations that the Supreme Court is no longer under law but above it.

Impact of the Reformation

Of course, if there is no fixity in law and no reference point, then law can be what a judge says it is. If, however, there is a fixity to law, there is some absolute basis upon which judgment can be made. This was part of the belief system that the American colonists inherited from the Reformation thinkers.

To fully comprehend the Reformation and its impact, it must be understood that two movements were underway almost simultaneously, both with roots in the fourteenth century. As Francis Schaeffer comments in *How Should We Then Live?:* "in the south, much of the High Renaissance was based on a humanistic ideal of man's being the center of all things, of man's being autonomous; second, in the north of Europe, the Reformation was giving an opposite answer."[11] Important is the fact that while the Reformation and the Renaissance overlapped historically and addressed the same basic questions concerning God and man, they gave completely different answers and had completely different effects upon their culture.

A pivotal thinker in the High Middle Ages was Thomas Aquinas, the greatest of the medieval theologians. His view of the effect of the historic space-time Fall of man led to much of what was to follow in the fourteenth, fifteenth, and sixteenth centuries in Latin Europe. Aquinas did not believe in the total depravity of man—the Fall affected man substantially but not to the same degree in every part. To Aquinas, man was indeed fallen, but his intellect was left uncorrupted. Although flawed, it was still very capable indeed.

This was a sharp break with the position up to that point in history. Until then men had tended to distrust the ability of the intellect to arrive at any finally significant truth unaided by biblical revelation. Once Aquinas accorded greater scope to the intellect, the effect was profound. People projected Aquinas's thought further and increasingly believed that they could rely on their own human understanding without reference to the Bible on many important problems. They were free to mix the truths of the Bible with truths reached by non-Christian philosophers, not merely with respect to the world of nature but with regard to spiritual matters as well. This is what Paul was warning about in Colossians 2 when he said, "Beware lest any man spoil you through philosophy and vain deceit, after the tradition of men, after the rudiments of the world" (v. 8). Now there was a synthesis of biblical and pagan teaching.

Although the Bible remained authoritative, it was only part of a larger structure of knowledge. The implication of Aquinas's idea was that man could discover at least some truth without revelation. The Bible was no longer the ultimate reference point for truth; the synthesis of revelation and human reason became higher and more comprehensive.

The Reformation thinkers of the sixteenth century, notably Martin Luther and John Calvin, fought against Aquinas's concept of the Fall. They revived the old Christian suspicion of human reason and once again made the Bible the sole reference point for truth. They denied even the relative autonomy of human reason. Despite its ability the human intellect is easily deluded, Calvin wrote. Only the Bible has ultimate authority. Like the medieval Catholics, the Reformers accepted the Bible as the literal Word of God. But they went beyond the Roman Catholics in reaffirming its sufficiency and its essential clarity. Because the Bible is clear on fundamental matters, it can serve as a reference point for truth to all, not merely to the theologians and priests.

Nothing was considered equal to the Bible in authority. It was final. Man and all his institutions, including the state as well as the church, were *under* the authority of the Bible. The decisive word became *sola Scriptura,* by Scripture only.

Such thinking reformed the principles of government and law since the church had long since come to define the theory of government and the state. Despite the claims of the papacy, the states of Renaissance Europe were becoming autonomous and absolutist. Where it triumphed, the Reformation reversed that trend.

The Reformers stressed that it was the Bible, not the Keys of St. Peter, that gave a base to law and government. This meant that the ruling authorities were *under* God's law in a meaningful way, just as the people were. The Bible, not another human such as the pope, was the final authority. In fact, once the Bible was translated into ordinary language, the reformers

"I guess it was only a matter of time!"

showed that laymen could read it and judge a ruler's actions by its light.

The Reformation taught that freedom is a gift from God, and that each individual man and woman may approach God and obtain salvation directly, by faith, without the need of recourse to a hierarchy.

The Reformation did not bring perfection, but it did introduce a vast and unique improvement in the principles and practice of government. In a time of social and political upheaval, it provided the framework for political freedom unknown up to that time, thanks to the fact that the standard of reference, the Bible, was placed in the hands of the people. Freedom could exist without license and without chaos.

It became apparent that whenever a culture establishes its institutions upon the teaching of the Bible, it is able to have freedom in society and government. These principles logically led to a culture that brought about the civil freedoms and benefits Western Europe and the United States have enjoyed for centuries.

Chapter Two

The
Christian
Idea

We live in a world that is structured by ideas. Our presuppositions and ideas create our world view, the grid through which we view the world. More importantly, our presuppositions are the basis upon which we act. As a man "thinketh in his heart, so is he" (Prov. 23:7).

We are more than mere products of our environment. Men and women project their inward thoughts out into the external world where, in fact, their thoughts affect their environment. Ideas thus have consequences, which can be productive or destructive—depending upon their basis or foundation.

Ideas are seldom neutral. For example, we are hearing such ideas as "separation of church and state," "individual autonomy," "right to abortion," "death with dignity," or even "the death of God" expressed with increasing frequency. Each of these phrases portrays something that could initially be characterized as objective or neutral—the expression of an abstract "idea." Their supposed neutrality is belied by their very real and often physical impact in the external world. Words are important since they reveal the faith of the speaker, and all men have faith, consciously or unconsciously, in some basic world view.

What Is the Christian World View?

The Reformation taught that the Bible has something to say about every area of life. Man should base his world view, the Reformers taught, upon the principles of the Bible. The Bible is the grid through which man should view the world.

The Christian world view teaches a unified view of truth. Its principles deal in absolutes that do not vary according to circumstances but should, in fact, govern the actions of man as he responds to constantly changing conditions.

Although biblical principles represent absolute norms, they have never been applied perfectly because people, being fallen, have never carried them out perfectly. However, when biblical principles have been administered with some consistency, they have brought about positive results. In fact, as one views the diminishing number of countries that have any vestige of political freedom, the line between free countries and unfree ones can be seen to correspond to that between those countries that were strongly influenced by the Reformation and those that were not. We may include those Roman Catholic countries such as France that were influenced by Reformation thinking.

An even clearer line can be drawn between the countries that have never had any Christian base (whether Roman Catholic or Reformation in character). Poland has raised the aura of freedom through the Solidarity Union in its resistance to Communist Russia. This was made possible because of the strong influence of Roman Catholicism in Poland. So much of the Eastern Orthodox world is now under communism that Orthodoxy constitutes an exception.

The Christian world view teaches that man is created in the image of God. The implications of man made in God's image can be summarized by saying that man, like God, has personhood, a measure of self-transcendence, intelligence, morality, love, and creativity.[1] In essence, to say that man bears God's image affords man a dignity above and beyond all other creatures.

The fact that man and woman were made in the image of God is intimately connected to the concepts of authority and of power to govern and man's relationship to the revealed law of God. In Genesis 1:26 we read, "God said, Let us make man in our image, after our likeness: and let them have dominion . . . over all the earth, and over every creeping thing." In 1:28 the grant of dominion is reiterated with the added emphasis that man is to "replenish the earth, and subdue it." In the light of the Christian world view, we see that man's dominion is a delegated authority under God. Adam's naming of every creature in Genesis 2:19 was his first authoritative act.

The commands in Genesis 1 (vv. 26 and 28) are commonly called the "cultural mandate"—the mandate from God as revealed to Adam, yet unfallen, to utilize and direct the earth's resources to the glory of God. This mandate has not been withdrawn from fallen man. But only regenerate individuals—that is, Christians who truly love the Lord—can understand and carry out its implications.

Christians are called to apply God's revelation to all areas of life and to all disciplines. Unfortunately, what we have been witnessing in the last century is the non-Christian's usurpation of the cultural mandate against the terms of the Bible. When exercised contrary to the principles of the Bible, the cultural mandate becomes a pretext to manipulate man and his environment. Adam's delegated authority did not include the power to manipulate others, for Adam himself was under the law as expressed by God.

Adam was told by God that he could eat of all the trees of the garden but one: the tree of the knowledge of good and evil. If he ate that fruit, the penalty was death. Adam heard God's command. Thus he had received the law as revealed by God, and understood at least in principle, the difference between right and wrong in absolute terms: in terms of life and death. Having a free will, he could do either of two things: keep God's law or, breaking it, assume an autonomous attitude and thus formulate his own laws without reference to God. Adam chose the latter, thus becoming the first humanist.

This deliberate disobedience we call the Fall. Christian theism holds that man is flawed in his total being: there is no part of man that was not tainted by the Fall. Simultaneous with Adam's fall, nature was blighted. Moreover, the flawed character of Adam was subsequently passed on to all humans. This points to man's tremendous significance: one man's act not only affected him but also extended to all his descendants and to the world surrounding him.

Christian theism explains the present abnormality of man in terms of the flaw caused by the Fall. The humanist thinkers of the Renaissance had no answer for the fact that man's noble attributes are vitiated by selfishness, cruelty, and vice. They tended to close their eyes to man's flaws, and dwell on his virtues. Modern man, more deeply aware of the flaws, sometimes sees himself as absurd and futile.

Christian theism provides the answer in the atoning work of Christ. The fatal infection of sin is cured, though symptoms and effects remain. The Christian is substantially healed by Christ's work, but he is never perfect in this life. Therefore, Christian man is in need of the absolutes of the Bible to order and direct his fallen nature.

Christian theism teaches that man is held accountable to his Creator. Absolute standards exist by which all moral judgments of life are to be measured. With the Bible, there is a standard of right and wrong. These fundamental principles made up the Reformation world view. They were passed on in substance and without significant alteration to the American colonies through the influence of a book written by Samuel Rutherford, *Lex, Rex or, the Law and the Prince (1644)*.

Government under Biblical Law

Lex, Rex challenged the fundamental principle of seventeenth-century political government in Europe: the divine right of kings. This doctrine held that the king or state ruled as God's appointed regent. Therefore, the king's word was law. (Although Scripture was seen as normative, it was the king alone who interpreted and embodied that norm.)

Counterbalanced against this position was Rutherford's assertion that the basic premise of government and, therefore, of law must be the Bible, the Word of God rather than the word of any man. All men, even the king, Rutherford argued, were *under* the law and not above it. This religious concept was considered both heresy and treason and punishable as such.

Lex, Rex created an immediate controversy. It was banned in Scotland and was publicly burned in England. Rutherford, a Presbyterian minister who was one of the Scottish commissioners at Westminister Abbey in London and rector of St. Andrew's Church in Scotland, was placed under house arrest and summoned to appear before the Parliament at Edinburgh where probable execution awaited him. He died shortly before he could be made to comply with the order.

But Rutherford's ideas lived on to influence later generations. His basic presupposition of government based upon the absolutes of the Bible was finally realized in colonial America through the influence of two sources: John Witherspoon and John Locke.

Witherspoon, a Presbyterian minister who had been educated at Edinburgh University, brought the principles of *Lex, Rex* into the writing of the Constitution. The only clergyman to sign the Declaration of Independence, Witherspoon was a member of the Continental Congress from 1776 to 1779 and from 1780 to 1782. He played a key role on a number of the committees of the first Congress. Witherspoon's students, profoundly influenced by him, also reached positions of eminence in the Constitutional Convention and in early United States history. They included a president, James Madison; a vice president, Aaron Burr; ten cabinet officers; twenty-one senators; thirty-nine congressmen; and twelve governors, as well as other public figures.[2]

James Madison was particularly influenced by Witherspoon. Col-

"Well, if our life-style must change, it's nice somebody is doing it with class!"

umbia University professor Richard B. Morris writes in *Seven Who Shaped Our Destiny:* "Most influential in shaping Madison's . . . outlook was Princeton's president, John Witherspoon, a leading empiricist of his day . . . whose expositions of the doctrines of resistance and liberty quickly established him throughout the Continent as an imposing intellectual."[3] The Witherspoon influence later played a major role in the drafting of the Constitution. In fact, Madison has been labeled "The Father of the Constitution" for his contribution in writing the founding document.

Two principles enunciated in *Lex, Rex* were drawn upon by the colonists in declaring their independence from Great Britain in 1776. First, there was the concept of the covenant or constitution between the ruler and

God and the people. This covenant, Rutherford argued, could not grant the state absolute or unlimited power without violating God's law. Taking the cue from Rutherford the colonists asserted that King George had violated his covenant with God by transgressing their God-given rights.

Rutherford's second principle declared that all men are created equal. Since all men are born sinners, Rutherford reasoned that no man is superior to any other man. He established the principle of equality and liberty among men, which was later written into the Declaration of Independence.

Although John Locke secularized the Reformed tradition, he nevertheless drew heavily from it.[4] He elaborated fundamental concepts such as unalienable rights, government by consent, the social compact (a constitution between the people and the government), separation of powers, and the right to resist unlawful authority. The biblical base for these concepts is set forth in Rutherford's *Lex, Rex*. As Francis Schaeffer has noted, many "of the men who laid the foundation of the United States Constitution were not Christians in the [full] sense, and yet they built upon the basis of the Reformation either directly through the *Lex, Rex* tradition or indirectly through Locke."[5]

It is important to understand that our political institutions have their base in this Reformation thinking. When we contrast this fact with the increasingly arbitrary nature of our modern civil government, we see that we have, in effect, come full circle. Today, in many ways, our "democratic" institutions reflect the governmental viewpoints of those absolute monarchists who condemned Samuel Rutherford. There is one vital difference. The monarchs of that day acknowledged the sovereignty of God, at least in theory. The Bible was held in high respect, and to challenge the monarch's prerogatives on biblical grounds—as Rutherford did in *Lex, Rex*—was considered a dangerous threat as well as heresy. If *Lex, Rex* were published today it might very well be ignored and labeled another irrelevant Christian statement in a society that respects neither the Bible nor the church.

The Influence of Blackstone

The renowned, eighteenth-century English jurist William Blackstone also played a leading role in forming a Christian presuppositional base to early American law. Because the American colonists and Blackstone shared the same background of Reformation thinking, Blackstone's ideas on law were readily accepted in the colonies.

Blackstone, who was a lecturer at law at Oxford, embodied the tenets of Judeo-Christian theism in his *Commentaries on the Laws of England,* published between 1765 and 1770. The *Commentaries* were popular in

Great Britain, but by 1775, more copies of the *Commentaries* had been sold in America than in all England.[6] So influential were the *Commentaries* that historian Daniel Boorstin writes: "In the first century of American independence, the Commentaries were not merely an approach to the study of the law; for most lawyers they constituted all there was of the law."[7]

Blackstone, a Christian, believed that the fear of the Lord was the beginning of wisdom. Thus he opened his *Commentaries* with a careful analysis of the law of God as revealed in the Bible. He defined law as a rule of action, which is prescribed by some superior, and which the inferior is bound to obey. To illustrate this definition Blackstone expressed the presuppositional base for law as he saw it:

> The doctrines thus delivered we call the revealed or divine law, and they are to be found only in the holy scriptures.
>
> Upon these two foundations, the law of nature and the law of revelation, depend all human laws; that is to say, no human laws should be suffered to contradict these.[8]

Blackstone took it as self-evident that God is the source of all laws, whether they were found in the Holy Scriptures or were observable in nature. His presuppositions were thoroughly Christian, founded upon the belief that there existed a personal, omnipotent God who worked in and governed the affairs of men. In consequence, man was bound by those laws, which were in turn a system of absolutes. Why? Because man is a derivative being. Blackstone wrote:

> Man, considered as a creature, must necessarily be subject to the laws of his Creator, for he is entirely a dependent being. . . . And, consequently, as man depends absolutely upon his Maker for everything, it is necessary that he should in all points conform to his Maker's will.[9]

Blackstone argued that the cultural mandate given to Adam and Eve in Genesis 1 is the basis for man's possession of property. This divine mandate was the only true basis for the right to hold private property or, for that matter, any right. In Blackstone's view, and in the eyes of those who founded the United States, every right or law comes from God, and the very words *rights, laws, freedoms,* and so on are meaningless without their divine origin.

Blackstone's influence is clearly expressed in the Declaration of

Independence. The colonists argued that it is "the Laws of Nature and of Nature's God" that entitled them to independence and to an equal station among nations. Blackstone had some years earlier written that the "will of Maker is called the law of nature."[10] And in echoing *Lex, Rex* the colonists proclaimed that "all men are created equal."

In seeking independence from Great Britain the colonists declared to the world their belief in a personal, infinite God—"their Creator"—who endowed them with "certain unalienable" or absolute rights. To the men of that time, it was self-evident that if there were no God there could be no absolute rights. Unlike the French revolutionaries a few years later, the American colonists knew very well that if the unalienable rights they were urging for were not seen in the context of Judeo-Christian theism, they were without content.

The Declaration of Independence, therefore, is structured upon a Judeo-Christian base in two fundamental ways. First, it professes faith in a "Creator" who works in and governs the affairs of men in establishing absolute standards to which men are held accountable. Second—and even more fundamentally, since all Western nations of that era professed a belief in the Creator—there is the idea that man is a fallen creature and, hence, cannot be his own lawgiver and judge. In the end it is God to whom the appeal must be made. In this sense, the law cannot be simply what a judge or a fuhrer says it is. It is what God says it is.

Chapter Three

From a
Judeo-Christian
America to—?

The framers of our nation understood the need for Christian content in the system they were developing. The knowledge of God as revealed in the Bible was widely diffused in colonial America, although the America of the eighteenth and early nineteenth centuries was not Christian in the sense that great multitudes had a personal relationship with Christ. But it was Christian to the extent that the American citizenry thought and acted from a biblical (or Judeo-Christian) base. This fact has been noted by many historians, among them C. Gregg Singer in his *A Theological Interpretation of American History:*

A Christian world and life view furnished the basis for this early political thought which guided the American people for nearly two centuries and whose crowning lay in the writing of the Constitution of 1787. This Christian theism had so permeated the colonial mind that it continued to guide even those who had come to regard the Gospel with indifference or even hostility. The currents of this orthodoxy were too strong to be easily set aside by those who in their own thinking had come to a different conception of religion and hence of government also.[1]

Alexis de Tocqueville, the French historian who wrote one of the definitive works on early America, *Democracy in America,* remarked:

America is still the place where the Christian religion has kept the greatest real power over men's souls; and nothing better demonstrates how useful and natural it is to man, since the country where it now has the widest sway is both the most enlightened and the freest. . . .[2]

A dominant aspect of the Christian influence on early nineteenth-century America was the interest and energy it displayed toward the external world and society. This was a result of the application of the cultural mandate. But the gradual dominance of the pietist movement in Christianity changed all this. Philip Jacob Spener, and his successor August Hermann Francke, turned Protestant Christianity inward; Christians began to abandon the cultural mandate to pursue the development of their interior spiritual life.

Although it began as a renewal movement, Pietism ultimately tended to degenerate into mere personal religiosity without much direct influence on society and culture. Religion became ''privatized'' and ceased to affect public life. The foundation laid by the colonists and the founding fathers was so strong that Christianity continued to pervade society for decades after Pietism. But eventually such influence began to wear off as the new generations of Christians turned inward and ceased any attempts to shape their society.

Although Christianity cannot survive if it neglects personal commitment and the spiritual life of the individual, it also inevitably declines if it devotes itself solely to the inward life. To be effective, Christianity must be both. The inward redemption must flow outward and affect the temporal world.

In *Redeemer Nation,* Ernest Tuveson, professor of English at the University of California at Berkeley, notes that the dominant influence of early American Christianity began with the idea that God was "redeeming both individual souls and society in parallel course."[3] The religious revivals that dominated the early nineteenth century, as Harvard historian Perry Miller points out in *The Life of the Mind in America,* were not aimed merely at saving souls but also at redeeming the physical aspects of the community.[4] Simply put, colonial Christianity saw God as working in the whole culture, not merely in the hearts of men.

This attitude led to the abolition of the slave trade in Great Britain and effectively began the train of events that saw slavery abolished in the

"Notice how some people always have to bring religion into Christmas!"

United States. William Wilberforce and others in England spent a lifetime fighting evils such as slavery because of their Christian faith and their determination to apply that faith's principles to the external world. In America Christian groups such as the Quakers fought slavery, applying their Christianity externally.

Even the early pietists were active social reformers. Unfortunately, the later wave of the pietistic movement looked inward. Their focus was, and still is, on the areas of life that were believed to be spiritual as opposed to the secular or worldly, including both politics and the arts. This view eventually led to a reduction of the Christian influence on the external world, leaving the field increasingly open to domination by those with non-Christian views.

Pietism, especially in its present form, stresses only the personal "salvation" experience. Bible study becomes simplistic, and any form of intellectualism is considered unspiritual. Pietism inevitably resulted in the church adopting a religious form of Platonism, the belief that the spiritual world is somehow superior to and above the physical-temporal world. It created an unbiblical dichotomy between the spiritual and temporal worlds.

The Civil War and Its Aftermath

Another force that diminished the influence of Christianity was the American Civil War (1861-1865), which played havoc with virtually every aspect of society. The social and spiritual upheaval it brought paved the way for the humanistic movement, which resulted from the introduction of Charles Darwin's theory of evolution by natural selection. Darwin himself never fully abandoned the conviction that there is a God. But by making man the product of "natural selection" rather than God's direct handiwork, he helped to rob man of a sense of responsibility to his Creator and of all obligation to heed the Creator's laws. Darwin himself remained a bourgeois, Victorian Englishman of traditional behavior and morality, but he effectively undermined traditional morality for the next generation.

Darwin's book, *The Origin of Species by Means of Natural Selection or the Preservation of Favoured Races in the Struggle for Life,* was published on November 24, 1859. All 1,250 copies were sold on the day of publication. Darwin set forth the concept that all biological life evolved from simpler forms by a process called "the survival of the fittest." Darwin's idea was popularized by Thomas Huxley. Herbert Spencer, who actually coined the phrase "survival of the fittest," extended the theory of biological evolution to all areas of life, including ethics.

In addition to removing the origin of man from God's direct supervision, Darwinism further undermined any normative, divine order to nature because now nature itself was evolving. The best is yet to come, so we cannot discern right principles of conduct from the natural order as it now exists.

George Bernard Shaw said that "the world jumped at Darwin."[5] In a sense, the world was waiting for a world view with scientific prestige to render the Bible obsolete, because the church, now so involved in Pietism, was not answering society's basic questions about the world and its meaning.

With the spiritual and philosophical vacuum created by the Christian retreat from society, humanistic thought (which had its roots in earlier eras, the late Renaissance, and the eighteenth-century Enlightenment) moved unopposed into all areas of life and became entrenched as a dominant thought form and force in American society. This led to the Victorian era of unadulterated, capitalistic rule at its best and worst, capitalism that knew how to develop the country both economically and scientifically but without compassion. It was, as historian Amaury de Riencourt noted in *The Coming Caesars,* a "merciless . . . age when social Darwinism ruled supreme. . . . With Roman-like ruthlessness, these Spencerian apostles confused mechanical expansion with historical progress and the very success of industrialization contributed to ensnare them in their own intellectual traps."[6]

As a consequence, J. D. Rockefeller could justify his industrial monopoly without restraint: "The growth of a large business is merely a survival of the fittest."[7] Likewise, Andrew Carnegie could expound on his conversion to Darwinism: "Light came as in a flood and all was clear. Not only had I got rid of theology and the supernatural, but I found the truth of evolution."[8]

Without the Judeo-Christian base, people were manipulated by the humanistic industrializers in what became, and still is, a pagan form of the biblical cultural mandate.

What, Then, Is Humanism?

The concept of humanism is somewhat elusive, particularly since some of its earlier forms were neutral or even positive. If one thinks of humanism as emphasizing the dignity of man, Christianity is in a sense humanistic, for it teaches that man is made in the image and likeness of God.

But humanism can quickly negate the Christian belief in man's fallen state and his need for God's revelation in the Bible. Erasmus of Rotterdam, the leading classical scholar of the early sixteenth century, supported some of the Reformation's cries against the Catholic church on the grounds that Catholicism was no longer true to the text of the Bible. But he came to oppose Martin Luther and the Protestant Reformation because he vehemently objected to Luther's understanding of the Fall of man and its consequences. Even the relatively mild, "Christian" humanism of Erasmus and others objects to any emphasis on man's fallen condition and his resulting depravity. Christian humanism all too often turns into a belief that man can arrive at ultimately valid and important truths on his own without recourse to God's revelation in the Bible, which is open rebellion against God and his sovereignty.

The term *humanist* was originally applied to those scholars who revived the study of "humane" as opposed to "sacred" literature—that is, the works of pagan antiquity. Beginning with the reasonable suggestion that pagan literature was of some value, humanism, under the influence of Aquinas, went on to place it on the same level as Scripture and then to ultimately rank it as superior. Humanism often begins with what appears to be an innocuous, altogether reasonable, interest in the classics of antiquity, but it almost invariably ends in the deification of man and rejection of God. The Italian Renaissance rediscovered the beauty of Greek and Roman antiquity. For a time the Catholic Church sensed the Renaissance's doubtful and even dangerous characteristics and resisted the movement. Ultimately, Roman Catholics very largely compromised with humanism, leaving the criticism of humanism to the Protestants of the Reformation.

But modern humanism has lost even a tenuous connection with God by denying that there is any order to nature, and insisting that man is totally autonomous. Because of its connection with classical literature and art, early humanism often appeared much more urbane and sophisticated than biblical Protestantism. Today's humanism, however, has lost much appreciation for classical culture and is scarcely more appreciative of the *Laws* of the philosopher Plato than of the law of God as revealed in Scripture. The humanism that we encounter today is almost exclusively opposed to Christianity and indifferent to the pagan classics. But this sometimes escapes detection because there have been Christians in the past who were favorable to the older humanism.

For our present purposes, humanism can be defined as the fundamental idea that men and women can begin from themselves without reference to the Bible and, by reasoning outward, derive the standards to judge all matters. For such people, there is no absolute or fixed standard of behavior. They are quite literally autonomous (from the Greek *autos,* self, and *nomos,* law), a law unto themselves. There are no rights given by God. There are no standards that cannot be eroded or replaced by what seems necessary, expedient, or even fashionable at the time. Man is his own authority, "his own god in his own universe."

Historian Ralph Henry Gabriel has explained the connection between the humanism that appeared subsequent to the Civil War and the effects of Darwinian thought on Judeo-Christian theism:

> The appearances of an aggressive humanism, a new religion of humanity, immediately after the end of the Civil War is one of the more significant events in the history of American democratic thought. The objective of the religion of humanity was to secure and to protect a larger human freedom and to make men understand that liberty implies responsibility. Like Morgan, the post-Appomattox humanists turned to science. When the anxieties of war relaxed, there was a sudden impact of Darwinism upon Chris-

tian orthodoxy. Auguste Comte, who died in 1857, gave the world a positivist philosophy which affirmed that the theological stage in the progress of humankind had ended as had also the succeeding stage of rationalistic philosophies. Mankind, thought Comte, had entered, in the nineteenth century, the age of science; in this new intellectual world man was destined to become the master of his own destiny. Comtean positivism affected American thought at the moment when Darwinism was challenging the old religious doctrines of the nature of man.[9]

"Our lecture today will be on contract demands and the science and formation of effective picket lines!"

During the nineteenth century humanists were thrusting their ideas into education, science, and the arts. Revivalistic piety, however, with its emphasis on the inner self, virtually abandoned these areas.

Unfortunately, the church has been all too willing to use the categories of "secular" and "religious" when no such distinction exists in reality. All things have been created by God. Thus, all things have their origin in God and should be under Christ's lordship. The pietist renunciation thus raises a core issue: the *lordship of Christ*.

To the true Christian, Christ cannot be Savior and not Lord. Christ is Lord over *all* areas of life—not merely the spiritual. Indeed, it is incorrect to make a fundamental distinction between spiritual and secular. Christ is Lord of the intellectual life, the business life, the political life.

If Christ is not Lord over the arts and science, then man is. This is humanism in practice. It was difficult for the church to dispute humanistic ideology because the church itself was practicing humanism by separating the spiritual from the totality of life and reality.

The Tension

We are all captives, to a greater or lesser extent, of the age in which we live. In our case we are locked into an age where humanism has come to full flower and is now confronting Christianity with a fierceness as never before.

Autonomous, secular humanism has replaced Christianity as the consensus of the West. This has had devastating effects, especially in the way man views himself. Now man has become only one part of the larger cosmic machine, some sort of dot in an improbable futuristic never-never land as posed in Carl Sagan's *Cosmos*. Perhaps man is interesting as a piece of evolving machinery, but certainly man is nothing that can command any final dignity, love, or respect.

Humanism, contrary to popular belief, is not a tolerant system. It preaches against religious "dogmatism," but imposes its own. Professor Harvey Cox of the Harvard Divinity School has noted in his work *The Secular City* that humanism, or secularism as he calls it, is an "ideology, a new closed world view which functions very much like a new religion. . . . It is a closed ism."[10]

Humanism is not only indifferent to alternative religious systems, but as a religious ideology it is opposed to any other religious system. Moreover, Cox believes that secularism is a menace to freedom because it "seeks to impose its ideology through the organs of the State."[11] The humanistic consensus is interested in eliminating Christianity, because individual Christians have an absolute standard by which to judge the system. Despots know very well the consequence of ideas.

The church's response has been inadequate, as Professor Berman has noted: "The significant factor in this regard . . . has been the very gradual reduction of the traditional religions to the level of a personal, private matter, without public influence on legal development, while other belief systems— new secular religions ('ideologies,' 'isms')—have been raised to the level of passionate faiths for which people collectively are willing not only to die but also . . . to live new lives."[12] As a result, Christianity has lost much of its public character as well as its political strength. Says Berman:

For the most part, people go to church as individuals, or as individual families, to gain spiritual nourishment to sustain them in activities and relationships that take place elsewhere. . . . We are thus confronted with a combination of a "religionless Christianity" and what may be called a "Christianity-less religion."[13]

This problem has been multiplied by the fact that the Christian community, by and large, seems intent on only emphasizing such spiritual quests as personal evangelism. Although personal evangelism is an important aspect of Christianity, it cannot be the only aspect of the faith. The modern

"We made the change after we started having more abortions than live births."

church seems to have—to mix metaphors—won some souls but lost the battle for society.

There have, of course, been exceptions to this rule of passivity. Francis Schaeffer's activity against abortion-on-demand is a good example. However, as Harold O. J. Brown states in the *National Review:* "It is certainly significant, and in some ways unfortunate, that the symbolic leaders of middle-of-the-road evangelicalism have not seen fit to identify with the concerns of Schaeffer . . ."[14]

The failure of Christianity to influence society has resulted in an America that is saturated with a new system of arbitrary absolutes, a philosophical relativism that changes with opinion but that demands absolute submission to its arbitrary will of the moment.

A Speaking Church

The solution to the humanistic crisis in values is a return to the Christian foundation that was reestablished and strengthened in the Reformation. It is a return to truth not simply for truth's sake but because the truths of the Creator work in the real world God has created—a world conceived to produce beauty, humanity, compassion, and dignity in his creation.

The silent church can no longer hide under the cloak of noninvolvement, as though it were neutral. Noninvolvement is choice. It is choosing to allow humanism to proceed unrestrained. Noninvolvement is, therefore, negative involvement. If the church continues its silence, the only option will be to capitulate and be dominated by a humanistic culture that will not tolerate Christianity. As this humanistic culture crumbles, we will no doubt see a continued return to the cruelty that characterized past pagan civilizations. In the end, we will come to be at the arbitrary disposal of a judge, a court, or even a fuhrer, preferring arbitrary laws to no law at all.

Chapter Four

Law Without an Anchor

The shift in the basic foundations of American life from a biblical to a humanistic base has had a marked influence in every discipline. This fact is no less true of the legal profession, which moved from one of little recognition in early colonial America to a profession that was highly regarded to one that is now losing its revered status.

Although reverencing law itself, Perry Miller has written that early colonial Americans held a distrust for lawyers. For example, the *Fundamental Constitutions of Carolina* (1669) declared it "a base and vile thing to plead for money or reward." In Massachusetts, the *Body of Liberties* (1641) permitted anyone who could not plead his own cause to retain someone else for assistance "provided he give him noe fee or reward for his paines." This popular detestation of lawyers was based in part on the biblical view that justice was of God and that it should not degenerate into a business.

But this early disrespect for lawyers soon changed. As Perry Miller noted in *The Life of the Mind in America*, "A phenomenon of fundamental importance for both the social and intellectual history of America is the amazing rise, within three or four decades, of the legal profession from its chaotic condition of around 1790 to a position of political and intellectual domination."[1] One reason for this change was that the legal profession developed into one of the most cultivated portions of early American society.[2] Prime examples of cultured lawyers were Alexander Hamilton and Thomas Jefferson, both framers renowned for their scholarship; John Marshall, chief justice of the Supreme Court from 1801 to 1835 and a giant of the law; or even Daniel Webster, a great orator who was the subject of much literary attention.

There is a certain lament today that the cultivated lawyer has been lost to society. In his stead, the culture is producing legal technicians who have little appreciation for the broader aspects of the law. Today the law student is surrounded by thousands of law books, which he is supposed to digest and read. The student is instructed to become a technician in every area of business: contracts, corporations, and commercial transactions. He also may become an analytical expert in courtroom tactics, but he often works with little consideration of what the public looks for in the courtroom: justice.

Yale law professor Fred Rodell expressed these concerns in 1939:

> In tribal times, there were the medicine men. In the Middle Ages, there were the priests. Today there are the lawyers. For every age, a group of bright boys, learned in their trade and jealous of their learning, who blend technical competence with plain and fancy hocus-pocus to make themselves masters of their fellow men. For every age, a pseudo-intellectual autocracy, guarding the tricks of its trade from the uninitiated, and running, after its own pattern, the civilization of its day.
>
> It is the lawyers who run our civilization for us—our governments, our business, our private lives.[3]

Over two-thirds of those men who have held the office of president have been lawyers or have been connected with the legal profession. Also, between one-half and two-thirds of the seats in Congress have usually been filled with lawyers. Unfortunately the presuppositional foundation that undergirds the law profession has now been shifted from a Judeo-Christian base to a humanistic one.

"Ours is a sick profession," commented Supreme Court Chief Justice Warren Burger in an address to the American College of Trial Lawyers. A profession marked by "incompetence, lack of training, misconduct, and bad manners. Ineptness, bungling, malpractice, and bad ethics can be observed in court houses all over this country every day."

At the American Bar Association's annual meeting in St. Louis, Burger further commented: "The American public is aware of the moral and professional deficiencies of lawyers, is hurting and doesn't know what to do about it, but wants to do something." In fact, a 1973 Harris Poll found that

"Honesty is the best policy, men. . . . When you offer somebody a 10 percent kickback, make sure they get the whole 10 percent."

only 18 percent of the public had confidence in lawyers, a somewhat lower approval rating than that of garbage collectors.

The moral and professional decline of lawyers is a threatening phenomenon because lawyers through the various government agencies and the courts literally run the country. French journalist Alain Clement commented in 1980 that American lawyers are "the ruling class." Says Clement: "About 40,000 lawyers work in Washington, double the number 10 years ago. Eight of 13 cabinet members are lawyers, 8,000 participate in government." Moreover, Clement writes: "The exceptional position of the American lawyer derives from the power of American judges. Their power in turn springs from their role in interpreting the Constitution."[4]

The legal profession, because of its power to mold laws (and even the Constitution) has become the eye of the storm, so to speak, in terms of social change. An aggressively humanistic legal elite seems to be determined to change the basis of law.

The Evolving Law

The vital point in any discipline is the education system that undergirds it. The ideas that people absorb from their teachers more often than not are applied in the culture at large. This is even truer in legal education since law school is a vigorous inculcation of principles over a three-year period. An entire world view can be altered by such an indoctrination.

The legal profession itself is molded in the law schools. What is occurring in law and government today is merely the fruits of what was taught to the law students of yesteryear.

This shift began with the application of Darwinism to law—all law. Julian Huxley once noted that the evolutionary belief system encompasses the disciplines such as "law and religion. . . until we are enabled to see evolution as a universal, all pervading process. . . . Our present knowledge indeed forces us to the view that the world of reality is evolution—a single process of self transformation."[5] Moreover, Huxley wrote: "There proceeded during the 19th Century, under the influence of the evolutionary concept, a thoroughgoing transformation of older studies like History, Law and Political Economy; and the creation of new ones like Anthropology, Social Psychology, Comparative Religion, Criminology, Social Geography."[6]

Likewise, in 1952 Fred Cahill, professor of political science at Yale University, wrote: "The appearance in the mid-nineteenth century of the concept of evolution was an event of transcending importance to the development of American jurisprudence. . . . This involved . . . a shift . . . from the rationalistic, deductive pattern, characteristic of the pre-Darwinian period, to the empirical, evolutionary approach that is followed . . . today."

This shift began in the 1870s when Christopher Langdell, dean of the Harvard Law School, began to apply Darwinian thought to legal education. Langdell introduced the "case method" of teaching law, which as law professor Herbert Titus of the O. W. Coburn School of Law (Tulsa) has noted, "revolutionized the study of law in the United States."[7]

However, Langdell's real impact on law education was his belief that the basic principles and doctrines of the law were the products of an evolving and growing process over many years. Langdell believed that this evolution was taking place in the opinions written by judges. This meant that what a judge said was law, and not what the Constitution said.

Before Langdell's influence became dominant in the legal education system, the law had primarily been taught by practicing lawyers in law offices throughout the country. William Blackstone's *Commentaries* were often the basic legal treatise. The prevailing opinion was that the principles and doctrines of the law were unchanging: law was based upon absolutes in the biblical sense. All the student had to learn was to apply those legal principles and doctrines. Beginning with Langdell, however, law education shifted to the classroom, where students were taught that the principles and doctrines of the law were being developed in the appellate courts by judges

"Personally, I wish they would teach creation along with evolution. . . . I never did believe in the literal interpretation of Darwin."

across America. Justice Hughes was merely echoing Langdell's philosophy when he remarked that "the Constitution is what the judges say it is."

Langdell's system was effective in attacking Blackstone's belief that the judges' opinions in appellate cases were not sources of law, but merely "evidence" of law. The fact that Blackstone is not studied in law schools today most likely stems from his presuppositional differences with the predominant relativistic, evolutionary approach taught in contemporary legal education. Modern legal scholars have rejected the views of Blackstone because they have rejected his faith in God and his reliance upon the Genesis account of creation and the origin of man and the universe.

The method of teaching used by Langdell, though accepted with enthusiasm by his pupils and soon adopted by his colleagues, met with criticism both from the bar and from law professors in other law schools. However, as his students issued forth into the legal profession and assumed positions in law schools throughout the country, Langdell's philosophy began to predominate. Today his ideas and belief system have prevailed.

For example, the eminent Harvard law school dean, Roscoe Pound, a successor of Langdell's who is said to have had a profound effect on our legal system,[8] wrote: "It must be borne in mind that 'nature' did not mean to antiquity what it means to us who are under the influence of evolution."[9] He taught "that no current hypothesis is reliable, as ideas and legal philosophies change radically and frequently from time to time."[10]

Pound also proclaimed: "I am skeptical as to the possibility of an absolute judgment."[11] By the time of Pound, the teaching that law was based upon absolutes was gone. Blackstone was merely an interesting antiquity to be studied in an elective course on jurisprudence.

Under Langdell's application of evolution, the Constitution itself becomes a document that is at the disposal of the opinion of judges. Harvard law professor Laurence Tribe, an influential constitutional spokesman who is often cited by the Supreme Court in its decisions, writes that "the constitution is an intentionally incomplete, often deliberately indeterminate structure for the participatory evolution of political ideals and governmental practices."[12]

As such, Tribe writes that "the highest mission of the Supreme Court, in my view, is not to conserve judicial credibility, but in the Constitution's own phrase, 'to form a more perfect Union' between right and rights within that charter's necessarily evolutionary design."[13] A Constitution, which is called a "living" or evolving instrument, is then what the Supreme Court says it is.

Jurisprudence

Modern legal theorists define the term *jurisprudence* as meaning the science of the law. Jurisprudence, however, encompasses more than a vague generality such as that. The Latin term *juris* means right or just. *Prudentia,* another Latin term, is defined as practical skill in the management of business affairs. In other words, jurisprudence has to do with the administration or weighing of justice or right values.

A jurisprudential view of law is expressed in the Declaration of Independence when it asserts that "the Laws of Nature and of Nature's God" establish the basic principles upon which man is to base life. As Blackstone admonished in his *Commentaries,* the laws of nature and of nature's God are expounded upon and clarified by the Bible. In terms of the judge, he is to exercise a jurisprudential application of man's law in relation to the higher law.

Sociological Law

Roscoe Pound is credited with initiating a movement toward *sociological jurisprudence*, which as René Wormser noted in *The Story of Law*, "has radically affected, sometimes directly and sometimes indirectly, the thinking of American jurists, judges, and lawyers. It has also made itself felt throughout the entire international field of Western jurisprudence."[14]

"Very nice. . . . I'll take it!"

Sociological law presupposes that no absolutes exist upon which law or laws can be based. Law is seen as evolutionary in character, and it is based upon a system of arbitrary absolutes. Concerning sociological law, Francis Schaeffer and C. Everett Koop write in *Whatever Happened to the Human Race?*:

> [L]aw is only what most of the people think at that moment of history, and there is no higher law. It follows, of course, that the law can be changed at any moment to reflect what the majority currently thinks.
>
> More accurately, the law becomes what a few people in

some branch of the government think will promote the present sociological and economic good. In reality the will and moral judgment of the majority are now influenced by or even overruled by the opinions of a small group of men and women. This means that vast changes can be made in the whole concept of what should and what should not be done. Values can be altered overnight and at almost unbelievable speed.[15]

Law has become utilitarian. It can be what the majority conceives as law, or it can be what an elite says it is. There is no absolute. In the end, it is always what a court or judge says it is.

The Langdell Progeny

Once the foundation for sociological law was laid in the classroom, it was only a matter of time before it would find expression through the judges who sat on the courts. One such person was Oliver Wendell Holmes, a contemporary of Pound and a Supreme Court justice from 1902 to 1932. In his most extensive piece of scholarship, *The Common Law,* Justice Holmes proclaimed: "The life of law has not been logic; it has been experience."[16]

Professor G. Edward White has interpreted Justice Holmes's use of the word *logic* to mean:

the formalistic, religion-based logic that reasoned downward syllogistically from assumed truths about the universe; the proposed counter-system was "experience," the changing "felt necessities" that reflected current social values and were altered by time and circumstances. . . . [This was] merely a fatalistic acceptance that law was not so much the embodiment of reason as a manifestation of dominant beliefs at a given time.[17]

The nineteenth-century logic of Christian theism, which found its source of law in the written revelation of the Bible, was an anathema to Holmes. Law could not be seen in absolute terms since law for Holmes "was simply an embodiment of the ends and purposes of a society at a given point in its history."[18] If there are no absolutes through man in the form of unalienable rights, then the will of the state, as Holmes posited, is the law.[19] Laws under Holmes's view are considered "beliefs that have triumphed" and no more.[20]

The idea that God endows man with absolute rights, such as life, liberty, and the pursuit of happiness are lost within the Holmes framework of sociological law. The implications of sociological law are disturbing when executed by someone with despotic power, such as an Adolf Hitler or a Joseph Stalin. Whether that power emanates from an individual or a majoritarian vote, the substitution of sociological law for law based upon biblical absolutes is alarming.

Under the impact of sociological law, justice, together with law, is made the creature of the state. God and the Bible are nowhere involved in the lawmaking process and, in fact, are discouraged from becoming a reference point for society by the legal system. Thus, the legal profession and the courts and numerous agencies that intimately affect our daily lives become a more

and more exclusive preserve for those who have the political muscle to make their sociological ideas prevail. These ideas become, in effect, the world view forced upon the majority, willingly or unwillingly.

"Truth," Holmes said, "[is] the majority vote of that nation that could lick all others."[21] He declared that "when it comes to the development of a *corpus juris* [or body of law] the ultimate question is what do the dominant forces of the community want and do they want it hard enough to disregard whatever inhibitions may stand in the way."[22]

In other words, whatever the dominant forces say is law is law, even if they have to disregard those who "may stand in the way." The system in power is thus intolerant and closed to alternative points of view.

With the loss of absolutes and with the application of evolutionary principles, the dignity of man is severely diminished. Concerning the nature of man, Holmes remarked:

> I see no reason for attributing to man a significance different in kind from that which belongs to a baboon or a grain of sand. I believe that our personality is a cosmic ganglion, just as when certain rays meet and cross there is a white light at the meeting point, but the rays go on after the meeting as they did before, so, when certain other streams of energy cross at the meeting point, the cosmic ganglion can frame a syllogism or wag its tail.[23]

The logical conclusion of man's significance being no greater than "a baboon or grain of sand" found its expression in the Supreme Court's decision in *Roe* v. *Wade,* which upheld the right to abortion-on-demand. To the Supreme Court the unborn child, as a nonperson, had little significance.

Having rejected the Judeo-Christian heritage, the courts have replaced law with politics. The only absolute that remains in the system of sociological law is the insistence that there is no absolute. The Christian base has been eliminated because of its insistence on absolutes.

The Courts as a Negative Factor

It has been a common fallacy to attribute twentieth-century conceptions to the minds and intentions of the framers of the Constitution. At the time of the Constitution's adoption, the notion that judges could make law was alien to colonial thinking. In fact, "fear of judicial discretion had long been part of the colonial political rhetoric."[24] The judicial role, in colonial thinking, was limited to policing constitutional boundaries.

Harvard professor Raoul Berger writes that for "150 years the Court was content with the policing function; even the headstrong laissez-faire Court merely acted as a nay-sayer. It fell to the Warren Court to take the lead in deciding what national policy ought to be when the legislative and executive failed to act. But the failure of Congress to exercise legislative power does not vest it in the Court."[25]

The judicial branch of the federal government was provided in Article III of the Constitution. The Constitution itself established only the Supreme Court, but it gave Congress the authority to establish lower federal courts as deemed necessary. As it has developed, the American system of courts has three levels of jurisdiction (the power to hear cases). The first, or lowest, level is made up of the district courts, where most cases are tried and settled. The second level is that of the court of appeals, where appeals from district court decisions are heard. The third, and highest, level is the Supreme Court.

It was never intended by the framers that the Supreme Court and its lower federal courts should exercise the national power they now possess. Alexander Hamilton in *Federalist Papers* No. 78 stressed that the federal courts were to serve as "bulwarks of a limited Constitution against legislative encroachments." The framers thus contemplated the courts' role as being "negative"; it was the function of the courts to check legislative excesses in order to prevent a usurpation of power by Congress. The framers saw Congress, the federal legislature, as the great threat to liberty.

The Court was thus posed as a balance against the possibility of legislative tyranny. This principle was inherent in the separation of powers of the legislative, judicial, and executive branches. However, if the Supreme Court, by way of sociological jurisprudence, can decide the law upon which the other branches operate, the Constitution is what the Supreme Court says it is.

This is exactly what has happened. The Supreme Court's distortion of the concept of judicial review has transferred immense powers to the federal court system and, ultimately, to the federal bureaucracy. The establishment of sociological law affords the courts great discretion with little restriction.

Judicial Review

A decade after the Constitution went into effect, the Supreme Court was an institution of little notice. However, in 1803 the Court received the impetus to become one of the most powerful institutions known to the history of man. The case was *Marbury* v. *Madison*.[26]

William Marbury was one of many justices of the peace for the District of Columbia named by President John Adams during a rash of last-minute judicial appointments at the end of his Federalist administration. These commissions had been signed by Adams and Acting Secretary of State John Marshall (the same man who would later decide the matter as chief justice of the Supreme Court), but they had not been delivered to Marbury and the other appointees by the end of Adams's last day in office. Therefore the incoming Jefferson administration chose to disregard them.

Marbury and some disappointed colleagues went directly to the Supreme Court asking that a writ of mandamus (an order that compels a public official to do some act within his duty) be served on Jefferson's secretary of state, James Madison, to compel him to deliver their formal commissions.

The Judiciary Act of 1801, passed by Congress, had given the Supreme Court the right to issue a mandamus, but John Marshall's opinion held that this part of the law was unconstitutional. This was the first time that any legislation, state or federal, had been held unconstitutional by the Supreme Court, and it was not to occur again until the *Dred Scott* case just before the Civil War. However, the principle was established: the Supreme Court had the right to pass on the constitutionality of an act of Congress. This was the breakthrough.

Marshall held that it was the duty of the Supreme Court alone to decide whether or not the other branches of government—the legislative and executive—were acting contrary to the Constitution. Thus, if Congress passed a law, which in the opinion of the Supreme Court justices was repugnant to the Constitution, the Supreme Court could void that law.

The legal term for this doctrine is *judicial review,* and it is the bedrock of the power of the Supreme Court and the lower federal courts. This case is also the foundation for the study of constitutional law in legal education.

The *Marbury* case opened the door. *Marbury* was a unanimous decision, but since that time numerous laws of both the state legislatures and Congress have been overturned by the Supreme Court on a simple 5-to-4 majority. Marshall, however, cannot be blamed for the excesses of the contemporary judiciary. Marshall himself was a student of Blackstone and advocated rule of law.

"Judicial power," Marshall wrote in *Osborn* v. *The Bank,* "as contradistinguished from the power of the laws, has no existence. Courts are mere instruments of the law, and can will nothing. . . . Judicial power is never exercised for the purpose of giving effect to the will of the judge; always for the purpose of giving effect . . . to the will of the law." But with the substitution of sociological jurisprudence for the Judeo-Christian base, the doctrine of judicial review has become a tyrannous device. It places the entire government under the authority of the Supreme Court, which can void an act if in the *opinion* of five of the nine justices that act is unconstitutional.

Professor Edward Corwin, a constitutional authority, has noted that the concept of judicial review was not articulated with clarity by the framers in the Constitutional Convention.[27] There may have been some notions among the framers on the power of courts to review legislative acts of Congress but only in terms of direct violations of the Constitution itself—never in terms of social policy based upon some vague public opinion.

By placing the ultimate source of constitutional authority in the hands of the Supreme Court, the Court has in effect become the living or speaking Constitution in an evolving sense. Students who study constitutional law in reality study Supreme Court decisions. Attorneys themselves, as Professor Corwin has said, have been "prone to identify the judicial version of the Constitution as the authentic Constitution."[28]

A dangerous aspect of the assumption that "the Supreme Court is the Constitution" is that decisions of the Court have come to be viewed as the final statement on an issue—unless it reverses itself. Therefore, it is now accepted that once the Court decides an issue, it must be followed as if it is law.

"I'm not feeling very infallible today!"

For example, the Court invalidated, by way of judicial review, the abortion laws of virtually every state in the Union in *Roe* v. *Wade*. Although the outcries against legalizing abortion-on-demand were justified, equally as important in the decision was the fact that the Supreme Court fixed its opinion as irrevocable law across the nation (with no means of appeal of its decision except by constitutional amendment). Thomas Jefferson had long ago argued against such power:

> Nothing in the Constitution has given them [the Supreme Court] a right to decide for the Executive, more than the Executive to decide for them. The opinion which gives to the judges the right to decide

what laws are constitutional, and what not, not only for themselves in their own sphere of action, but for the Legislative and Executive also, in their spheres, would make the judiciary a despotic branch.[29]

Fifty years after *Marbury* the Supreme Court decided the *Dred Scott* case,[30] in which it held a second act of Congress unconstitutional. In this case the Supreme Court held that a black person was chattel property, and that Congress could not bar slavery from the newly established territories. Therefore, the Missouri Compromise (which barred slavery in the unorganized territory that later became the northwestern and midwestern states) was unconstitutional. In his First Inaugural Address in 1861, in partial response to the Dred Scott decision, Abraham Lincoln noted that "the candid citizen must confess that if the policy of the Government upon vital questions affecting the whole people is to be irrevocably fixed by decisions of the Supreme Court, . . . the people will have ceased to be their own rulers, having to that extent practically resigned their Government into the hands of that eminent tribunal."[31]

We have not heeded the advice of Jefferson and Lincoln. Consequently, we have paid dearly for it. We are now at the mercy of the nine people who sit on the Supreme Court. And as *Roe* v. *Wade* indicates they have power over life and death.

Chapter Five

The Legal Revolution

Even to the casual observer it should be obvious that a legal revolution has occurred. It came quietly. It was clear that it was coming, but there was little resistance.

This revolution is possibly best illustrated by what is occurring through the courts today, especially the federal courts. Although what follows in this book is critical of the direction the federal judiciary has taken, the author realizes that the federal courts, when they operate constitutionally, are an asset to the administration of justice. The federal courts have been a positive influence in many cases. There are federal judges who undoubtedly regret the spread of humanism and have been successful in dispensing justice in terms of the Constitution. Unfortunately, I feel that in recent years the negative consequences of the federal judiciary outweigh the positive results. In this book I intentionally focus on the negative aspects, with hopes of raising an awareness that will provide solutions.

The students of Christopher Langdell's thesis that basic law is made through court decisions now sit on the courts of our land. Instead of waiting patiently for the natural flow of evolution, the courts have become active in their development of the law. Judicial activism is now a recognized fact. The courts make law. The written Constitution has little value except as a shibboleth used by the courts to justify their intrusions into the lives of the people.

Through this activist approach, the Supreme Court has disturbed long-standing institutions in American society. James A. Kidney, associate editor of *U.S. News & World Report,* has commented: "Despite growing unease among the public and legal experts, judges . . . are reaching into areas once considered the exclusive preserve of legislators, public administrators and the family."[1]

For example, in 1962 and 1963 the Court ruled that devotional prayer and Bible reading were unconstitutional practices in the state-supported public schools. One may wonder if these decisions contributed to the apparent deterioration in the quality of American public education. Such deterioration is certainly consistent with the removal of the moral and ethical force for good, which had been present in the form of prayer, Bible reading, and the recognition of man's relationship to God. Although it is oversimplistic to lay the blame at the door of these rulings, it must be recognized that the Court's decisions gave strong support to other humanistic infiltration (and dominance) in public education.[2]

The Supreme Court's 1973 abortion decision was an instance of judicial activism. With no true constitutional basis, the Court fashioned out a national law on abortion. It held that pregnant women have a "right" to abortion. There is no such right in the Constitution. The Court created it.

Congressman John Ashbrook notes further examples of judicial activism:

> In Atlanta, parents, outraged by "head shops" pushing drug paraphernalia aimed at youngsters, persuaded the Georgia legislature to outlaw such sales. But . . . a federal judge voided the law as "vague," even though similar wording had been upheld in laws outlawing counterfeiting, gambling and bootlegging paraphernalia. So drug paraphernalia reappeared in the head shops.
>
> Outside Albany, New York, high school students sought

to hold a voluntary prayer session in their classrooms before the start of the school day. Outlawing the practice as "too dangerous to permit," federal judge Irving R. Kaufman argued that it "might indicate the state has placed its imprimatur on a particular religious creed.[3]

The list goes on and on.

All authority has virtually been transferred to a state institution: the

"I wouldn't want this to get around, but my wife's going to have a baby!"

Supreme Court and its inferior federal courts. The courts, under the present system of arbitrary absolutes, have power over every facet of our lives—even our life and death itself.

This is *statism,* the concentration of power in the hands of a centralized state. It was statism that the framers feared. It was statism that brought them into conflict with Great Britain. Now statism has reared its head in our time, and is finding its expression in varying forms through the state and its agencies. The courts as agencies of the civil government have in large part transformed the loose confederation of states, which once existed in America, into a highly centralized bureaucracy where, instead of law, the ever-changing opinions of men reign supreme.

A Judicial Philosophy

The modern sociological, judicial philosophy of Langdell, Holmes, and others has truly come home. Like icons they stand staring over the shoulders of those who wield the power in the courtrooms today. The federal judges, appointed for life, exercise a dominating influence in nearly every facet of American life. They make law and enforce it, functions which were never intended to be the province of the courts ´

This rise of activism didn't happen overnight. It wasn't until the sixties and seventies that the federal court system assumed an open, active role in what appeared to be a revolution in American culture. This was, in part, a reflection of what was happening in the streets and on the university campuses.

Unfortunately now a significant number of the judges who sit on the federal courts are activists. Instead of deciding the issue before them in a particular case, they often go beyond the situation and dictate new rules or law. Added to this was the sharp surge in the appointment of activist judges when President Jimmy Carter signed the Omnibus Judgeship Act of 1978 into law.

This act created 152 new federal judgeships, an increase of nearly one-third, in the 525 federal court judgeships that existed in the United States prior to the passage of this act. Before President Carter had left office in 1981, he had appointed nearly all of the allotted 152 judges. An article in *U.S. News & World Report* concerning Carter's federal court appointments commented that the "newcomers are apt to give the Federal courts a markedly more activist approach to law. The shift comes at a time when some scholars and other critics are warning that the judiciary has gone too far in assuming executive and legislative power over a side array of public policy matters."[4]

In recent years much concern has been voiced over the role of federal judges as they operate in American society. With "the octopus-like growth of the government, and United States Supreme Court decisions expanding the parameters of the Constitution, U. S. District judges—all appointed for life—are being called upon to make decisions that touch every facet of our lives,"[5] complained managing editor Edward Whelan in the *Cleveland Magazine*. As another journalist has noted, the courts "have entered the classrooms to second-guess teachers and school officials with decisions overturning the suspension of students in which constitutional rights are being extended to minors battling adult authority."[6] The federal courts have decided everything from length of hair to the proper dress attire of students to what books school boards may include in school libraries.

Noting the potentiality of the Carter appointments, a columnist for the *Washington Post* said: "A president can be elected to no more than two terms. Nevertheless, Jimmy Carter—even should he last only one term in the White House—has the power to shape the lives of Americans for years to come through the federal courts. . . . What happens to our society is being determined by appointees not subject to our vote."[7]

Appointments to the federal judiciary are for life. Once an appointment is made, it by and large irrevocably fixes a pattern of decision making. It is virtually impossible to have a federal judge removed. In fact in the two hundred years since the ratification of the Constitution only five federal

"Am I apathetic about the election? What election?"

judges have been impeached, and of those five, only two have been convicted. It is probable that the current activist posture will continue in the courts for some time.

Moreover, the erosion of the constitutional process will continue. In fact, elected officials have less and less power in the face of an imperial judiciary. Those who place hope in changing the country through the election of officials must realize that a back door now exists in the political process. It stands wide open to the manipulation of the entire country through nonelected, permanent government officials who are virtually free to alter the face of the nation as radically as they choose.

By constitutional authority, the Senate confirms judicial appointments made by the president. Unfortunately in some cases Senate confirmation has become little more than a "rubber stamp." This must say something about a Congress that has allowed the judicial system to assume its legislative function and has, in many instances, deferred to the courts in its constitutional duty of lawmaking.

However, many of the Carter appointments were contested in the Senate, but to no avail. One controversial appointment was that of Patricia Wald to the Circuit Court of Appeals for Washington, D. C. This court has been termed "the second most important court in the nation" because it literally looks over how the country is run.[8] Mrs. Wald, a member of the Board of Editors of the *American Bar Association Journal*, had no prior judicial experience before her appointment was made. She has, however, been very vocal on various issues, especially in the areas of children's rights.

Comparing the "institution of children" to the "institution of slavery," Patricia Wald advocates that children need legal representation independent of their parents.[9] In a 1976 article in the *Journal of the Child Welfare League of America* she wrote: "In situations where the interests of the child and parents are likely to conflict and a serious adverse impact on the child is likely to be the consequence of unilateral parental actions, the child's interests deserve representation by an independent advocate before a neutral decision maker. . . . A child should have access to free or paid legal services on a confidential basis to discuss his personal grievances."[10]

Rejecting the design of the biblical family, Wald argues for the "equality of all family members."[11] Concerning school and work, Wald advocates: "From the age of seven on, a youth should be able to exercise increasing control over his choice of school and work or, at the very least, to participate fully in making decisions affecting this vital area of life. . . ."[12]

On medical care, Wald states that "[c]ertainly from 12 on, a youth ought to be able to seek medical or psychiatric care of his own."[13] Concerning parental notification of such care, Patricia Wald notes: "In some instances (contraception, abortion, drugs, VD, psychiatric help) disclosure may spell disastrous consequences for the child within his family and thus deter him from ever seeking help. Incest, a psychotic parent, or even a *frantically moralistic one* [emphasis added], are cases in point."[14]

To eliminate confusion between parental rights and children's rights concerning medical care, Wald proposes legislation "vesting rights to engage in such services in youth, rather than in their parents."[15] In claiming the need for an "emancipation proclamation . . . for teenage children,"[16] Wald states that "youth ought presumptively to enjoy a whole range of civil rights."[17]

During Wald's confirmation hearings before the United States Senate, Senator Gordon Humphrey of New Hampshire said:

> Wald, who belongs to that activist band known as "child advocates" and who terms herself a "fierce" civil-libertarian, wants to fundamentally change the American family. . . . the Wald nomination is a case which is outrageous. Here is a nominee who would radically alter the traditional family structure by virtually abolishing parental authority and who would empower a child to formally

"I love you, Cindy. . . . Will you marry me for a year or two?"

> challenge his parents whenever in the child's opinion the parents were violating his civil rights. Here is a nominee who would give political power to mere children. . . . Sweden recently passed a law prohibiting parents from spanking their children or even scolding them. Indeed, the Government has prepared television spots to inform children of their right to disobey their parents. Is that what we want in our country?[18]

Despite the protestations, Patricia Wald was confirmed by the Senate and now sits on the United States Circuit Court of Appeals.[19]

The great danger in the advocacy of children's "rights" is the devastating impact it can have on the traditional family. The importance of the family as the basic institution in society cannot be underscored enough. The family emerges from the pages of the Bible as the basic unit. In the family man first learns religion and self-government and his basic world view.

Not only does the family prepare future citizens and leaders, but traditionally it has served as a buffer (a safety zone) between the individual and the state. It affords members of the family protection from total statist control. However, with the breakdown of family autonomy—accompanied by state interference into family affairs—the buffer is fading. If this continues the individual will be left naked against the state.

George Gilder, in answering the various feminist attacks on the family in *Sexual Suicide,* recognizes that "there has emerged no institution that can replace the family in turning children into civilized human beings or in retrieving the wreckage of our current disorder."[20] In the face of the impending doom that is engulfing American society, Gilder writes that the family "is most indispensable to overcoming our present social crisis."[21] If children have rights independent of parents, an obvious conflict will exist within this unit.

An illustration of this is found in the case of *In re Snyder,* a 1975 case decided by the Washington Supreme Court. In this case a fifteen-year-old girl who was antagonistic toward her parents asked a juvenile court to declare her incorrigible and place her in a foster home.

However, the girl had no police record and there was no evidence that she was incorrigible in the traditional meaning of the word. She had lived all her life with her natural parents in a typical middle class family. In an early phase of the case, the parents had been found to be "fit" parents in the statutory sense. But the family had experienced friction because of difference of opinion between the parents and the girl concerning her dating, her friends, and her desire to smoke.

The Washington Supreme Court framed the issue as "whether there is substantial evidence to support a finding that the parent-child relationship had dissipated to the point where parental control is lost and therefore Cynthia is incorrigible." Later the court ruled the girl was incorrigible because it said it had found a "total collapse" in the parent-child relationship.

The *Snyder* case implies that a dissatisfied child can be permitted, as any adult would, to leave the family at her own request. Cynthia Snyder decided that she preferred not to be subject to the authority of her parents, and her choice was upheld. This case is an argument for the proposition that a child can divorce (or at least achieve separation from) his or her parents on grounds of incompatibility.

The fact that these types of things are now happening should concern us, especially when someone such as Harvard law professor Laurence Tribe is arguing that when the parents "threaten the autonomous growth and expression of [family] members . . ." there is no longer any reason to continue to protect family authority.[22] Who is going to determine when children are "threatened by the family"? In the humanistic society, the state will become the parent, and all family members will be its creatures.[23]

The child is thus not required to possess an allegiance to or alliance with the family, but can seek an alliance with the state. In such an instance, the

"I'll tell you one thing. As soon as I'm thirteen I'm gonna stop!"

child becomes an informer for the government over and against the parents much in the same vein as is depicted in George Orwell's *1984*. This paragraph from his book may all too soon be possible:

> The family could not actually be abolished, and, indeed, people were encouraged to be fond of their children . . . . The children, on the other hand, were systematically turned against their parents and taught to spy on them and report their deviation. The family had become in effect an extention of the Thought Police. It was a device by means of which everyone could be surrounded night and day by informers who knew him intimately.[24]

It is no coincidence that the family is attacked by those who object to ''the limits and restrictions placed on their personal freedom of choice'' by Christian values and absolutes. They obviously realize what countries like the Soviet Union have known for years: If one can destroy the traditional family unit—set child against parent and give the ultimate authority in child rearing to the state—the basic institution that stands between total state control of the citizenry is eradicated. And the freedom of thought passed down by the family from generation to generation is lost.

All this is not to say that children do not have rights, but that the advocacy of children's rights, apart from the biblical base, could lead to the destruction of the family unit. Of course, children who are physically abused or otherwise mistreated should have the protection of the law. In fact, the church should strive toward establishing programs to care for and protect such children.

With the humanist makeup of the Supreme Court and lower federal courts, many are concerned that the United States is coming perilously close to enacting a federal judicial policy that is antagonistic toward Judeo-Christian theism as a whole. This would mean that attorneys advancing arguments in support of Christian values would find it extremely difficult to prevail before such courts. Clearly, the activist nature of the federal courts would militate against an impartial hearing on issues of Christian concern.

The Legiscourt

The judicial action in the last two decades ''adds up to a radical transformation of the role and function of the judiciary in American life,'' remarks Harvard law professor Abram Chayes. ''Its chief function now is as a catalyst of social change with judges acting as planners of large scale.''[25]

Whether particular decisions are just is not the ultimate issue. The key to a constitutional government is that the people supposedly possess a written document to which an appeal can be made against statist interference. A written constitution is in itself a restriction and limitation on the state. But if the Constitution can be disregarded or ''interpreted'' to fit the social desires of a particular judge, then its value as a governing document is greatly diminished, and the power of the state, acting through its judge, is increased.

Unfortunately many of the American people accept the court system's usurpation of rights. As Professor William Forrester, former dean of the Cornell Law School, aptly noted: ''The Court has assumed, gradually, the role of deciding the problems on its own and . . . the American people and their selected officials gradually have accepted the Court as the political instrument for lawmaking.''[26]

The research of Dr. Peter A. J. Adam, an associate professor of pediatrics at Case Western Reserve University, shows how far a Supreme Court decision can be taken. Six months after *Roe* v. *Wade* Dr. Adam reported to the American Pediatric Research Society on research he and his associates had conducted on twelve babies who had been born alive by hysterotomy abortion up to twenty weeks. These men took the tiny babies and cut off their heads—decapitated the babies and cannulated the internal carotid arteries (that is, a tube was placed in the main artery feeding the brain). They kept the diminutive heads alive, much as the Russians kept the dogs' heads alive in the 1950s. Take note of Dr. Adam's retort to criticism:

> Once society's declared the fetus dead, and abrogated its rights, I don't see any ethical problem. . . . Whose right are we going to protect, once we've decided the fetus won't live?[27]

In making a national law on abortion in *Roe* v. *Wade,* the Supreme Court assumed a power to legislate. Bob Woodward and Scott Armstrong clearly recognized the legislative implications of *Roe* in their book, *The Brethren:*

> The clerks in most chambers were surprised to see the Justices, particularly Blackmun, so openly brokering their decision like a group of legislators. There was a certain reasonableness to the draft [opinion], some of them thought. But it derived more from medical and social policy than from constitutional law. There was something embarrassing and dishonest about this whole process. It left the Court claiming that the Constitution drew certain lines at trimesters and viability. The Court was going to make medical policy and force it on the states. As a practical matter, it was not a bad solution. As a constitutional matter, it was absurd. The draft was referred to by some clerks as Harry's abortion.[28]

The fact that the Supreme Court as well as the lower federal courts make legislation through court decisions is disturbing when the Constitution in Article 1 gives the authority to make laws only to the federal legislature. In describing the Supreme Court as a "Legiscourt" Dean Forrester states:

> We have failed to see that the Supreme Court has evolved into a new institution—one that is even more unique and unprecedented than commonly supposed. Indeed, the institution can no longer be

described with accuracy as a court, in the customary sense. Unlike a court, *its primary function is not judicial but legislative. It is a governing body* [emphasis added] in the sense that it makes the basic policy decisions of the nation, selects among the competing values of our society, and administers and executes the directions it chooses in political, social, and ethical matters. It has become the major societal agency for reform.[29]

Forrester goes on to note that this power "is legitimate because it has been accepted implicitly or at least acquiesced to by the American people as well as by the other departments of government and the states."[30] If the majority agrees, according to Forrester, then an unconstitutional act is made legitimate.

Finally, in Forrester's analysis he states, "note well that it is not an act of condemnation or disapproval to say that the institution is not primarily a court. It is a matter of healthy recognition that a new kind of governmental institution has evolved—one probably unique in the history of governmental institutions."[31] Thus Forrester, too, approves the usurpation of power he describes.

Such power is wrong historically. It runs contrary to the philosophy of such men as William Blackstone and John Marshall. It is a return to something closely akin to the divine right of kings, wherein the king's word was law—except now it is not the king but a different elite, the Court, acting arbitrarily. The implication is that law becomes law for the sake of the elite.

The Collective Conscience

It is clear that the Supreme Court has become the final arbiter of social issues on a national level. This is sociological jurisprudence in its purest form. As constitutional authority Alpheus Mason notes, the Supreme Court sits as a "super-legislature" in safeguarding certain rights.[32] The Supreme Court and lower federal courts now announce policies to which the country must align itself. From the lowest level state courts to the federal appellate courts, the Supreme Court's word is law.

Some legal scholars would have the Court serve as a "national conscience"* and, therefore, as "an educational body [that] teaches in a vital national seminar."[33] Justice Arthur Goldberg in a decision in 1965 articulated the national conscience doctrine: "In determining which rights are funda-

---

*This concept is similar to Jean-Jacques Rousseau's theory of the "general will" which is discussed in the Appendix, Essay I.

mental, judges are not left at large to decide cases in light of their personal and private notions. Rather, they must look to the 'traditions and (collective) conscience of our people'."[34]

But the Court's reading of the general will has resulted in cruelty and injustice. Consider the Japanese relocation cases, in which the Supreme Court during World War II upheld so-called "war powers" under the Constitution. In reacting to a West Coast hysteria concerning the Japanese and the possibility of sabotage, the Court read the nation's conscience and allowed the American military to herd 70,000 Japanese Americans, many of whom were

"Hey, I know how we can shut them down. . . . Let's tell the Supreme Court the dancers always open their act with prayer!"

American citizens, into places that were, in reality, concentration camps.[35] Many of those carted away to Relocation Authority camps were aged persons as well as children.[36]

Yale law professor Eugene Rostow termed the action by the federal government as one of "the worst blows our liberties" have ever sustained.[37] Professor Rostow wrote:

> They were arrested in any area where the courts were open, and freely functioning. They were held under prison conditions in uncomfortable camps, far from their homes, and for lengthy periods—several years in many cases. If found "disloyal" in

administrative proceedings they were confined indefinitely, although no statute makes "disloyalty" a crime . . . [38]

Rostow then went on to say that this "step converts a piece of war-time folly into a political doctrine, and a permanent part of the law."[39]

Lieutenant General J. L. DeWitt, who issued the order to relocate Japanese citizens, said that the Japanese citizens living on the Pacific Coast were an enemy race and that "we must worry about the Japanese all the time until he is wiped off the map. Sabotage and espionage will make problems as long as he is allowed in this area—problems which I don't want to have to worry about."[40]

Interestingly enough, through 1945, when this order was issued, no resident Japanese Americans had been convicted of sabotage or espionage while many white persons had been arrested and convicted as Japanese agents.[41] Being fully cognizant of these facts, the Supreme Court acquiesced to setting what amounts to a dreadful precedent for racial concentration camps. Why? Because the Supreme Court deemed this to be the general will.

The Guardians

The legal academe once castigated the Court for its inaction—during the era when the Court took a laissez-faire approach to law. Professor Arthur Sutherland explained that between 1920 and 1940 the academe "viewed the federal judiciary with dismay" and was "deeply imbued with faith in majorities." However, a "change of political theory developed" between 1938 and 1948, because of "Hitler's popularity among the German people, public support of the Un-American Activities Committee and McCarthy Hearings," and so on. Suddenly it was realized that "unrestricted majorities could be as tyrannical as wicked oligarchs."[42]

Because of the failure of the national conscience to be as enlightened as the judges, the Court now had to decide issues as an elite for the betterment of man. In essence, then, Supreme Court justices have come to view themselves as the guardians of society—philosopher kings, so to speak. This led Archibald Cox to remark that the Warren Court (named after Chief Justice Earl Warren) "behaved even more like a Council of Wise Men and less like a Court."[43] In *The Supreme Court Under Earl Warren* Leonard Levy observed that to "both the Court's admirers and critics . . . the Justices seemed to consider themselves as movers and shapers of the country's destiny rather than as impersonal spokesmen for the law."[44]

Justice Hugo Black in his later years stated that "any broad unlimited power to hold laws unconstitutional because they offend what this Court conceives to be the 'conscience of our people' . . . was not given by the Framers, but rather has been bestowed on the Court by the Court."[45] Early in his career, Justice Black himself had been characterized as an "overpowering advocate" who believed that he "had a mission to impose his convictions on the nation."[46] However, in the latter part of his career, Black saw that the judicial excesses were leading to the embodiment of all power and authority in the Supreme Court. The Court and lower federal courts would become active participants in formulating the law themselves. In the end the Supreme Court becomes the Constitution.

"How do I know this is a good honest bribe and not one of those underhanded Abscam things?"

The New Oligarchy
The men who sit on the federal judiciary are not elected but are appointed by the president to sit on the courts for life. They become in effect a form of permanent government—an oligarchy that answers to no one.

These new rulers, however, have stepped outside the written Constitution to make fiat law. James Madison, who played a major role in the drafting of the Constitution, said that those "who overleap the great barrier which defends the rights of the people . . . are tyrants."[47] British historian Edward Gibbon wrote in *The History of the Decline and Fall of the Roman Empire* that "the discretion of the judge is the first engine of tyranny."

I fear that power in government has indeed passed to those who act tyrannically. The decision in *Roe* v. *Wade* should have raised the red flag. Law, like clay, can be molded to fit the desires of the judge.

The disregard of the Constitution by the Supreme Court has even been passed on to the other branches of government. In the Watergate scandal Donald E. Santarelli, an associate deputy attorney general in the Nixon administration, described himself as in charge of "an idea shop," which worked "on concepts" and "plans" for the president. He stated:

> [The] Constitution is flexible. . . . Your point of view depends on whether you are winning. The Constitution isn't the real issue in this; it is how you want to *run the country,* and achieve national goals. The language of the Constitution is not at issue. It is what you can interpret it to mean in light of modern needs. In talking about a "Constitutional crisis" we are not grappling with the real needs of running the country but are using the issues for the self-serving purpose of striking a new balance of power. . . . Today, the whole Constitution is up for grabs.[48]

An attorney, Mr. Santarelli was in all probability expressing a position he had learned in law school, and which the Supreme Court had been articulating in their practice for some time.

All authority has passed to a centralized federal bureaucracy. The state, not the law protecting the individual, is supreme. This is statism. The centralized state has become in many ways the great provider as well as the arbiter of what values are important and should be provided to the masses. Self-government by the people in the United States has literally been wrested from them by a legislating judiciary. The door has been opened to the massive federal machine, and it will continue to grow and enlarge because its humanistic base philosophically cannot control it. The door to statism cannot be closed unless the foundation is altered.

There is no longer consent of the governed. The governed don't have a chance to consent or even object. As Professor Raoul Berger asks: "How long can public respect for the Court [as well as all courts], on which its power ultimately depends, survive if the people become aware that the tribunal which condemns the acts of others as unconstitutional is itself acting unconstitutionally?"[49]

In this respect, Berger pleads: "Return the government to the people. They have a right to govern themselves and to make their own mistakes."[50]

Chapter Six

What
Is the
Higher Law?

Law in the Judeo-Christian sense implies something more than form. Law has content in the eternal sense. It has a reference point. Like a ship that is anchored, law cannot stray far from its mooring. If the anchor chain breaks, however, the ship drifts to and fro. Such is the current state of law in our country.

Law in the true sense is bibliocentric, concerned with justice in terms of the Creator's revelation. Of course, not all issues that should be covered by the law are areas of black and white. Fallen men disagree as to what the Bible says about certain subjects. However, the principles of the Bible are reference points upon which law may be formulated. Although men may disagree, it does not mean that they cannot assemble and formulate law, which is not in contradiction to the Bible.

The Greeks also envisioned a higher law, but it was based in nature, which being both mute and fallen cannot be an effective base to law.* Nature, especially as perceived in the light of evolution, is not normative, and, therefore, cannot provide an absolute. It is both cruel and noncruel; it contains irregularities as well as regularities.

The older natural law was not based on nature alone, at least not in the Christian era. It was based on the doctrine of Creation, the conviction that an all-wise Creator had established the world and its order. The difficulty today is that the doctrine of Creation and of the Creator has been denied. "Nature" in Jefferson's sense has been replaced with an evolutionary process. What is "unnatural" at one point in time—such as infanticide or euthanasia—may be "natural" at another. Law based in nature is then like a ship without an anchor. It is destined for shipwreck.

The bottom line is that man's law must have its origin in God's revelation. Any law that contradicts biblical revelation is illegitimate. Illegitimate law, as the colonists protested to King George, was "of none effect." After all, it is the Creator who endows man with rights, which the law is to protect. Succinctly put, there is a law, a system of absolutes, derived from biblical principles that transcends man and his institutions. It existed before man and will exist after him.

However, I do not mean to imply that the United States should be a theocracy (government of a state by immediate divine guidance). The founding fathers made clear in the First Amendment that they were not suggesting a theocracy. As Francis Schaeffer writes in *A Christian Manifesto*:

> In the New Testament, with the church being made up of Jews and Gentiles, and spreading over all the known world from India to Spain in one generation, the church was its own entity. There is no New Testament basis for a linking of church and state until Christ, the King, returns. The whole "Constantine mentality" . . . making Christianity the official state religion opened the way for confusion up till our own day. . . . We must not confuse the Kingdom of God with our country. To say it another way: "We should not wrap Christianity in our national flag. . . ." None of this, however, changes the fact that the United States was founded upon a Christian consensus, nor that we today should bring Judeo-Christian principles into play in regard to government. But that is very different from a theocracy in name or in fact.[1]

*Law and nature are discussed in detail in the Appendix, Essay I.

The Three Basic Law Systems

Essentially societies utilize and are based on three types of law systems, all of which are sustained by a common thread—the higher law seen dimly in nature and expressed plainly in the Bible.

The first type of law is the *fundamental law* upon which the culture and society are established. This fundamental law may be equated with the "higher law," which should be "the Laws of Nature and of Nature's God." The higher law is clearly expressed in God's revelation as ultimately found in the Bible. In this the higher law has its sustenance.

The second type of law, *constitutional law,* provides the form of civil government to protect the God-given rights of the people. The people can base their institutions upon constitutional law, in conjunction with the higher or fundamental law. Although the Constitution is undergirded by an absolute value system, it is not a source of ultimate values.

"The Constitution is an instrument whereby fundamental values can be protected, defining procedures, principles, and methods whereby government can function to allow the people to give content to their lives," says Harold O. J. Brown in *The Reconstruction of the Republic.* "But the Constitution itself cannot give that content."[2]

The Declaration of Independence, by contrast, does express ultimate values. It explicitly witnesses to "the Laws of Nature and of Nature's God" as the presupposition upon which the emerging nation is to be founded. Not even the Declaration, of course, is the ultimate source of values. The Declaration, which explicitly witnesses to what we have called the higher law, thus forms the necessary bridge to the Constitution. And, as pointed out in detail in chapter eight, the higher law values of the Declaration are incorporated into the Constitution by its preamble.

If we recognize that the Constitution presupposes the Declaration and the higher, fundamental law to which the Declaration witnesses, then we will understand the Constitution and it will serve us well. Such biblical principles as federalism, separation of powers, limited authority, and liberty of conscience found in the Constitution then make sense.* They did not arise from a vacuum. If we see the Constitution as standing alone, and forget or deny that it presupposes the Declaration, we will misunderstand the Constitution and allow it to become a vehicle for the exercise of tyranny over us. The difference between seeing the Constitution as based on the Declaration and seeing it as standing entirely autonomous is analogous to the difference between a constitutional monarch such as the Queen of England and an absolute dictator such as Joseph Stalin.

Third, there are laws enacted by the political body having legislative power. The very term *legislator* means not one who makes laws but one who moves them—from the divine law written in nature or in the Bible into the statutes and law codes of a particular society. Just as a translator is supposed to faithfully move the meaning from the original language into the new one, so the legislator is to translate laws, not make new ones. When legislation loses sight of its fundamental limitation (the fact that it is to be carried out in reference to the fundamental, higher law) it becomes lawmaking.

Whether laws are pronounced by a monarch, an elite, or a democratic assembly, it is vitally important to preserve the classic principle: "Law is found, not made." In the last analysis, we would be far freer under an absolute monarch who saw his authority as subject to God's law in the Bible and in nature than under a democratically elected assembly that took the arbitrary will of the majority as its highest value.

If the legislative power is performed in reference to the fundamental law, the person acting as an elected representative should enact no law that contradicts the higher law. The representative is obliged to follow the mandates of the higher law even if it means contravening the claims of a majority. This check is a hedge against majoritarianism or mob rule. The system just does not work unless this common thread or reference point is maintained.

The Common Law and the Ten Commandments
Essentially common law is an age-old doctrine that developed by way of court decisions that applied the principles of the Bible to everyday situations. Judges simply decided their cases, often by making explicit reference to the Bible but virtually always within a framework of biblical values. Out of these cases rules were established that governed future cases.

The common law was important in the constitutional sense in that it was incorporated into the Constitution by direct reference in the Seventh Amendment. This amendment reads: "In suits at common law, where the value in controversy shall exceed twenty dollars, the right of trial by jury, shall be preserved; and no fact tried by jury, shall be otherwise re-examined in any court of the United States than according to the rules of common law." By implication this means that the framers intended to be governed in practice as well as in principle by the higher law. There are numerous examples of the common or higher law being applied in court decisions by early American judges.*

To understand the common law, it is necessary to consider its foundation in some detail. The biblical prophet Isaiah (sixth/seventh century

*The common law is discussed in detail in the Appendix, Essay II.

B.C.) proclaimed: "For the Lord is our judge, the Lord is our lawgiver, the Lord is our king" (Isa. 33:22). And the Roman philosopher Cicero (106-43 B.C.) declared that first there is a universality in laws and, second, that the lawgiver is God. This is the Bible's position: the true God is the final lawgiver. Even the classical pagan understood the necessity of law being rooted in his concept of God—even if his gods were not sufficient.

The fact that this principle carried over into the early life of America is apparent by the natural way the summary of biblical law, the Ten Commandments, functioned as a pattern and a guide both in court decisions and in

the framing of individual pieces of legislation. Episcopalian theologian T. R. Ingram has observed that the reference point for the common law was in the Ten Commandments: "Christian men have always known that what we might call political liberty as part of all Christian liberty is a consequence of upholding the common law. . . . the Ten Commandments."[3]

In 1978 one state, Kentucky, sought to bring this realization home to its young citizens by requiring that the Ten Commandments be posted in its public school classrooms. The law required the following statement on these posters: "The secular application of the Ten Commandments is clearly seen in its adoption as the fundamental legal code of Western Civilization and the Common Law of the United States."

In a 1980 decision, however, the Supreme Court struck this law down as being in violation of the First Amendment's prohibition against establishing a religion. What it really violated, of course, was the justices' implicit claim that they are the sources of all fundamental values and have no higher standard over them. This case is an example of the Supreme Court's continuing repudiation of the biblical basis of American society.

Americans, who have been fed the false political dictum of the absolute separation of church and state, will probably be surprised to discover that even the first four of the Ten Commandments, those having to do with man's "religious" duty toward God, were once included without question in the law of America. They were not perceived as creating an unconstitutional "establishment of religion." In many states there were laws against blasphemy. Although we may not agree with such laws, they were originally designed not only to honor God but also to uphold the authority of the state to act with the Bible as its reference point.

The Old Testament Decalogue is two-pronged in that the first four commandments (three, according to the Lutheran and Catholic numbering) set forth man's duty toward God. The next six commandments establish man's duty toward man. Christ conveniently summed up the basic structure of the Ten Commandments in the Book of Matthew by saying: "Thou shalt love the Lord thy God with all thy heart, and with all thy soul, and with all thy mind. This is the first and great commandment. And the second is like unto it, Thou shalt love thy neighbor as thyself. On these two commandments hang all the law and the prophets" (Matt. 22:37-40). Both "tables" were carried over into the common law and embodied in many specific statutes.

The First Commandment mandates: "Thou shalt have no other gods before me." This includes gods of wood, stone, and metal. "Other gods" also refers to angels or spiritual powers or even to "superhuman" authorities, which rule over nations. It includes anything put in the place of God. Therefore, to allow any ruler absolute power is to worship another god contrary to this commandment.

As T. R. Ingram relates: "Tyranny may not be a specific crime but there are plenty of legal and procedural safeguards in any governmental system designed to keep the ruler within the bounds of right and justice so that tyranny is unlawful."[4] The word *tyrant* from the Greek term *tyrannos* means a secular ruler—one who rules without the sanctions of religious law and one whose authority religion had not established.[5] The First Commandment was incorporated into the American legal system with our acceptance of common law, which recognizes a higher law that prohibits the exercise of absolute, arbitrary power by the state.

Idolatry is condemned in the Second Commandment. "Thou shalt not make unto thee any graven image." This is a different offense from that detailed in the First Commandment, and it is best illustrated by pornography and vice. Idolatry is something that proceeds from man—a product of man's hands. We have no statutes against idol worship, but if we recognize that often idolatry deals with that which is sexually defiling, we see that forms of idolatry have been prohibited. Vice—homosexuality, prostitution—represent idolatry and can never be justified even if "legalized" by the state. Attempts to do so repudiate the Second Commandment.

"Mark my words. After putting prayer back in schools and getting creation science okayed, somebody will really louse us up by suggesting we follow the Ten Commandments!"

The Third Commandment in essence prohibits the taking of an oath in the name of God falsely.[6] "Thou shalt not take the name of the Lord thy God in vain." It basically identifies the crimes of perjury and heresy, both of which are false swearing. Ingram notes that "God himself is said to take vengeance on false swearing, but so does man. All authority would collapse if God's authority were not upheld in this way; there could be no court procedure, no hold on officials who violated their offices, no punishment of crime."[7] Even today people are expected to swear upon the Bible as they take their oath in court.

The Fourth Commandment declares a legal holiday, one day in seven to commemorate God's work of creation. "Remember the sabbath day, to keep it holy.'' Interestingly, it is a legal holiday on practically a universal level despite some variances. This rest from labor is an act of faith for the Christian, for it signified a belief that God is in control. No matter what the business, it will be accomplished through God's providential outworking in history. Unfortunately, in 1961 the Supreme Court secularized the religious significance of the day of rest by holding that the purpose of Sunday ''blue laws'' were not religious but practical: to set aside Sunday as a day of rest and recreation. Although these laws were Christian in origin, the Court ruled that the state had a legitimate secular goal in providing a day of rest for its citizens. The original purpose of such laws to honor the Creator was denied.

The mandate to ''honour thy father and thy mother'' is found in the Fifth Commandment. This principle may be included in the first table of the law because parents, father and mother, represent God's basic authority on earth in the form of the family, to honor them is to acknowledge God. It is a delegated authority with allegiance owed to the Creator. Parental authority is universally recognized in statute law around the world. However, it has been seriously eroded by American court decisions in recent years.

The second table (the last six commandments) concerns man's duty to man. Human beings are created in the image of God and, although flawed, they are to be treated with dignity and respect. Laws upholding human life, liberty, and property are included.

The second table contains laws against adultery, and thus establishes the sanctity of marriage and the necessity of keeping the bond within the family unit. There are also laws against bearing false witness, which is the dishonesty at law by which a man may be deprived of life, liberty, or property. Even covetousness is covered. Covetousness is internal, but when externalized, it results in the crime of fraud—that is, of depriving another of what is his by deceit or treachery.

Much of the criminal law of the state is outlined in the Ten Commandments. Today the law is moving away from this outline in two opposing directions. The first table of laws (which recognize the sovereignty of God and prohibit dishonoring him, his name, and his laws) is being abolished under the pretext that it represents an unconstitutional establishment of religion. In other words, things that should be criminal because they represent an affront to the very foundations of society and of justice are declared legitimate.

When fundamental principles of law are undermined, public confidence in law and public willingness to abide by law are also sapped. And when nonfundamental regulations are elevated to the status of solemn, absolutely binding law, public confidence and trust tend to disappear entirely.

The Eighteenth Amendment to the Constitution, the "Prohibition Amendment," ratified in 1919, is an example of this second development. Its counterpart in federal law, the Volstead Act, outlawed the possession of alcoholic beverages and also their manufacture. To enforce this amendment, the state authorities had to conduct numerous unlawful searches and seizures of property.

However, under the common law it was a punishable offense for anyone unlawfully to seize or take what belonged to another. Thus it was even unlawful for police authorities to put a man under arrest without an arrest

"Good news. . . . I whittled it down to where you should only get two and a half years!"

warrant or personal knowledge of a criminal act. In the prohibition era, however, numerous police raids on private property were conducted—sometimes on mere suspicion. The result was an intuitive recognition by the people that they no longer enjoyed the protection of the law. Gangsterism was the result. There was a collapse of respect for law provoked by an exercise of unlawful statist power.

The contemporary counterpart to the prohibition era is the Internal Revenue Service's wide sway of authority to conduct searches and seizures without warrants. The Internal Revenue Code itself is virtually unenforceable except by force. This has resulted in a widespread tax revolt movement. *Tax Revolt 1980: A How-To Guide* by Sheldon Engelmayer and Robert Wagman is one of a number of books written in recent years to foster a tax revolt. The IRS has responded to resistance with police state tactics. Again, the people intuitively recognize they no longer enjoy the protection of the law. Thus there is wholesale evasion of the law.

The Ten Commandments embody the basic principles upon which the laws necessary to keep peace and order can be structured. They were the absolute reference point under the common or higher law, and in most cases, the judge was compelled to identify the Ten Commandments and apply them.

Chapter Seven

A Law
Unto
Themselves

Before God revealed the Ten Commandments and the rest of the written law, Moses judged the people of Israel according to the unwritten or higher law of God. The people brought their disputes to Moses, and he resolved those disputes: first, by making known the laws of God, then by validating those rules as the living prophet or oracle of God. On these two principles Moses, prompted by his father-in-law Jethro, established a judicial system for the new nation of Israel (Exod. 18:13-26). "Sir William Blackstone justified the common law judicial system of England on the same principles,"[1] wrote professor Herbert Titus.

Blackstone wrote in his *Commentaries* that, "The common law of England is an 'unwritten law' (or higher law) made known and validated by judges."[2] Consequently, Blackstone did not include judges in his list of lawmakers,[3] but placed judges in a special category as "the depositories of the laws; the living oracles . . . who are bound by an oath to decide according to the law of the land."[4]

Guardian of the Covenant

From the example of Moses and Samuel as judges in the Old Testament, we find a biblical pattern for the judicial office. In Moses' time the judge resolved disputes among the people at their request according to the law of God. After the appointment of a king for Israel, the judge interpreted and applied the law of the covenant and specific legislative acts. As a judge, Samuel was the guardian of the covenant that had been made with Saul as king. In fact, it was Samuel who drafted the covenant, which set forth "the manner of the kingdom" and "the rights and duties of the Kingship" (1 Sam. 10: 25). This covenantal basis of governmental authority was adopted and urged by Samuel Rutherford in *Lex, Rex,* and was carried to America by the early pilgrims.

Early in the history of the United States, Chief Justice John Marshall in *Marbury* v. *Madison* established the authority of the Supreme Court and other courts to review the constitutionality of legislative and executive acts. The Supreme Court became the guardian of the covenant (or Constitution) in the days of President Thomas Jefferson as Samuel had been in the days of Saul. Our Constitution is a covenant between the people (collectively in the states) and the United States government.

In *Marbury* Marshall stressed: "The government of the United States has been emphatically termed a government of laws, and not of men." From this, Marshall argued that the Supreme Court must interpret and apply the law, and if a law contradicts the basic covenant (that is, the Constitution), then the law should fall. In this way, the Court was the guardian of the written law, a written law interpreted in light of the higher law.

However, once the Court lost its mission to interpret the covenant in light of the higher law, then what was a government of laws became a government of men. The covenant became what the judges wanted it to say. A document written to secure liberty is now sometimes interpreted to restrict freedom. Every man is doing what is right in his own eyes, just as the Israelites did in the last three chapters of the Book of Judges. This is a pretense of deity.

Unlike today, the idea of the higher law was assumed by the late eighteenth- and early nineteenth-century American judiciary. Justice was seen in terms of the higher law and its application in the everyday life of the people. As a consequence, in early America the courts were commonly referred to as *courts of justice,* not courts of law—the distinction being between God's law and man's law as applied in the courtroom. Because the Bible was the final authority, the practice of requiring witnesses to take an oath on the Bible before testifying was begun. However, with the rise of sociological law and the loss of biblical absolutes, the courts have become courts of law where man's law is the final authority. As a consequence, the courts are no longer guardians of the covenant, but are, instead, arbitrary decision makers.

The judge stands in a unique position in any society. He is to administer justice. This is the demand of the higher law. For example, the Bible in the nineteenth chapter of Leviticus states:

> Ye shall do no unrighteousness in judgment: thou shalt not respect the person of the poor, nor honour the person of the mighty: but in righteousness shalt thou judge thy neighbour (verse 15).

The judge must not show favoritism to either the rich or the poor. He is to be just in terms of the higher law. The judge is not to be an activist, as are many contemporary jurists. Again, in the sixteenth chapter of the Book of Deuteronomy (verse 19) the higher law admonishes that judges "not respect persons . . ." Why? The Bible makes it explicit in Paul's Epistle to the Romans: "For there is no respect of persons with God" (2:11).

Reformation leader Martin Luther observed that the Creator "lays down his rule to . . . judges and officers: they are to judge justly, that is, according to the Law of God and not according to their own understanding."[5] The judge thus has a reference point he must follow, and he must not proceed under his "own understanding." Since the judge, as a civil officer, must continually deal with various issues affecting the whole person, the necessity for impartiality in all matters is always before him.

A New Deity

Because man is fallen and thus flawed, even the most sincere judge will be fallible and erring. However, with a reference point in the higher law, the judge has a basis upon which to decide without total reliance on his fallen nature. In contrast, the judge who aligns himself with the sociological view is left to his own opinion and, too often, will represent a faction or class.

In Romans 13:1-4 the apostle Paul declares that all civil authorities are ministers of God. The judge, then, as a civil authority is charged by the Bible to use the higher law as his ultimate reference point. If, in fact, the court is to act as a minister of God, then every court could be considered a religious establishment. Any legal system, humanistic or Christian, necessarily has a kind of "religious" foundation.

All pronouncements of right and wrong—laws—are, after all, moral concerns. Such issues have always been at their base religious, even if this religion is the belief system of materialism, humanism, and rationalism. As such, a moral order will maintain that foundation by some form of hostility, subtle or otherwise, to any other religious moral order. Real tolerance among religious systems (in the sense of one system accepting another as equally true) is, as history teaches, nonexistent. For this reason, the new "religion" of secular humanism cannot and will not be tolerant of the biblical, Judeo-Christian values still embodied in the American legal and social structure. As Professor Harvey Cox insists, humanism is a closed system: It will not tolerate alternative points of view.

But man cannot escape his religiousness. This principle is inherent in the Second Commandment, prohibiting idolatry. In it the concern is not with atheism but with the fact that all men, Christian or not, seek something outside themselves to deify. As Calvin points out, men would rather worship an idol than admit that they have no knowledge of God.

One contemporary idol is humanity itself or some portion of humanity—such as women in what we may call the "religion" of feminism, children in the "religion" of child rights, profit in the "religion" of capitalism, or whatever else has been put in the place of a real and living faith by secular humanists. In this vein, Mao Tse-Tung could proclaim: "Our God is none other than the masses of the Chinese people."[6]

The concept of man's naturally religious orientation is looked upon with some scorn by the secularist who thinks himself beyond such superstition. But this disdain is inappropriate. The person who calls himself a secularist, or even an atheist, may suppose that the secular label affords him an air of objectivity and impartiality. We must note, however, that even an atheist must exercise "faith" in order to assert that there is no God. If we cannot prove that God is there, no one can prove that he isn't. It is amusing that well-known atheists such as Madalyn Murray O'Hair travel back and forth across America proclaiming that there is no God. She expends a great deal of effort in fighting something that supposedly doesn't exist. This, too, is an act of "faith."

The Supreme Court assumes a posture of objectivity. It would like us to believe that it is somehow above the issues. In the various cases in which the Court has ruled that Judeo-Christian traditions are unconstitutional in public places, it has with the same breath proclaimed a benevolent neutrality toward religion.

However, the very phrase "benevolent neutrality" as used by the courts should alarm us. In actuality, it means that Christianity and all religions exist at the pleasure of the state. In other words, through the benevolence of the state, the people are permitted to worship their God on Sunday. Gone is the concept that religious freedom is a God-given right. It is now a privilege granted by the state. This is very reminiscent of ancient Rome's polytheistic environment. Rome also presumed to be divine.

The Supreme Court uses this fiction of neutrality as a sugarcoating to make palatable to us the bitter pill of the abandonment of Christian values

and of the moral order that accompanies them. "Of course," we are told, "we cannot legislate morality." This totally overlooks the fact that all substantial laws—as opposed to mere regulations, such as specific traffic rules—necessarily involve judgments between right and wrong. Therefore, they involve moral principles and establish what is necessarily a kind of religious concern (although it may not be that of Christianity or any other organized religion).

Jurisprudence or Legisprudence?

The fact that courts were once seen as institutions of justice (not legislating bodies) cannot be underscored enough. The court's function was to arrive at a just result, but in terms of the higher law. Thus the courts were not obliged to enforce a law that was unjust in terms of the Bible. Or they were not obliged to uphold acts, which ran contrary to Christian theism or to natural law.

This is well illustrated by a series of Supreme Court cases in the late nineteenth century, in which congressional acts against bigamy were upheld. Those laws were aimed at the practice of polygamy then current among Mormons. Underlying the Court's approval of this legislation was the fact that polygamy was contrary to Christian moral standards. The Court's decisions were thus premised upon what was right or wrong according to its reference point in the Bible. This was a "jurisprudential" view of the law: the prudence of seeking justice with the Bible as the final reference point.

With the current trend of the courts acting as applicators of law and, eventually, as the legislators, the jurisprudential view of law has declined. It has been replaced by a legisprudential view of law and civil government. *Lex* is the Latin word for law. The term *lex* literally means the rules of political society—in the Greek, *politika,* as distinguished from *ethika* or ethics. Legisprudence is the acceptance of what many term *legal positivism* or, more properly, the idea that we need not seek for "justice" but only for law—for the commands or regulations or laws of the state, its agents, officers, or agencies.

Legal positivism is the idea that law is established or recognized by state authority. The law sets the standard for justice. What is legal is by definition just. Once the law is enacted, it is obligatory. There is no higher or transcendent law by which to measure it because the state is the ultimate source of the law. Positive law is not only arrogant, it is expansive. Virtually, it seems there isn't an area of concern that escapes the mind of the bureaucrat who writes the myriad of regulations that control American society.

The crucial question is really one of epistemology—the theory of knowledge. If man cannot know, according to a higher law, what is just or right in a given situation, he cannot protest and criticize legitimately any particular course of action as unjust. Therefore, questions of right and wrong are resolved, in the legisprudential view, by the political process. As Notre Dame law professor Charles Rice in *Beyond Abortion* notes, during the Nazi era in Germany positivism disarmed the German jurists against law of an arbitrary and criminal nature. The very same thing has now happened in America.

In recent years we have witnessed numerous marches on Washington in which one group or another has demanded new "rights." Frequently, such rights have not meant freedom from state control, but rather entitlement to state action, protection, or subsidy. In the process of yielding to the "will of the people" and creating new rights, the state inevitably enlarges itself and its bureaucracy. Each new right seems to demand a new agency to guarantee it, administer it, or deliver it.

As the state creates new rights for some, it necessarily diminishes some rights for others. Someone has to lose, but there can be no appeal to any outside criterion of justice in a system where there is no god but Caesar. Legisprudence, as opposed to jurisprudence, does not seek what is just, but only what is legal, which depends entirely upon the arbitrary will of the state.

In contemporary society it is coming to be assumed that the state grants rights to the American citizen. This is dangerous thinking. Government is not God, to create rights, but is God's minister to protect the rights God has given man.

Moreover, in this respect, the term *civil rights* is a contradiction in terms. *Civil* basically means government created. If something is government created, it cannot legitimately be a "right" in the old sense but should only be an exercise of privilege. Freedom of worship is a right. Food stamps and social security benefits are privileges. An illegitimate government is in the business of assuming the prerogative of granting so-called civil rights.

The Tax Police

An agency which may best serve as the example of the new legisprudential view of government is the Internal Revenue Service. The IRS, headquartered in Washington, D.C., has seven regional and fifty-nine district offices throughout the United States. It employs 13,500 field agents, 4,460 office auditors, 2,800 special agents as well as 66,000 other full-time employees. The IRS, with a budget of over $2 billion, has at its disposal massive computer banks that are cross-indexed and possess information on virtually every citizen. Unfortunately the IRS has distorted its power to assess and collect income tax under the Sixteenth Amendment.

Journalist Blake Fleetwood, writing in the *Saturday Review* says: "Agents of the regime routinely seize homes, businesses, cars, bank accounts—even before the victims are told what they have been accused of. . . . If they feel like it, they can prosecute you for doing exactly what they told you to do. And if the regime is after you, there's nothing it won't stoop to: It will bug phones, pick locks, hire women to prostitute themselves, and use a variety of methods to spy on your private life."[7]

Fleetwood documents various cases to support what appears to be a systematic harassment of citizens suspected of evading taxes.

Consider the case of Stephen and Mona Oliver, who were assaulted by agents in full view of dozens of onlookers and news photographers. While they sat in their Volkswagen, the agents smashed the car windows and then dragged the couple over the broken glass, leaving them bruised and bloody. A tow truck hauled their car away. The IRS assessed them $4,700 for their 1977 taxes without giving a reason and moved immediately to seize their car.

Or consider Michael Wolstencroft, the resident manager of the Castle Bank in Nassau. In a recent affidavit he testified that he had sexual relations with a certain woman. This woman was a paid IRS informant. On one particular night her assignment was to keep Wolstencroft busy so that other agents could photocopy the contents of his briefcase.

Several Congressmen who have realized IRS abuses and attempted to curb its power have had their political careers ruined by the agency. In the mid-sixties Senator Edward V. Long conducted an exhaustive three-year probe into the IRS. The subcommittee he chaired found that the IRS defied court orders, criminally picked locks, stole records, illegally tapped phones, opened mail, and that much of this lawlessness was encouraged by highly placed Washington officials.

"The IRS," Long said, "has become morally corrupted by the enormous power which we in Congress have unwisely entrusted to it. Too often it acts like a Gestapo preying upon defenseless citizens."[8]

What happened to Senator Long? His tax returns were illegally leaked to *Life* magazine months before his reelection campaign in 1968. All sorts of irregularities were suggested. Long was cleared by a Senate subcommittee and never did have any tax problems. But his thirty-eight-year political career was destroyed. Although he had never been beaten in a political race before, he lost the Democratic nomination to Thomas Eagleton. The same fate later befell Senator Joseph Montoya of Watergate fame who also challenged IRS authority. Moreover, the list of victims goes on and on.

Would the founding fathers have approved of such governmental tactics? I hardly think so, since they threw tea into the Boston Harbor in protest of a tax.

Jerome Kurtz, former commissioner of the IRS, in an address made in January 1978, stated that "[w]e have almost no specific statutory guidance."[9] Without congressional guidance, the IRS promulgates literally thousands of *regulations,* which direct such things as what kind of people private schools admit to what indicia constitutes a valid church. This is disturbing since Article I of the Constitution mandates that only Congress is to exercise legislative power. The fact of the matter is that Congress has delegated its power to a body of nonelected IRS officials who not only possess the power to assess and collect taxes but also to write laws. The citizenry, however, never votes on these regulatory laws. What has evolved is a form of taxation without representation. And the people are without recourse if Congress does not exercise its authority over the IRS. "Until this changes," Fleetwood writes, "the IRS will keep terrorizing the citizens of America."

This is all part of the giant bureaucracy that has developed in the federal government. Charles Peters, editor-in-chief of the *Washington Monthly,* in his book *How Washington Really Works* states:

"Before we go over your return, I'd like to read you your rights!"

There is a permanent government in Washington that consists of people whose power does not depend on election results. It includes the courts, the military, and the foreign services as well as those unofficial but powerful branches, [such as] the press and the lobbies. But the largest part of the permanent government is the bureaucracy, which has over two and a half million federal civilian employees. Ten times that number are funded by the taxpayers, either through government contracts, as employees of state, county, and municipal governments, or as members of the military. . . . With one in ten of our citizens working for government, it is not surprising that the bureaucratic presence is increasingly dominant in our lives.[10]

The Roman historian Tacitus recognized in the first century that the "more corrupt the government, the greater the number of laws." More importantly, the laws enacted by the contemporary regulatory agencies do not derive their undergirding values from Judeo-Christian theism but from the humanistic consensus that is prevalent in the present statist philosophy. Some members of these regulatory agencies are humanist activists who deliberately use the regulations and agencies to further their own philosophy in an aggressive manner. The IRS abuses cited above attest to this fact.

A permanent, nonelected government thus has entrenched itself in America. The power it exercises is sometimes alarming. The Supreme Court has given the bureaucracy sanction in its use of power against citizens. The case of *United States* v. *Euge* is a good example.

In the *Euge* case, the IRS was conducting one of its numerous investigations and audits of a taxpayer. During an investigation of Mr. Euge's alleged income tax liability, an IRS agent issued a summons requiring Euge to appear and execute handwriting samples. The IRS was trying to determine if deposits in certain bank accounts not registered in his name represented income attributable to him.

Believing that the IRS had gone too far, Euge protested that having to produce the handwriting samples was an illegal search and seizure under the Fourth Amendment, and that such was testimonial evidence protected by the Fifth Amendment. The Supreme Court disagreed, giving the IRS broad powers to compel citizens to give over vast amounts of personal and private information on mere allegation of suspicion by the IRS.

Justice Thurgood Marshall noted the importance of the Fifth Amendment's protection against state interference, in his dissent to this decision: "Fifth Amendment privilege is rooted in 'the basic stream of religious and political principle [and] reflects the limits of the individual's attornment to the state.' "[11] Justice Marshall saw very clearly that the door is opened to a totalitarian-type intervention into privacy if there are no limits on arbitrary power.

From time to time individual justices have recognized the direction the Court as a whole is taking in its assumption of absolute lawmaking power and bitingly dissent from a majority decision. Since there is no standard (other than their own will) by which they can be judged, these occasional flashes of clarity offer no protection against the autocratic trend of the court. They only show that the justices are to some extent conscious of what they are doing. In terms of modern law there seems to be little justice. The judges are no longer guardians of the law but legislators. There is no hedge against arbitrary power. No higher law. No appeal—except to "raw judicial power."

Chapter Eight

Whatever Happened to the First Amendment?

Whenever the Christian community becomes involved in the political arena or a teacher in a public school requests the right to pray on school premises, the hue and cry has been, "This is a violation of the First Amendment. This disrupts the 'separation of church and state.' "

     However, as with most areas of constitutional law, this so-called wall is an arbitrary phenomenon. If a teacher wants to pray in the public school, the state often presents an absolute separation of church and state argument. However, when the state is attempting to interfere with and regulate the church, the state argues there is no absolute separation of church and state. To say the least, the state and its attorneys argue both sides of the coin well.

Thus, in the eyes of state officials, there may be a wall of separation, but it is a wall they can move and cross at will. Thus it is a false political dictum.

Franky Schaeffer V has written: "It has been convenient and expedient for the secular humanist, the materialist, the so-called liberal, the feminist, the genetic engineer, the bureaucrat, the Supreme Court justice, to use this arbitrary division between church and state as a ready excuse. It is used, as an easily identifiable rallying point, to subdue the opinions of that vast body of citizens who represent those with religious convictions."[1]

Christianity As the Base of Freedom

Religious liberty was a prime issue in the colonists' dispute with Great Britain. John Adams cited the attempt by parliament to force the establishment of the Church of England on the colonies as responsible "as much as any other cause" for the break. He said: "The objection was not merely to the office of a bishop, though even that was dreaded, but to the authority of parliament, on which it must be founded."[2] Historian Carl Bridenbaugh wrote: "It is indeed high time that we repossess the important historical truth that religion was a fundamental cause of the American Revolution."[3]

The framers of the Constitution well understood the danger of statist expansiveness and, therefore, provided that the First Amendment specifically limit the power of the federal government in several areas of man's basic rights: freedom of religion, speech, press, and assembly. It is not surprising that religion was listed first, since the guarantee of religious freedom was seen as paramount to the framers. Religious freedom, in effect, forms a base for the exercise of other freedoms. This was the Reformation heritage inherent in Martin Luther's assertion of the priesthood of all believers, which came to be known as the liberty of conscience.*

Roland Bainton in *The Travail of Religious Liberty* writes that "all freedoms hang together. . . . Civil liberties scarcely thrive when religious liberties are disregarded, and the reverse is equally true. Beneath them all is a philosophy of liberty, which assumes a measure of variety in human behavior, honors integrity, respects the dignity of man, and seeks to exemplify the compassion of God."[4] The eminent jurist James Kent, a giant of early American law, in his classic *Commentaries on American Law,* commented that "The free exercise and enjoyment of religious profession and worship may be considered as one of the absolute rights of individuals, recognized in our . . . law."[5] This was the heritage of the Reformation. It was developed

*Luther's early development of the liberty of conscience is discussed in more detail in the Appendix, Essay III.

from Blackstone by James Kent. For example when Kent published his *Commentaries,* not only did he adapt a title and structure parallel to Blackstone's, but he shared Blackstone's faith in the divine origin of the law.

The religion spoken of by Bridenbaugh, Bainton, Kent, and other historians who have made like comments is not religion in general or some nebulous Eastern religion or cult. They were talking about biblical religion—Judeo-Christian theism. Other religious faiths were virtually nonexistent in colonial America. Thus the religion of early America was Judeo-Christian theism, and it was considered to be the basis of freedom. It was the glue that held liberty and society, as a whole, together.

God and the Constitution

The text of the Constitution itself makes no reference to God. However, the Constitution is a technical document, a contract (or covenant) between the federal government and the people (collectively in the states). The framers left religion out of this contract because they did not want the federal government to have any authority over the church and religion. John Witherspoon and the other Christian leaders—having observed the British monarchy and hierarchy as both the head of the church and the state—did not want a connection between their church and the new federal government. They considered such an association a calamity and a curse. But at the same time, the knowledge of God as revealed in the Bible was so commonly diffused that it was probably not anticipated by colonial Americans that the Constitution might be made to operate on non-Christian principles.

Although God is not mentioned, the preamble of the United States Constitution incorporates the theistic principles of both the Declaration of Independence and the individual colonial constitutions. A preamble is by definition a statement that explains and gives credence to what is to follow. The preamble reads:

> WE THE PEOPLE of the United States in Order to form a more perfect Union, establish Justice, insure domestic Tranquility, provide for the common defence, promote the general Welfare, and secure the Blessings of Liberty to ourselves and our Posterity, do ordain and establish this Constitution for the United States.

Notice that the Constitution was ordained to "secure" the blessings of liberty that already existed in 1789. Where did these blessings exist? They were present in the individual states which were openly Christian. For example, the Massachusetts Constitution of 1780 proclaims in its preamble:

> We . . . the people of Massachusetts, acknowledging with grateful hearts, the goodness of the great Legislator of the Universe, affording us, in the course of His providence, an opportunity, deliberately and peaceably, without fraud, violence, or surprise, of entering into an Original, explicit, and Solemn Compact with each other . . .

All states of the United States of America have expressed either in their preambles or the body of the state constitution itself dependence on God for their preservation and strength. This biblical ideal was woven into these constitutions when the leaders of the different states were planning the structure of their civil governments. Therefore, when the federal constitution was drafted, the principle of faith in God was presumed to be a universal for healthy civil government.

The First Amendment

Various factions were not satisfied with the Constitution as it was originally drafted. There was fear that too powerful a government had been created. In particular, the clergy demanded a specific limitation or amendment concerning religion. Thus the First Amendment came into being.

A central concern of those who drafted the First Amendment was to prevent the federal government from establishing a national denominational church. This protected the state-established or state-preferred Christian denominations that existed in many of the colonies of that era. In the words of James Madison, the First Amendment was prompted because the "people feared one sect might obtain a preeminence, or two combine together, and establish a religion to which they would compel others to conform."[6]

Thus the philosophical base of the First Amendment was that of *denominational pluralism*–a healthy coexistence between the various Christian denominations. Such practical denominational pluralism is not to be confused with the new concept of pluralism, which commands complete acceptance of all views, even secular humanism.

At the time of the ratification of the First Amendment in 1791, many of the colonies were supporting a single church or religion. As Supreme Court Justice Hugo Black grudgingly acknowledged in the Supreme Court's 1962 decision banning devotional prayer from the public schools: "Indeed, as late as the time of the Revolutionary War, there were established churches in at least eight of the thirteen former colonies and established religions in at least four of the other five."[7] Moreover, this trend in some form continued in the individual states throughout the early part of the nineteenth century. For example, Massachusetts paid the salaries of the Congregational ministers in that state until 1833.

The fact that the early American states had Christianity as their foundation does not mean that they were theocracies (the government of a state by officials who are regarded as divinely guided). It meant that their laws and civil governments were based upon biblical principles. The state governments did not dictate how one should worship. Instead, man in his political actions was governed by laws that had the Bible as the reference point. Liberty of conscience thus was upheld while restraining external acts considered to be

"It said another bad word!"

non-Christian. For example, a usual law on the books in most states was one that prohibited blasphemy. Such a law had nothing to do with worship but proscribed something the colonists believed to be inimical to good order and civil government.

Supreme Court Justice Joseph Story, a leading Unitarian of his time who served on the Supreme Court from 1811 to 1845, wrote:

> Probably at the time of the adoption of the Constitution, and of the first amendment to it . . . the general if not the universal sentiment in America was, that Christianity ought to receive encouragement from the state so far as was not incompatible with the private rights

of conscience and the freedom of religious worship. An attempt to level all religions, and to make it a matter of state policy to hold all in utter indifference, would have created universal disapproval, if not universal indignation. . . . The real object of the amendment was not to countenance, much less to advance, Mahometanism, or Judaism, or infidelity, by prostrating Christianity; but exclude all rivalry among Christian sects, and to prevent any national ecclesiastical establishment which should give to a hierarchy the exclusive patronage of the national government.[8]

The Constitution separated the institution of the church from the institution of the state but not the Christian religion from the federal state—far less Christian individuals from any meaningful activity within the state and society at large. At that point in our history, the idea that a Christian should be excluded from practicing his Christian principles except in church and at home would have been unthinkable.

In particular, the First Amendment states: ''Congress shall make no law respecting an establishment of religion, or prohibiting the free exercise thereof.'' The word *Congress* has been interpreted to mean the federal government. *Respecting* is literally defined as ''having anything to do with.'' And *establishment* has historically meant ''government support of a single church or government preference of one creed or denomination over another.'' Therefore, the First Amendment would read like this if it were stated in contemporary language: ''The federal government shall make no law having anything to do with supporting a national denominational church, or prohibiting the free exercise of religion.''[9]

The term *religion* as used in the First Amendment is also important. Basically, the founders defined religion in terms of Judeo-Christian theism. James Madison, for instance, termed religion as ''the duty we owe our Creator.''[10] Thus, the religion that was originally meant to be protected under the First Amendment had its reference point in God. However, this God-centeredness of the First Amendment has now been altered by Supreme Court interpretation.

Originally the First Amendment, as well as the entire Bill of Rights, placed restrictions on the federal government and not the states. The Supreme Court, however, through interpretation of the Fourteenth Amendment, passed shortly after the Civil War, has determined that the Bill of Rights should restrict the individual states in their actions. This has given the Court the broad power to apply its dictates nationwide. For example the Supreme Court has prohibited all fifty states from allowing their public schools to conduct devotional prayer and Bible reading, or even the posting of the Ten Commandments in its public schools. As such, this interpretation of the Fourteenth Amendment is one of the great distortions of American constitutional doctrine.* In the process, an amendment that was originally established to protect the freedom of theistic religion has been turned on its head and now excludes, in many instances, individual Christians from exercising their beliefs and influencing the society in which they live.

*A detailed discussion of the Supreme Court's misinterpretation of the Fourteenth Amendment is found in the Appendix, Essay III.

"Put me down for 'No Comment' on that one. . . . I really haven't read enough polls on the subject to form an opinion!"

The Wall of Separation

The phrase *wall of separation,* indicating an impassable gulf between church and state, is nowhere to be found in the United States Constitution. In fact, the term *church and state* is lacking in the First Amendment.

The phrases had their origin in a letter written by Thomas Jefferson in 1802 to a group of Baptists and Congregationalists in Danbury, Connecticut, who had attacked him when he ran for president, calling him an infidel, an atheist, and a few other uncomplimentary names. In effect, Jefferson told them to stay in their places, saying that there should be "a wall of separation between church and state." However, in 1805 in his Second Inaugural Address, Jefferson said: "In matters of religion I have considered that its free exercise is placed by the Constitution independent of the powers of the General [federal] Government. I have therefore undertaken on no occasion to prescribe the religious exercises suited to it, but have left them, as the Constitution found them, under the direction and discipline of the church or state authorities acknowledged by the several religious societies.''

In this Inaugural Address, Jefferson rightly places a wall of separation around the church to protect it from any infringements by the federal government. That places him in line with the other founders, who feared the federal government and its possible attempts to establish a national church. Religion was to be a state concern, not a federal one.

However, as early as 1879 the Supreme Court had declared that Jefferson's wall-of-separation phrase was "almost an authoritative declaration of the scope and effect of the [First] Amendment."[11] From there the Supreme Court has gone on to hold that various Christian practices are unconstitutional if they occur in the public schools or other public places. One of the Court's major arguments in eliminating prayer and Bible reading from the public schools was Jefferson's so-called wall-of-separation philosophy. But Thomas Jefferson had nothing to do with the writing of the First Amendment. He was in Paris in 1791 when it was written.

Jefferson has often been cited as being hostile to biblical theism. That is not altogether true. As founder of the University of Virginia he recommended that students be allowed to meet on the campus to pray and worship together, or, if need be, to meet and pray with their professors on campus.[12] He was the author of the first plan of public education adopted for the city of Washington,[13] which included the Bible and the Isaac Watts Hymnal as the principal books to teach reading to students.[14] Obviously some of the founding fathers' religious views have been distorted.

As constitutional law authority Edward S. Corwin points out in *American Constitutional History,* the purpose of the First Amendment was "to exclude from the national government all power to act on the subject . . . of religion."[15] And in the words of James Madison: "There is not a shadow of right in the general [federal] government to intermeddle with religion. . . . This subject is, for the honor of America, perfectly free and unshackled. The government has no jurisdiction over it."[16] The First Amendment, therefore provides freedom *for* the Christian religion, not *from* the Christian religion.

Unfortunately as Dr. James Kennedy, pastor of the Coral Ridge Presbyterian Church, stated in 1980, "Something has been turning that around. . . . So that 98 percent of the times when you hear the phrase 'the separation of church and state,' what has been talked about? One thing. What the church shall not do. That's 180 degrees off from the First Amendment of the Constitution.''

Chapter Nine

Is Religion Whatever The Supreme Court Says It Is?

The term *religion* as found in the First Amendment is important in light of the protection it affords the various and sundry religions and religious belief systems today. As noted, the principal religion to be protected by the First Amendment was Judeo-Christian theism. The Supreme Court, however, has altered that historical fact.

History has not been one of the Supreme Court's better subjects. History loses its importance in a relativistic system that stresses an evolving law through court decisions. A contemporary example of the Supreme Court's nonhistorical approach is the attitude that marked the years that Chief Justice Earl Warren served on the Supreme Court—from 1953 to 1969. Many of the history-altering decisions on religion took place under his helm.

Law professor Fred Rodell of Yale lauded Warren in a 1966 article in *The New York Times Magazine* for being a Supreme Court justice who "brush[ed] off pedantic impediments to the results he felt were right." He was not a "look-it-up-in-the-library" intellectual, and was "almost unique" in his "off-hand dismissal of legal and historical research from both sides and in [his] pragmatic dependence on the present day results. . . ."[1] In fact, Rodell concludes, "Warren was quite unworried that legislative history, dug from a library, might not support his reading."[2] This was the judicial mentality that viewed, analyzed, and "interpreted" the religion clauses of the First Amendment. Now it is appropriate to ask, "What is religion?" within the context of the Constitution.

The Christian Definition of Religion
The Supreme Court did not undertake an extended interpretive examination of the religion clauses of the First Amendment until the 1870s. Prior to that time *religion* was assumed to be Christian theism. However, the heated controversy concerning the early Mormon Church forced the Court to define *religion*.

We must understand that the framers never intended that the federal government (or a court) define religion. In fact, the term *religion* as used in the First Amendment is used in its jurisdictional sense. It was meant to restrict the federal government's jurisdiction (or authority) in relation to religion.

Unfortunately, the courts have disregarded this fact and have undertaken to define religion. As we shall see, this has resulted in a constitutional interpretation contrary to the intentions of the framers.

In *Reynolds* v. *United States*, the Supreme Court made its initial inquiry into the religion clauses of the First Amendment. Congress passed a law making bigamy a criminal offense in any territory under the jurisdiction of the federal government. Richard Morgan in *The Supreme Court and Religion* has written that the legislation was clearly aimed at the Mormon practice of polygamy, which conflicted with Christian theism's tenet of monogamy.[3]

George Reynolds, a Mormon, was indicted and convicted of bigamy. Reynolds claimed the right to practice polygamy, a tenet of faith in his religion, as a guarantee of the First Amendment. In reply the Court said:

> Laws are made for the government of actions, and while they cannot interfere with *mere religious belief and opinions* [*emphasis added*], they may with practices. Suppose one believed that human sacrifices were a necessary part of religious worship, would it be seriously contended that the civil government under which he lived

could not interfere to prevent a sacrifice. . . . So here, as a law . . . of the United States, it is provided that plural marriages shall not be allowed. Can a man excuse his practices to the contrary because of his religious belief? To permit this would be to make the professed doctrines of religious belief superior to the law of the land, and in effect to permit every citizen to become a law unto himself. Government could exist only in name under such circumstances.[4]

The Court in *Reynolds* presupposed that the United States was

"Why can't I sleep? Because I took a sleeping pill, that's why!"

Christian in character. As historian and theologian R. J. Rushdoony has recognized: "The structure of a state represents, implicitly or explicitly, a particular religion. Implicit in the Court's decision was the equation of Christian moral standards with civilization. The legal structure they defended was implicitly Christian. It is *other* religions that are restricted to 'mere opinion' when they are in conflict with the religious establishment of American law."[5]

The *Reynolds* rationale has great First Amendment implications when it is realized that the Christian theistic religious practices that the *Reynolds* Court presupposed have now judicially been reduced to "mere opinion" or belief. Christianity has lost its historically preferred position.

The Mormon cases following *Reynolds* represent no substantial departure or addition to the reasoning of *Reynolds*. Eleven years after *Reynolds* the Supreme Court, in *Davis* v. *Beason*, held that the Mormons' "opinions" concerning polygamy were not religious tenets, and that not only the practice but also the teaching or counseling of polygamy constituted criminal actions.[6] The importance of *Davis* lies in the Supreme Court's definition of the term *religion* and its reaffirmation of Christian theism. In referring to "the general consent of the Christian world," the Court said: "The term 'religion' has reference to one's views of his relations to his Creator, and the obligations they impose for reverence for his being and character, and the obedience of his will."[7]

Religion, as defined in *Davis*, involves a belief in a "Creator" which, the Court held, imposes certain obligations upon each individual. This definition of religion mirrors that understood by James Madison and those within the historical milieu that drafted the First Amendment. It is both historically and constitutionally accurate. Madison termed religion as "the duty which we owe to our Creator, and the manner of discharging it."[8]

Following the Mormon cases, it was not until 1931 that the Supreme Court again defined religion. In that case the Court said: "The essence of religion is belief in a *relation to God* involving duties superior to those arising from any human relation. . . . One cannot speak of religious liberty, with proper appreciation of its essential and historic significance, without assuming the existence of a belief in supreme allegiance to the will of God."[9] This view of religion mirrors the definition of religion given in the *Davis* case.

The Humanistic Definition of Religion
Beginning in the 1940s, Christian theism came under increasing attack. The federal courts began to broaden and diversify the definition of *religion* until by the end of the 1960s the judicial definition of religion was altered from *sustenance of belief* (belief in and obligation owed to the "Creator") to the *impact* of the belief on the *life* of the person expressing and holding it. It is interesting to note that this personalization of religion mirrored what had happened within the church and Christian leadership itself, with their emphasis on pietistic faith and inward spiritual values.

Moreover, this judicial transformation of "religion" was corresponding to the change that was taking place in a previously theistic society. The basis of truth was shifting from Christian theism's emphasis on God-centeredness to humanism's emphasis on man-centeredness.

The signaled departure from theistic religion came in the 1941 case of *United States* v. *Kauten*. Mr. Kauten sought exemption from military service as a conscientious objector. He argued that as a matter of "religious conscience" he could not take up arms to defend the United States but admitted that his position was not based upon a "belief in Deity." The federal court of appeals accepted Kauten's assertion that his belief was a "religion" by stating:

> Religious belief arises from a sense of the inadequacy of reason as a means of relating the individual to his fellow men and to his universe—a sense common to men in the most primitive and the

"Eat your dinner, Arthur. Don't you want to grow up to be big and strong like your mother?"

> most highly civilized societies. . . . It is a belief finding expression in a conscience which categorically requires the believer to disregard elementary self-interest and to accept martyrdom in preference to transgressing its tenets. . . . [Conscientious objection] may justly be regarded as a response of the individual to an inward mentor, call it conscience of God, that is for many persons at the present time the equivalent of what has always been thought a religious impulse.[10]

The *Kauten* decision represents an intense and dramatic shift in emphasis. As one legal commentator, writing in the *Harvard Law Review*, said: "Whereas *Davis* saw religion as relating man to God, *Kauten* examined the relationship of man to the broad universe and to other men. . . . The Second Circuit [Court of Appeals] focused on the psychological function of the belief in the life of the individual."[11] That the *Kauten* case was a sharp break is demonstrated by remembering the Mormon cases, in which it was held that certain Mormon practices were not protected within the context of the First Amendment. The Mormon Church in many ways mirrors the Christian religion with its belief in the Creator and moral absolutes. However, this was not good enough for the Supreme Court justices of the late nineteenth century. In 1941, by contrast, an assertion of "religious conscience," apart from God, was sufficient to be protected by the First Amendment.

Although *Kauten* concerned the interpretation of the Selective Service Act of 1940, beginning with *United States* v. *Ballard* the Supreme Court began to shift its inquiry and analysis of religion. In *Ballard* the Court held that the truth or verity of a person's religious doctrines or beliefs could not be considered by a judge or jury without running afoul of the First Amendment.[12] The Court concluded that only the particular adherent's *sincerity* of belief may be examined. In *Ballard* the Supreme Court made it clear that the classification of a "belief" as a religion does not depend upon the tenets of a creed, but rather upon the *sincerity* of the belief. Consequently, in the eyes of the Supreme Court justices, the characterization of a belief as religious would seem to be beyond the competence of anyone other than the adherent. The Supreme Court has adopted a humanistic concept of religion, which emphasizes the centrality of man. This is, in fact, a secular or pagan application of Christian pietism. It is the other side of the coin.

In 1965 the Supreme Court made its latest and most definitive statement on "religion" and "conscience." In *United States* v. *Seeger,* the Court upheld the conscientious objector status of three men, despite the fact that their religious beliefs did not conform to the concept of religion as defined in the Selective Service Act.[13] The Act only granted exemptions to objectors whose religion was directly related to their belief in a Supreme Being. The Court examined the legislative history of the Act and through interpretation concluded that Congress had intentionally provided a broad definition of *religion*. The Court reasoned that Congress's utilization of the term *Supreme Being*, rather than the term *God* indicated their intent to broaden the meaning of the word *religion*.[14]

The *Seeger* Court attempted to define *Supreme Being* by consulting several progressive theologians, most notably Paul Tillich. Tillich's view is that the essence of religion is "ultimate concern," and, therefore, religion is itself "ultimate concern."[15] Further, Tillich postulates that the term *God* does not define religion; rather it is "ultimate concern" that defines the term *God*. In *The Shaking of the Foundations,* he wrote:

> The name of this infinite and inexhaustible depth and ground of all being is *God*. That depth is what the word God means. And if that word has not much meaning for you, translate it, and speak of the depth of your life, of the source of your being, of your ultimate concern, of what you take seriously without any reservation. Perhaps, in order to do so, you must forget everything traditional

"All I'm asking for is a chance to go to Washington to get a cushy committee assignment, my share of freebie junkets, make a few good connections for my retirement years, . . ."

> that you have learned about God, perhaps even that word itself. For if you know that God means depth, you know much about Him. You cannot then call yourself an atheist or unbeliever. For you cannot think or say: Life has no depth! Life itself is shallow. Being itself is surface only. If you could say this in complete seriousness, you would be an atheist; but otherwise you are not. He who knows about depth knows about God.[16]

Tillich's thesis is that the concerns of any individual can be ranked according to their importance to the individual, and that, if probed deeply enough, the individual will discover the underlying concern, which gives meaning and orientation to a person's whole life. Under the belief-as-ultimate-concern theory professed by Tillich, everybody has a religion. Obviously, Tillich's theory minimizes the importance of a belief in the God of the Bible. With dependence upon Tillich and the progressive theologians, the Court in *Seeger* determined that a belief is valid if it is "sincere and meaningful [and it] occupies a place in the life of its possessor parallel to that filled by the orthodox belief in God of one who clearly qualifies for the exemption. Where such beliefs have parallel positions in the lives of their respective holders we cannot say that one is 'in relation to a Supreme Being' and the other is not."[17]

Therefore, a "belief" is constitutionally protected if it is in a "parallel position" to that of a belief in the Judeo-Christian concept of God. The *Seeger* decision defined religion as all sincere beliefs "based upon a power or being, or upon a faith, to which all else is subordinate or upon which all else is ultimately dependent."[18] Thus, according to the justices in *Seeger, religion* includes atheism and agnosticism.

As professor Robert Rabin of Northwestern University has noted, the logical conclusion of the *Seeger* decision is that "[a]bsolute vertical disbelief in the traditional sense—disbelief in God—is irrelevant" to First Amendment considerations.[19] In other words, belief or disbelief in the Christian view of God is no longer relevant in defining religion under the First Amendment.

The definition of religion-as-belief is a radical departure from the historical definition of religion. Furthermore, the judicial definition of religion-as-belief is a sharp break with the early Supreme Court cases that defined religion as man's relationship to his Creator. From a preferred position within the religion clauses, Judeo-Christian theism has been relegated to the level of all other systems of belief—and of unbelief.

Secularizing the First Amendment

In 1961 in the case of *Torcaso* v. *Watkins*, the Supreme Court in exercising judicial review struck down a Maryland constitutional provision that required all public officers and employees to declare their belief in God. The Court held that this declaration invaded Roy Torcaso's "freedom of belief and religion" and that the "power and authority of the State of Maryland . . . is put on the side of one particular sort of believers—those who are willing to say they believe 'in the existence of God'."[20] In this case, the Court went on to define and recognize specific nontheistic creeds as religions (including its specific mention of secular humanism). The Court said that "neither a State nor the Federal Government can constitutionally aid all religions as against non-believers, and neither can aid those religions based on a belief in the existence of God as against those religions founded on different beliefs.''[21]

By repudiating Maryland's theistic preference and, thus, leveling all religions, the Court in *Torcaso* rejected Judeo-Christian theism as the religion and foundation of the United States. The mischief was compounded because of the Court's edict that its First Amendment rulings are binding on all the states (and local governments) uniformly. Thus in two hundred years we have come full circle to where it is the centralized federal state through its agency, the Supreme Court, that dictates what is and what is not religion. This is in direct contradiction to those who drafted the First Amendment. Religion was meant to be a province of the states to guard against the federal machine dictating what is and is not religious. The Supreme Court dictates in these areas are ''unconstitutional'' in and of themselves.

Several examples point up the Court's secularizing of the First Amendment. One concerns the 1963 Supreme Court decision in which it ruled that devotional Bible reading—using the Bible as a religious document—was an unconstitutional violation of the First Amendment. Justice William Brennan in his concurring opinion in that case captured the true meaning of the decision when he argued that the words *under God* could be kept in the Pledge of Allegiance. He said:

> This general principle might also serve to insulate the various *patriotic* exercises and activities used in the public schools and elsewhere which, whatever may have been their origins, *no longer have a religious purpose or meaning*. The reference to divinity in the revised pledge of allegiance, for example, *may merely recognize the historical fact that our Nation was believed to have been founded 'under God'* [emphasis added]. Thus reciting the pledge may be no more of a religious exercise than the reading aloud of Lincoln's Gettysburg Address, which contains an allusion to the same historical fact.[22]

The implication is that the words *under God* can be kept in the Pledge of Allegiance if they are not taken in the Christian sense, or if they have no reference to truth but only express a kind of historical museum.

Another example is provided by the Supreme Court's decision in *Stone* v. *Graham* on November 17, 1980. In that case the Court struck down, by way of judicial review, a Kentucky law requiring the posting of the Ten Commandments in public school classrooms. The justices ruled that the posting was a form of state-sponsored religious indoctrination prohibited by the First Amendment. The Court said that the Ten Commandments were "plainly religious" and may "induce the school children to read, meditate upon, perhaps to venerate and obey the Commandments." In other words, if they were taken seriously, in the Christian sense, they were against the law.

In this case the Court seemingly held that the First Amendment can allow only "secular" activity in the public schools of America. And this was precisely the dissenting argument of Justice William Rehnquist. He said that the posting should have been allowed because Kentucky "was permitted to conclude that a document with such secular significance should be placed before its students."[23]

As Charles Rice notes in *Beyond Abortion,* when the United States government, through the Supreme Court, declared its neutrality on the existence of God, the stage was set for *Roe* v. *Wade,* and the fate of millions of children was sealed. Not that the Supreme Court in the *Torcaso* case said anything about abortion; it did not have to. By 1961 the philosophy of American society had become thoroughly humanistic, its ultimate inhumanness held in check only by a lingering Christian memory.

However, when the Court declared its official indifference to God in *Torcaso,* the door was opened. The Court, and thus the civil government, had no further duty to adhere to a moral code any higher than that set by the Court. Thereafter, the Court would treat such issues as abortion only in so-called neutral and wholly amoral terms. Under those rules, the unborn child never had a chance.

Humanism and the Myth of Neutrality

Justice Tom Clark in the Supreme Court's 1963 Bible-reading decision stated that "the State may not establish a 'religion of secularism' in the sense of affirmatively opposing or showing hostility to religion, thus 'preferring those who believe in no religion over those who do believe'."[24]

The prohibition against the state establishing a "religion of secularism" was strengthened in *Torcaso* v. *Watkins,* in which the Supreme Court recognized that the First Amendment grants the same protection and imposes the same limitations on the religion of secular humanism as are applicable to theism. Therefore, it logically follows that the state is prohibited from establishing nontheistic or secular ideologies.[25] This would include the court systems and executive agencies.

Undergirding the state and its governmental agencies, however, is a law or legal system. Law in this country from the standpoint of legal positivism is a creation of the state. This is true whether the law is legislated by a representative body or whether it emerges from interpretations by the courts. All law, and therefore the legal system in its totality, is based upon moral principle. Jacques Ellul, a professor of law at Bordeaux in France, in *The Theological Foundation of Law* has written:

> In its origin law is religious. This is confirmed by almost all sociological findings. Law is the expression of the will of a god; it is formulated by the priest; it is given religious sanction, it is accompanied by magic ritual. Reciprocally, religious precepts are

"I didn't use my option for silent prayer this morning. . . . Could I take a minute now?"

> presented in judicial garb. The relationship with the god is established by man in the form of a contract. The priest guarantees religion with the occult authority of law.[26]

Historically morals have always been a religious concern. Therefore, because law establishes and declares the meaning of justice and righteousness, law is inescapably religious.

Just as Christian theism was once the foundation undergirding law and government, a religious origin in contemporary law exists by province of the Supreme Court, but it has shifted from biblical revelation to humanism. The denial of God does not eliminate the fact that there is an operative god in every religious system or faith. The religious motivation and impetus for the present American law and governmental system is humanism, which has become, in effect, a state-established religion.[27]

The Supreme Court, however, has mandated state religious neutrality. The state is to prefer no religion or religious group over and above another religion or group. The question is: How can the Supreme Court truly be neutral? Sir Walter Moberly in *The Crisis in the University* comments on the religiously "neutral" British universities:

> On the fundamental religious issue, the modern university intends to be, and supposes it is, neutral, but it is not. Certainly it neither inculcates nor expressly repudiates belief in God. But it does what is far more deadly than open rejection; it ignores Him. . . . It is in this sense that the university today is atheistic. . . . It is a fallacy to suppose that by omitting a subject you teach nothing about it. On the contrary, you teach that it is to be omitted, and that it is therefore a matter of secondary importance. And you teach this not openly and explicitly, which would invite criticism; you simply take it for granted and thereby insinuate it silently, insidiously, and all but irresistibly.[28]

Any legal system, secular or otherwise, must develop a religious foundation of law, and maintain that foundation by hostility to any other law order or it will falter.

The Supreme Court's theory of neutrality as we have seen is clearly erroneous. Court decisions, as well as statutory law, establish the morals of society. As discussed earlier, *Roe* v. *Wade* was clearly a moral decision which adopted the specific status of the unborn child called for by humanism. The myth of neutrality, however, postulates the idea that the state exhibits "a benevolent neutrality" over spiritual matters.[29] The state assumes an air of objectivity while acting as an umbrella under which all religions can operate and thrive. The state is seen as secular. But in such an instance, the state is religious, because its "ultimate concern" is the perpetuation of the state itself.

Inherent in the concept of state neutrality is the idea that no religion possesses absolute values. Instead, the state defines what is absolute and what is acceptable religion. And one absolute of the state is its abstinence from Christian theism. Neutrality then does not result in expansive freedom, rather it restricts religious expression to the private realm and removes it from the public arena—thus rendering it ineffective as it relates to the culture. Erik von

Kuehnelt-Leddihn in *Leftism* has written that once the state moves in the direction of adopting humanism as its religious and philosophical base, the result is "[e]ither complete hostile annexation of the Church or persecution of the Church by separation. Religion is then first removed from the marketplace and the school, later from other domains of public life. . . ."[30]

With the emergence of the relativistic idea of belief-as-ultimate concern, a new polytheism exists: the state tolerates many religions and, therefore, many gods. The position of the American state is increasingly that of pagan antiquity, in which the state as god on earth provides the umbrella

"He certainly resembles you, Martha. . . . Why his skin is the exact same shade of green as your eyes!"

under which all institutions reside. Religion is thus a department of the state as is all else.

We must be cognizant of the fact that in this new polytheism the rights of Christians are many times dependent upon the rights of other religious groups. For example, if the Supreme Court were to rule that it was illegal for the Hare Krishnas to evangelize in public places, then Christians and Jews would also be banned. Under the present judicial mentality, the constitutional principles will apply across the board. It is, therefore, incumbent upon the Christian community to defend the principle of free religious expression for all religious groups. Christians can be confident that "the truth of Christianity will prevail in an open marketplace of ideas."

The Return to Rome

Rome was ready on the whole to recognize almost any religion and to give it legal status, provided the new religion recognized the superior jurisdiction of the state as the essential and primary manifestation of the divine order. The officials of the Roman Empire did not force the Christians to sacrifice to any of the heathen gods, but to the genius of the emperor and the fortune of the city of Rome. The early Christians, however, refused to submit to Rome's jurisdiction. At all times this refusal was looked upon as a political offense, not a religious one. Francis Schaeffer in *How Should We Then Live?* has said:

> Rome was cruel, and its cruelty can perhaps be best pictured by the events which took place in the arena in Rome itself. People seated above the arena floor watched gladiator contests and Christians thrown to the beasts. Let us not forget why the Christians were killed. They were *not* killed because they worshipped Jesus. Various religions covered the whole Roman world. One such was the cult of Mithras, a popular Persian form of Zoroastrianism which had reached Rome by 67 B.C. Nobody cared who worshipped whom so long as the worshiper did not disrupt the unity of the state, centered in the formal worship of Caesar. The reason the Christians were killed was because they were rebels. This was especially so after their growing rejection by the Jewish synagogues lost for them the immunity granted to the Jews since Julius Caesar's time.[31]

Therefore, the Supreme Court's interpretation of the First Amendment and its definition of religion as belief is not new or innovative. Rather, it has initiated a return to a system of religious exercise that existed in antiquity. We are, so to speak, back on the road to Rome.

Chapter Ten

The Convenient "Right to Privacy"

The radical transformation of the First Amendment into an instrument of restraint on the citizenry was a foreshadow of what was to come in the area of privacy law. The outcries from the militant women's rights groups, homosexual organizations, and other small, but highly organized, interest groups for so-called "privacy" rights has found expression through a number of court decisions and, most notably, *Roe* v. *Wade*. As such, the humanistic concept of privacy is egocentric. It places man at the center with no other reference point. First God is set aside, then others (for example, the unborn child), until, in the end, everything is seen in utilitarian terms.

　　The basic argument advanced by these groups is that by their very nature human beings possess certain rights, among which is the right to privacy. This is in essence a natural law argument, and as such makes a plausible claim. It is an appeal to the higher law of which we speak. As such, these groups argue, the Constitution should protect their concept of the right to privacy, which is the base of the right to abortion-on-demand. The argument is mistaken because, in the last analysis, privacy is *not* a God-given, natural law on the same level as the right to life. But the Court in effect ignored the natural law argument and considered privacy a constitutional, man-made right.

The Question of Human Rights
The concept of human rights is a fertile source of confusion because of our persistent failure to be specific about the nature and source of what we call human rights. From a biblical perspective, "rights" as such do not exist but grow out of duties and limits. There is no explicit "right to life" in the Bible, but an explicit prohibition of the taking of innocent life, from which the right to life emerges. Indeed, even in the Bill of Rights, the first ten amendments to the Constitution, the rights are established by setting limits on the power of the federal government.

Within a purely secular framework, one might consider rights in terms of natural law. That is to say, human beings are destined by nature if not by "Nature's God" for certain ends and therefore are endowed with certain rights, which must be acknowledged and respected by law. This traditional approach to rights was recognized by the deistically inclined among the founding fathers and was compatible with the Christian view that rights are the specific endowment of the personal Creator God of the Bible.

But our modern secular framework has moved to a second concept of rights, which is totally incompatible with biblical views. The modern secular view holds that individuals have just such rights as the Constitution and other laws give them. From this humanistic base, the "struggle for rights" becomes, in effect, a conflict with other human beings to persuade—or force—them to generate laws entitling us to the rights we seek. Unless we succeed in clarifying what we mean by *rights,* that is, whether we mean what the Declaration of Independence means (an endowment by the Creator) or, what modern humanistic law means (a legal entitlement based on the arbitrary will of the lawmaking authority), we will neither be able to understand nor to influence what is going on in America today.

Properly understood, a *right* is a benefit or lawful claim granted by the law itself in recognition of principles of the biblical higher law. He who breaks no law has a right to live and operate without constraint as long as he stays within the limits of the law. However, if he transgresses the law, his rights of life, liberty, and property are placed in jeopardy. They are not absolute or autonomous.

Rights must have a reference point and a specific context or they are meaningless. The reference point determines the nature of the right exercised, defining the one who possesses it and setting limits to others who must respect it. Both the claim to and the exercise of a right, therefore, can be either valid or invalid depending upon its reference point. If the reference is the Bible, then there is an absolute base and a meaningful content to determine whether the right is indeed a right and whether the exercise of that right is proper.

"When we signed our live-in contract, I somehow missed section 3, paragraph 4, line 2!"

Rights, Duties, and Power

The question of rights and their exercise becomes a baffling one when we do not make careful distinctions. If rights are seen as endowments by the Creator, whose will is made plain in the Bible, then we can turn to the Bible in order to define our rights and their limits. If they originate in nature itself, we may still achieve a measure of certainty as long as we have a fair consensus concerning the order of nature. (Unfortunately, the effort to discern the order of nature becomes ultimately impossible if one refuses to acknowledge the hand of the Creator.) But there is no valid standard to determine rights if they are seen autonomously—either as the claim of the autonomous individual or as the gracious endowment of autonomous man through the will of the state.

Each man may be a law unto himself. In this case, anything goes and all actions are equally acceptable. If it is the individual who determines right and wrong, then it is up to each individual to determine what his rights are and to claim them. If it is the will of society as expressed by some authoritative body (whether a dictator, a legislature, or a court), then the question is not, "What is right?" but rather, "Who has the power to say?" As C. Everett Koop, surgeon general of the United States, writes: "Today we face a situation in which there is a chaos of rights."

It is widely held that individual rights may be exercised as long as they do not infringe on the similar rights of others: "Your freedom ends where my nose begins." This commonsense position may work fairly well as long as there is a ready understanding of what persons are. But it fails if someone usurps the right to define others—and their rights—out of existence.

When Hitler determined to exterminate the Jews, some German humanists objected on the basis of the sanctity of life and of natural justice. Hitler simply defined the Jews as less than fully human, and his critics were anesthetized. If the Jews were not human, then they did not have human rights. What a simple solution to an otherwise perplexing problem! The argument for rights, separated from any basis in a reliable frame of reference, becomes capricious and merely a matter of definition of terms by whoever has the power to make his definition stick.

The issue of autonomous rights is nowhere clearer than in the area of abortion and "personal choice." Proabortionists argue that they are defending the right to choose, not the right to kill. Their position is not proabortion; it is prochoice. Individual women claim to have a natural right to do whatever they please with their bodies. When abortion opponents object that in doing so they destroy other persons—unborn children—and deprive them of all their rights, the prochoice party simply resorts to having the competent power—the Supreme Court—declare that unborn children are not persons and hence have no rights to interfere with a woman's freedom of choice. This is a perversion of the terms *freedom* and *rights* to include the concept of absolute, unlimited freedom of choice.

Is There a Natural Justice?
Early in constitutional history certain jurists put forward a theory of natural justice, which divorced it from correspondence with the Bible and proposed that it could be used to overturn particular laws and indeed the provisions of the written Constitution itself. Initially, this argument was rejected, but it has now returned in the guise of sociological law. In its present manifestation, the

appeal to a kind of natural justice is far more dangerous than it was in the early nineteenth century, for nature is no longer seen as the purposeful handiwork of a wise Creator but as a process in flux.

In 1798, Supreme Court Justice Samuel Chase attempted to infuse a natural law concept into the Constitution in the case of *Calder* v. *Bull*. Chase wanted, in effect, to release the Supreme Court from the necessity of adhering to the written Constitution by placing the claims of natural justice above it.[1] Chase argued that the written Constitution could not bind the justices if they found its provisions to contravene their concept of natural justice.

The difficulty lies not in the concept that there is a limit to the authority of the Constitution, but in the idea that this limit lies in the opinion of the judges, untrammeled by any external, valid point of reference. The genius of the Constitution is its ability to limit the arbitrary authority of autonomous man. If a particular human agency can modify the Constitution at will, then free reign is once again given to autonomous man's arbitrary will. This is precisely the point made by Justice James Iredell in *Calder* v. *Bull:*

> The ideas of natural justice are regulated by no fixed standard; the ablest and the purest men have differed on the subject; and all that the Court could properly say, in such an event, would be that the Legislature (possessed of an equal right of opinion) had passed an act which, in the *opinion of the judges* [emphasis added], was inconsistent with the abstract principles of natural justice.[2]

Thus the concept of natural law and natural justice could be used to allow the authorized interpreters of natural justice, the members of the Supreme Court, to remake the Constitution.

The door to natural law theory was officially opened in 1905 in the Supreme Court's decision in *Lockner* v. *New York*.[3] In this case the plaintiff, an owner of a New York bakery, argued that a state labor law, which prohibited his hiring an employee to work more than sixty hours in one week, denied his liberty without due process of law under the Fourteenth Amendment. The Court sustained the bakery owner's claim on the basis of a *right to contract*. This right was raised to constitutional stature for the first time in *Lockner*.

However, the justices made no effort to show that the right claimed was found in the Constitution. Rather, the Court relied on a list of so-called Fourteenth Amendment "liberty" rights that it had recognized in a case eight years earlier.[4] The truth of the matter is that the so-called right to contract is not found in the Constitution or even the English common law. It was Court manufactured. It was presumably based on nature, but on nature in evolution, not on nature as reflecting God's order.

To his credit, Justice Holmes, dissenting in *Lockner*, said: "The 14th Amendment does not enact Mr. Herbert Spencer's Social Statistics."[5] Spencer, a social Darwinian, was an eighteenth-century philosopher who extended the theory of biological evolution to all areas of life. And in *Lockner*, Holmes implies that Spencer's statistics on behavior should not be the basis for law.

Holmes, however, went on in *Lockner* to posit that a law or a right would be within the parameters of the Constitution if it were *rational* according to the "fundamental principles as they have been understood by the traditions of our people and our law."[6] Even as he was trying to oppose the Court's trend to expand the term *liberty* to mean whatever the Court wanted it to mean, Holmes set the stage for further problems.

He argued that it was up to the justices to determine whether something was to be found in the Constitution, according to whether or not they believed it rational. He wanted to use the standards of "a rational and fair man" and traditional understanding to judge this rationality. But in the last analysis it is the justices who decide what a rational and fair man might think.

If the justices were forming their opinion of what is right on the basis of the Judeo-Christian tradition (the Bible), it would be possible to argue with them on that same basis. Even if they were operating on the basis of the older natural law, it would be possible to appeal to the order of nature against their arbitrary interpretations. But seeing as they appeal to the Constitution from the way they and they alone interpret it and expand it, the justices are in reality setting themselves up as the absolute authorities from which no further appeal is possible.

The Mysterious Right to Privacy

The cornerstone case for the right to privacy was a 1965 Supreme Court case, *Griswold* v. *Connecticut*. The executive director of the Planned Parenthood League of Connecticut had been prosecuted and convicted for aiding and abetting married persons who used contraceptive devices in violation of Connecticut law. In the exercise of judicial review the Supreme Court, citing *Lockner* and other cases that are the offspring of *Lockner*,[7] held the law unconstitutional on the basis that it violated the Fourteenth Amendment's prohibition against denial of liberty without due process of law.

Justice Arthur Goldberg, in a concurring opinion, grafted the principle of the right to privacy onto the Constitution. In essence he proclaimed that the right to contraceptives, which is based upon the right to privacy, was found in the Ninth Amendment.[8] This amendment states: "The enumeration in the Constitution of certain rights shall not be construed to deny or disparage others retained by the people." As one can very well see the Ninth Amendment does not mention a right to privacy. Goldberg wrote that in determining which rights, such as privacy, are fundamental, "judges . . . must look to the 'traditions and conscience of the people' to determine whether a principle is 'so rooted [there] . . . as to be ranked fundamental'."[9]

Thus he changed his argument in mid-flow from an appeal to the text of the Constitution (that is, the Ninth Amendment) to an appeal to the

opinions of judges. His appeal to history is only a subterfuge to conceal the fact that the Court is imposing its own preferences and making new law. Goldberg's opinion has since become a foundation of the constitutionality of the right to privacy.

Justice Hugo Black reacted to Goldberg's creation of this strange reincarnation of the theory of natural justice. In speaking of the Court's attempt at reading the conscience of the people to make their decisions, he said:

> Our Court certainly has no machinery of this age to take a Gallup Poll. And the scientific miracles of this age have not yet produced a

gadget which the Court can use to determine what traditions are rooted in the "conscience of our people." Moreover, one would have to look far beyond the language of the Ninth Amendment to find that the Framers vested in this Court any such awesome veto powers over law making, either by the States or by the Constitution.[10]

In *Griswold* Justice William O. Douglas, who wrote the majority opinion, admitted that the right to privacy could not be found in the Constitution. Instead, the right to privacy is to be found in the "penumbrae" (the partial illumination) formed by emanations from various guarantees found in the First, Second, Third, Fourth, and Fifth Amendments. Douglas acknowledged the extraconstitutional nature of the right to privacy. He said: "We deal with a right to privacy older than the Bill of Rights—older than our political parties, older than our school system."[11] Thus he took refuge in his idea of natural justice where the Constitution gave him no support. The Supreme Court has often found history—usually a very selective version of history—a convenient vehicle to enhance its positions, especially if what the justices are proposing cannot be found in the Constitution.

All this is not to say that there is no right to privacy, but merely—as Douglas admitted—that it is not in the Constitution. There is a right to privacy, but it is to be found in the ultimate reference point—the Bible with its doctrine of the dignity of man, made in God's image. The Supreme Court, however, has defined this "right" humanistically. As a consequence, the Court has disregarded the written limits of the Constitution, and the pronouncement of this new right has led to the slaughter of innocent, unborn children.

Mother Teresa of Calcutta, foundress of the Missionary Sisters of Charity, received a Nobel Peace Prize in 1979 for her work with the dying, the poor, and the children of India. When she accepted her prize, she named abortion as "the greatest destroyer of peace today."

"If a mother can kill her own child, what is left before I kill you and you kill me?" Mother Teresa asked the world.

Chapter Eleven

The
Abortion
Mentality

The right to privacy reached macabre proportions in the 1973 decision of *Roe* v. *Wade*. In its exercise of judicial review, the Court struck down a Texas criminal law, which proscribed procuring or attempting an abortion except on medical advice for the purpose of saving the mother's life. Justice Harry Blackmun, in relying upon *Lockner, Griswold,* and others, established the woman's right to abortion-on-demand as based upon the right to privacy. With arrogant audacity he stated: "The Constitution does not explicitly mention any right to privacy."[1]

He went on to say, however, that in "varying contexts the Court or individual justices have, indeed, found at least the roots of that right . . . in the concept of liberty guaranteed in the . . . Fourteenth Amendment."[2] Thus, the right to privacy upon which *Roe* v. *Wade* was based was "found" by the Court and its individual justices.

This is apparent even to those who favor abortion, such as Yale law professor John Hart Ely. In fact, Ely has written that the decision in *Roe* v. *Wade* is "frightening." Writing in the *Yale Law Journal,* he notes: "The problem with *Roe* is not so much that it bungles the question it sets for itself, but rather that it sets a question the Constitution has not made the Court's business. . . . It is bad because it is bad constitutional law, or rather because it is *not* constitutional law and gives almost no sense of an obligation to try to be."[3]

If anyone is doubtful that the decision in *Roe* v. *Wade* established abortion-on-demand, I refer them to the annual average of 1 million plus abortions performed in the United States since 1973. I would also point to Justice Byron White's dissent in *Planned Parenthood* v. *Danforth* in 1976: "In *Roe* v. *Wade* . . . this Court recognized a right to an abortion free from state prohibition."

Although the Supreme Court's fundamental tactic in *Roe* v. *Wade* was based on the right to privacy, the Court did protect itself against natural law arguments based on the right to life by also deciding that an unborn child is not a person within the meaning of the Fourteenth Amendment. As a nonperson, the unborn child can claim no rights to vie with the woman's right to privacy. Indeed, as a nonperson the fetus is a nonentity, with which the law may not concern itself. This conclusion is strange, indeed, because for at least a century, industrial corporations have been considered persons under the Fourteenth Amendment for purposes of lawsuits. They can be protected, although they are not living persons. Professor Ely states:

> [T]he argument that fetuses lack constitutional rights is simply irrelevant. . . . Dogs are not "persons in the whole sense" nor have they constitutional rights, but that does not mean the state cannot prohibit killing them: It does not even mean the state cannot prohibit killing them in the exercise of the First Amendment right of political protest. Come to think of it, draft cards aren't persons either.[4]

In other words, it is against the law to burn a draft card but not to kill an unborn child.

The new "right to privacy" was so sweeping that Justice Blackmun held that the Court did not need to resolve the question of when life begins. Nevertheless, he sought to forestall objections by protesting a hypocritically modest ignorance: "When those trained in the respective disciplines of medicine, philosophy, and theology are unable to arrive at any consensus, the judiciary, at this point in the development of man's knowledge, is not in the position to speculate as to the answer."[5] This is a strange conclusion in light of the fact that biologists, as a whole, consider life a continuum from conception to death.

Blackmun ultimately evaded answering the question of when life begins by giving the unborn child the biologically false definition of "potential life." Then he pronounced the Supreme Court's arbitrary moral judgment

"I had that one aborted!"

that potential life was protectable by the state only at the point of viability (when it is capable of normal life). This is an absurd limitation when dogs and corporations can be protected by the state.

C. Everett Koop in *The Right To Live; The Right to Die* writes: "When Mr. Blackmun said that the Court was not in a position to speculate on when life begins, he did us a great disservice. The Court really did decide when life begins in that life does not begin before live birth."[6] Both the Court's elevation of the right to privacy and its flat denial that life begins before birth look very much like special pleading to bolster the arbitrary views of the justices.

In *Roe* v. *Wade* arbitrary judicial principles decided a matter that was never intended to be a province of the courts. One absurdity led to another. Even the concept of viability on which the Court relied is subject to change. Harvard law professor Archibald Cox noted that the opinion reads:

> Like a set of hospital rules and regulations, whose validity is good enough this week but will be destroyed with new statistics upon the medical risks of childbirth and abortion or new advances in providing for the separate existence of a foetus. . . . Constitutional rights ought not be created . . . unless they can be stated in principles sufficiently absolute to give them roots throughout the community and continuity over significant periods of time, and to lift them above the level of the pragmatic political judgments of a particular time and place.[7]

By creating a new "right" the Court also created for itself new power to establish rules and regulations—regulations subject to alteration when the opinions of the justices change.

Finally, Blackmun said that "we do not agree that, by adopting *one theory of life,* Texas may override the rights of the pregnant woman that are at stake."[8] In effect, the Court held that no abortion law may be based upon any absolute moral value, either biblical or natural, about when life begins. Instead, any law concerning abortion must yield to the Supreme Court's arbitrary decree: that life cannot begin before the point of viability. This decree is rational in the view of the Court.

However, this so-called rationality is seen to be irrational when it is realized that in the second half of the twentieth century there is more precise scientific knowledge as to the exact nature of the unborn child than at any other time in history. Each passing week this knowledge builds to a more resounding argument that the unborn child is indeed a person in every sense of the word. With a fuller understanding of genetics, the technology concerning the emission of brain waves, and the intrauterine photography of fetuses (which has provided a close-up look at the developing baby), there is much less of an excuse today than there might have been in 1973 for a sweeping and arbitrary ruling such as *Roe* v. *Wade.*

Jerome Lejeune, M.D., professor of fundamental genetics at the University of Rene Descartes (Paris, France) testified before the Subcommittee on Separation of Powers of the United States Senate Committee on the Judiciary on April 23, 1981, concerning recent evidence about the unborn baby.

Dr. Ian Donald from England a year ago succeeded in producing a movie featuring the youngest star of the world, an eleven week old baby dancing in utero. The baby plays, so to speak, on a trampoline! He bends his knees, pushes on the wall, soars up, and falls down again. Because his body has the same buoyancy as the amniotic fluid, he does not feel gravity and performs his dance in a very slow, graceful and elegant way, impossible in any other place on the earth. Only astronauts in their gravity-free state can achieve such gentleness of motion.[9]

STAYSKAL
81 CHICAGO
TRIBUNE

"She had no right aborting me. . . . After all, it was my body."

Dr. Lejeune also described the fetus's early life:

At two months of age, the human being is less than one thumb's length from the head to the rump. He would fit with ease in a nutshell, but everything is there: hands, feet, head, organs, brain, all are in place. His heart has been beating for a month already. Looking closely, you would see the palm creases. . . . with a good magnifier the finger prints could be detected. Every document is available for a national identity card.

With the extreme sophistication of our technology, we have invaded his privacy. Special hydrophones reveal the most primitive music: a deep, profound, reassuring hammering at some 60-70 per minute (the maternal heart), and a rapid, high-pitched cadence at some 150-170 (the heart of the fetus). These mixed, mimic those of the counterbase and of the maracas, which are the basic rhythm of pop music.

We now know what he feels, we have listened to what he hears, smelled what he tastes, and we have really seen him dancing, full of grace and youth. . . . The human nature of the being from conception to old age is not a metaphysical contention; it is plain evidence.[10]

The indifference of the Court to scientific evidence is a basic example of the irrationality of the humanist. He claims to be rational and scientific, but blithely ignores scientific fact that is in disagreement with what he thinks are his rights as autonomous man.

In essence *Roe* v. *Wade* pits the supposedly constitutional, man-made "rights" of the pregnant woman against the God-given right to life of *her* unborn child. It is not too much to say that it pits the Court against God. The legacy of *Torcaso* v. *Watkins* has come home to roost. In that decision Christianity was officially scorned as the basis of law and government. Now the Supreme Court will not adopt "one theory of life"—Christianity—in right to life cases. From having been the foundation of American society, Christian values are now excluded on principle.

Supposedly this is objective and impartial. In fact, it represents a deliberate assault on Christian values. The lesson is clear. The only moral values that are constitutionally *im*permissible for a law to endorse are those resting upon Christian theism. As Dr. Koop notes: "Justice Blackmun . . . made it abundantly clear that if any religion was to be a guide to him it would be paganism. He alluded to the practice of the Persians, the Greeks, and of the Romans, but he ignored Christianity. The Hippocratic Oath, which has been taken by physicians for the past 2,000 years, specifically prohibits abortion and the suggestion of it. Justice Blackmun laid this aside as having no relevance today."[11]

The Mental Health Idea

Another Supreme Court argument for abortion was the impact of an unwanted child on a pregnant woman. Justice Blackmun said:

Maternity, or additional offspring, may force upon the woman a distressful life and future. Psychological harm may be imminent.

Mental and physical health may be taxed by child care. There is also the distress, for all concerned, associated with the unwanted child, and there is the problem of bringing a child into a family already unable, psychologically and otherwise, to care for it. In other cases, as in this one, the additional difficulties and continuing stigma of unwed motherhood may be involved. All these are factors the woman and her responsible physician necessarily will consider in consultation.[12]

The life of the unborn child thus is subordinated to the unhappy balance of the pregnant woman's mental health. It really becomes a matter of the mother's convenience. If the pregnant woman exhibits a preference for the nonlife of the unborn infant, then it supersedes any right to life the fetus may be deemed to possess.

Logically, the Court did not need to raise this issue since its view of the right to privacy and of the nonhumanity of the unborn child had already closed the case. But it is important to note that the Court did raise it, for the emphasis on mental health as more important than life itself shows where the abortion mentality is taking us.

As one would smash an annoying fly, one could for a similar annoyance terminate the life of the unborn infant. How long will it be before the youth of society begin exterminating their aged parents whom they consider an annoyance? Or, should euthanasia, too, be a matter of constitutional entitlement. And who is to claim it? The aged, or those who are being annoyed by them?

We are moving toward a society where only man's emotions and comfort are sacred. Personal peace has become the idol. Francis Schaeffer writes:

Personal peace means just to be let alone, not to be troubled by the troubles of other people, whether across the world or across the city—to live one's life with minimal possibilities of being personally disturbed. Personal peace means wanting to have my personal life pattern undisturbed in my lifetime, regardless of what the result will be in the lifetimes of my children and grandchildren.[13]

And it was for the sake of the personal peace of the pregnant woman that the Court decided *Roe* v. *Wade*. As a consequence, all of our lives are up for grabs.[14]

The Abortion Mentality and the Family

Roe v. *Wade* opened the door for other intrusions by the Court. The principles of this decision have been extended into the very heart of the family and threaten its existence as an institution.

In *Planned Parenthood* v. *Danforth* (1976), the Supreme Court ruled unconstitutional a Missouri law requiring the consent of the husband before the wife could have an abortion in the first twelve weeks of pregnancy and, in the case of an unmarried woman under the age of eighteen, the consent of a parent or guardian unless a doctor certified the abortion to be required to save the life of the mother.[15] The Court recognized that Missouri had an interest in promoting family and marital relationships. However, the Court implicitly rejected the Christian principle of the husband's or parent's responsibility for his family. Instead, the family must abide by a relativistic moral model.

The Supreme Court did not stop at *Danforth*. In 1977 it decided *Carey* v. *Population Services International* in which it held unconstitutional (based upon the right to privacy) a state law that restricted the sale of contraceptives to those over sixteen years of age, and then only by a licensed pharmacist.[16]

Two years later the Court decided the case of *Bellotti* v. *Baird*.[17] There the Court found unconstitutional a state law that required parental written consent before an abortion could be performed on an unmarried minor woman, but which provided that an abortion could be obtained under court order upon a showing of good cause if one or both of the parents refused consent.

In early 1981 in *H. L.* v. *Matheson*,[18] the Court upheld the constitutionality of a Utah statute that requires a physician to "notify, if possible" the parents of a dependent, unmarried minor girl prior to performing an abortion. The Court said: "As applied to immature and dependent minors, the statute plainly serves the important considerations of family integrity." This narrow decision does not give parents the authority to prohibit their children from having an abortion, but only provides notification of the intent to abort "if" it is possible at the time to contact the parents. Thus parents are reduced to the level of state-employed consultants.

The concern with these decisions lies in what they are saying about family and parental rights as a whole. *First,* the rights of parents are subordinate to the rights of privacy of their children to have abortions and sexual relations. Abortion introduces murder into the life of the family. The Supreme Court, however, has ruled that parents cannot stop the murder of their grandchildren. What decision could be more important? Yet it is illegal.

Second, the family is no longer the basic institution for determining values for children; instead, this is the state's province in and through its various agencies.

Of equal concern must be the groundwork that has been laid in the courts for even more intrusion into the life of the family. This is illustrated in the language of an important 1972 Supreme Court case. In this case, *Wisconsin* v. *Yoder*, the Supreme Court held that a school attendance law requiring parents to send their children to school until the age of sixteen violated Amish parents' freedom of religion and infringed their right to direct the religious

"It all started when she began watching Vegas, Dallas, Charlie's Angels, and Love Boat for the PTA!"

upbringing of their children. However, in his dissenting opinion, Justice William O. Douglas raised a question:

> If the parents in this case are allowed a religious exemption, the inevitable effect is to impose the parents' notions of religious duty upon their children. Where the child is mature enough to express potentially conflicting desires, it would be invasion of the child's rights to permit such an imposition without canvassing his views. . . . As the child has no other effective forum, it is in this litigation that his rights should be considered. And, if an Amish child desires to attend high school, and is mature enough to have that desire

respected, the State may well be able to override the parents' religiously motivated objections.[19]

In reply to the Douglas dissent, the majority of justices stated: "The dissent argues that a child who expresses a desire to attend high school in conflict with the wishes of the parents should not be prevented from doing so. There is no reason for the Court to consider that point since it is not an issue in the case."[20]

Therefore, the Supreme Court has left a question mark concerning whether or not a child has a constitutional right to refuse to follow parental direction in a myriad of instances. In light of the abortion and contraceptive cases, all decided since *Yoder,* the question mark looms even larger than originally thought.

The Doors Swing Wide

Through constitutional interpretation the basic institutions of society are being consumed by the state. The child is now the creature of the state. The Supreme Court even exercises the power of life and death over the unborn child. In its ostensible dedication to the recognition and creation of new liberties and rights (the right to contract, the right to contraceptives, the right to abortion) the state is making itself the absolute judge and custodian of all human values. We have arrived at the dead-end mentality of modern man: the disposable man.

Chapter Twelve

The Disposable Man

"There is a 'thinkable' and an 'unthinkable' in every era," state Francis Schaeffer and C. Everett Koop in *Whatever Happened to the Human Race?* "One era is quite certain intellectually and emotionally about what is acceptable. Yet another era decides that these 'certainties' are unacceptable and puts another set of values into practice. On a humanistic base, people drift along from generation to generation, and the morally unthinkable becomes the thinkable as the years move on."[1]

Many of us, I'm sure, can remember when the idea of legalized abortion was unthinkable. On January 22, 1973, it became thinkable—and the opposing view became "reactionary."

The abortion decision was the keystone of what is currently happening and will happen in the near future. As Schaeffer and Koop comment:

> The thinkable of the eighties and nineties will certainly include things which most people today find unthinkable and immoral, even unimaginable and too extreme to suggest. Yet—since they do not have some overriding principle that takes them beyond relativistic thinking—when these become thinkable and acceptable in the eighties and nineties, most people will not even remember that they were unthinkable in the seventies. They will slide into each new thinkable without a jolt.[2]

The idea that man is nothing more than a machine has generally become accepted by society. The current thinkables have become infanticide and euthanasia. Just over the horizon genetic engineering and the remaking of man await us. A machine can be tinkered with, and, if it malfunctions, the plug can be pulled and the lights will go out.

The Death of Meaning
The meaning of human life depends on an external reference point. As this reference point is denied in decisions such as *Roe* v. *Wade,* the meaning of life has been lost to modern society. Life is merely a function. Meaning belongs, it is held, to the old world of religion, which is really nothing but myth.

Man's new society must not be religious but technological, the humanist holds. Things must be judged, not in terms of good and evil, but in terms of utility and pragmatism. All things thus are relative to the purposes of society. If society says that it is better for the general welfare if you are in a prison camp, you will have no valid protest since there is no standard by which you can judge the actions of the state.

Man is here to be used and then discarded. Aleksandr Solzhenitsyn illustrates this principle in *The Gulag Archipelago*. If people were needed for a new construction plan in Siberia or elsewhere, as much as one fourth of Leningrad was arrested and transported to slave labor camps.[3] The people were impotent in the face of this. They tried to find the meaning of their arrests, but there was no meaning. There was only pragmatism, utility, and, in the end, terror.

The consequence of the loss of meaning in general is that man himself, who was once seen in the image of God, loses his meaning. He is seen only as a bundle of urges and drives seeking existential satisfaction. Man, like a throwaway pop bottle, is disposable.

René Descartes could say in the early seventeenth century: "I think, therefore, I am.'' The creative thought process demonstrated that man has spiritual reality and value. Now, Harvard behaviorist B. F. Skinner has written that man has a change in thought only as a consequence of his environment. Thought is, so to speak, a ''secretion of the brain,'' as bile is a secretion of the liver. Man, thus, has no self-initiating personality or creative thought process.

This doctrine of disposable man will ultimately prove suicidal. Since man is only a process, he has no true future, only the illusion of a technological hope. The growth of technology is leading people to substitute

"Well, it all started when they gave me a plastic heart. Then plastic kidneys, a plastic stomach, plastic leg, plastic . . ."

mechanical order for the life of the spirit, for the personal, and for God. There is thus a new idolatry: technolatry, the worship of scientific techniques.

Through technolatry man has been reduced to an abstract entity—a number in the computer—something that can be erased on the tape. Human beings are, therefore, an afterthought in a technology that merely views people in utilitarian terms. This is why we are beyond the thinkable in the areas of abortion, infanticide, and euthanasia. The new thinkable by way of genetic engineering is the transhuman: part man, part machine. It's the next logical step. Abortion is both a symptom of this disorder and the cause of further disorder—just as the high fever that is a symptom of infection may itself cause permanent brain damage.

The New Environment

Media analyst Marshall McLuhan writes in *The Social Impact of Cybernetics:* "We are never aware of our environment until it becomes the content of a new environment. The culture in which a man lives consists of structures based on ground rules of which we are mysteriously unconscious. . . . But any change in ground rules nonetheless modifies the total structure."[4] McLuhan is telling us that a society moves into a new environment or pattern of life before it realizes it. Clearly, then, when people fully realize that a horror has been created it may be too late to fight it.

The loss of the humanity of man is with us. It has become our new environment. When men such as Nobel laureate James Watson declare their beliefs in the appropriateness of infanticide, we are in the new environment.

"If a child is not declared alive until three days after birth, then all parents could be allowed the choice only a few are given under the present system," Watson said in 1973. "The doctor could allow the child to die if the parents so choose and save a lot of misery and suffering. I believe this view is the only rational, compassionate attitude to have."[5]

Likewise, another Nobel laureate, Francis Crick, remarked in 1978 that "no newborn infant should be declared human until it has passed certain tests regarding its genetic endowment and that if it fails these tests it forfeits the right to live."[6] These are just a few of numerous statements to this effect from leaders in both medicine and science. Such ideas have consequences, and they always translate into action.

The massive power of the humanistic media must not be underestimated in the creation of the atmosphere for the new environment. The organized media functions much like a nonelected bureaucracy. Presidents come and go, but the controlled press is always present. There may be no conspiracy to propagandize the news beyond recognition. However, when this group of highly powerful individuals share the same humanistic consensus, their weight takes on awesome proportions. Ideas put forth by active humanist groups are often trumpeted through the media. They are given public hearing through the courts, while facing almost certain success as the media locks in behind them to give the appearance of vocal and broad-based support. Much of the time, however, this support is not really there.

At the same time, groups or individuals who attempt to present alternative views on the issues are often denigrated. As the media analysts so well understand, truth is often a state of mind; the way something is perceived is the way it is believed to be. More and more cowed by the tremendous power of this organized machine in the courts, the bureaucracy, and the media, the public increasingly becomes bewildered and unable to cope with the challenge. This is when they are more easily moved into a new environment.

The new environment surrounds us. The hope is in the governmental and scientific elite. And the elite is out to remake man and, failing that, it will kill him.

Infanticide

Infanticide is the killing of a *born* child. It is killing whether it is accomplished by a direct act, or whether the child is allowed to die by indirect action such as refusing to feed him or her. In every state it is against the law to kill a born human being either by negligent action or by premeditation.

Yet "infanticide is being practiced behind the shielding facade of the hospital," says C. Everett Koop. "The law is strangely silent about what amounts to public confessions in reputable scientific journals by medical doctors who admit that they are indeed practicing it."[7]

The shameful state of the legal and medical professions is exhibited in the case of Dr. William B. Waddill, Jr. An obstetrician in California, Waddill was tried for allegedly strangling to death a baby born alive following a saline abortion. At a preliminary hearing in April 1977, Dr. Ronald Cornelsen testified that Dr. Waddill throttled the infant's neck and complained about what would happen if the baby survived.

"Waddill said that there would be lawsuits, that the baby would be brain damaged, and talked about stopping respiration by drowning or injecting potassium chloride," Cornelsen testified.[8]

At the trial in January 1978, Mrs. Joanne Griffith, a nurse at the hospital, testified that another nurse said Dr. Waddill ordered everyone to leave the baby alone and not do anything for the child. Dr. Cornelsen testified that when he first examined the baby, the heart was beating sixty to seventy times a minute with a regular rhythm. There was some discoloration on the baby's neck (allegedly from the first attempt at strangling). He further testified that while he was examining the baby, Dr. Waddill "stuck his hand back in [the isolette] and pressed the baby's neck again."[9]

The trial began to falter when the issue departed from whether or not Waddill had indeed strangled a living being and began to focus on the definition of death. Initially the judge had instructed the jury as to the traditional meaning of death: If the child was either breathing, had a heart beat, or there were spontaneous movements of voluntary muscles, the infant was alive. If none were present, the child was considered dead.

Later in the trial the judge introduced for deliberation the new California definition of death, which holds that lack of brain waves indicates death in the person. This difference in the definition of death caused confusion. Eventually the trial ended in a hung jury. A later retrial ended in another hung jury. A short while afterwards, the court involved dismissed the charges against Waddill.

The sense of right and wrong is lost in a system that seems to justify what could very well be murder. The child is at the mercy of a doctor who has a right to kill. And the courts will not enforce the law.

Lawyers should be frightened to condone infanticide. Even many of the lawyers who claim to be Christians do not take a vocal stand on abortion or infanticide. The church itself has forgotten God's view of the worth of human life. Schaeffer and Koop state: "If . . . theologians no longer believe in such a God, they should not use the church as a platform from which to propagate their discriminatory ideas."[10] The church has departed from the stand against abortion that the Christian church has taken from its earliest days. For example, Tertullian writes in A.D. 195:

> For us murder is once for all forbidden; so even the child in the womb, while yet the mother's blood is still being drawn on to form the human being, it is not lawful for us to destroy. To forbid birth is only quicker murder. It makes no difference whether one take away the life once born or destroy it as it comes to birth. He is a man, who is to be a man; the fruit is always present in the seed.[11]

The truly sad situation today is that a portion of the non-Christian world vocally objects to abortion while the church does little. The church should be out front and visible. Christians should be continually confronting the abortion clinics, the courts, the legislatures, and the media. The church should be *forcing* the issue.

Euthanasia

With the case of Karen Quinlan, the word *euthanasia* became a permanent part of our language. Karen Quinlan was delivered to an emergency room of a community hospital by friends. She was unconscious after having taken a combination of alcohol and drugs. Expert medical witnesses from various parts of the country said that she would never recover and that her life was being sustained only by the mechanical respirator, which breathed for her.

The situation broke nationwide when the parents of Karen Quinlan petitioned a court to direct the physicians caring for their daughter to terminate the operation of the respirator. Judge Robert Muir of the lower New Jersey court ruled that to disconnect the respirator would be an act of homicide, because Karen would be unable to support her own respiratory effort and would die. On appeal, however, the New Jersey Supreme Court reversed the lower court's decision and ruled that the plug could be pulled. Ironically, Karen didn't die when the respirator was disconnected.

It doesn't take much imagination to project what the future holds. Early in the history of the American welfare state, millions of young Americans supported a much smaller number of aged on various state programs. Today, the situation is reversed. Millions of aged people are being supported financially by a shrinking number of younger people. How long will it take for the youth of America who are continually bombarded with the abortion

"I knew I should have aborted you like all the rest, Leon!"

mentality to decide that the aged are really nothing more than useless eaters and quite unwanted? It isn't that big a leap.

Rational Suicide

Suicide is the ultimate assertion of autonomous man. It is also a denial of the goodness and power of God to sustain us in adversity and ultimately give us everlasting life. Since the mere word *suicide* has a depressing sound, nice-seeming adjectives are being added. The concept of "rational suicide"—a terminally ill patient's decision to take his or her own life—is rearing its ugly head. This concept, also termed "self-deliverance" and "voluntary euthanasia," began attracting attention in 1978 when Derek Humphrey, an

English journalist, wrote a book entitled *Jean's Way,* which describes how he aided his terminally ill wife to commit suicide. In the summer of 1980, Humphrey went even further and formed an organization called Hemlock in Los Angeles, which supports the right of the terminally ill to commit suicide. In an interview in the *American Bar Association Journal,* Humphrey explained that Hemlock "does not encourage people to die; we encourage them to hang on for as long as possible. . . . [but] if for medical reasons life becomes unbearable, self-deliverance is a civil right that patients should have."[12]

The media effectively brought the issue of rational suicide into focus when they aired the Public Broadcasting Service program "Choosing Suicide" in 1979. The program centered around Jo and Mel Roman, their family, and friends, as they discussed the contemplated suicide of Jo Roman. At one point in the program Mrs. Roman said: "I hope I'm going to get out before a stroke or before pain. . . . I don't want to have a minute of pain. I want to die on a day when I feel well and in command of myself, and where I can know that I am making my choice. It's my life canvas, and I am going to end it my way."

Mrs. Roman's statement was an explicit claim to total autonomy. Was her life really her canvas? Is suicide a biblical alternative to life? The answer is "No." Man is fearfully and wonderfully created to live. The ultimate example is Christ himself who obviously could have opted for suicide—perhaps even taking hemlock like Socrates—but instead chose to suffer the pain of the cross.

Pain is the human dilemma brought on by the Fall. Freedom from pain is not a real possibility. Pain is part of the human condition; suffering belongs to our way of life. This doesn't mean that man should not strive to end suffering and pain, but suicide—which means total despair—is not a biblical alternative. It is prohibited by the Sixth Commandment: Thou shalt not kill. Man is not to play God.

Rational suicide has brought about the right-to-die movement. Right-to-die bills have been introduced and become laws in a significant number of states. Moreover, state laws classifying attempted suicide as a crime have been largely eliminated. It has also been reported that "sentiment is spreading to reform laws against aiding and abetting suicides."[13]

Even influential members of the judiciary have accepted the idea that the right to die is a viable alternative to life. J. Skelly Wright, chief justice of the United States Circuit Court of Appeals for the District of Columbia, has said that the right-to-die movement is not a sign of moral decay "but that society is becoming more civilized, more sophisticated."[14] Pagan Roman society, which praised suicide, was very sophisticated indeed!

If this direction continues, the decision to die will ultimately be enforced by law through the courts. In the end, suicide will be controlled and augmented by the state. The door is opened to the *Brave New World* described by Aldous Huxley in 1936. If it is not closed, we can expect forced death some time in the future.

The Doctor as Killer

Francis Schaeffer and C. Everett Koop have written that a "doctor is responsible to God for the manner in which he works to save a single human life. It is a matter of stewardship. The surgeon is accountable for the way he uses the gifts that God has given him. He is also responsible for the life entrusted to his care. It is a question of moral principle."[15] Under God, the doctor is a minister of healing. But, as Koop notes, the "role of the physician is shifting from healer to killer."[16]

With abortion, infanticide, and euthanasia, the doctor ceases to be the protector of life and becomes a murderer, even if the Supreme Court says it is legal. A radical change is taking place in the medical profession. Instead of regarding life as sacrosanct—as wholly governed by God and beyond the doctor's province to destroy—doctors have begun to play God. The doctor becomes a murderer just as the judge who legitimizes abortion is a murderer.

The majority of the people may tolerate abortion, but they will never respect an abortionist. Even pagan cultures that practiced abortion freely despised the abortionist. Man, created in God's image, will always reflect some degree of the law of God. With the coming of abortion, the legal and medical professions have lost a great measure of respect.

The late anthropologist Margaret Mead pointed out in 1978 that in the days before Hippocrates and the Hippocratic oath, the patient never knew whether the approaching physician was coming in the role of the healer or the killer. Now that our country is in the hands of prodeath judges and doctors, we may face the same dilemma.

In a New Image

On June 16, 1980, the Supreme Court in *Diamond* v. *Chakrabarty* held that microbiologist Ananda Chakrabarty of the University of Illinois Medical Center was entitled to a patent for a strain of bacteria he developed through genetic crossbreeding.[17] Sidney Diamond, the United States commissioner of patents and trademarks, had refused Chakrabarty a patent, because Diamond did not believe that "living things" were patentable under the patent law. Without a hint of moral consideration, the Court stretched the patent law to include Chakrabarty's work.

Jeremy Rifkin, director of the People's Business Commission in Washington, D. C., said that "in 10 or 20 years, *Diamond* will be looked back on as one of the biggest decisions a court has ever made."[18] Rifkin, whose organization opposed the ruling, added that *Diamond* is "the patent decision of the century because it is the biggest opening. It says that any item manufactured by humans that performs a function is patentable; in other words, that anything is patentable."[19]

Moreover, Rifkin noted that holders of a patent on gene-splicing techniques "would be able to play God." The patentability of living organisms creates the potential for "the gene pool of this planet to be controlled by industry."[20] He warned that the patenting of genetically engineered organisms means that "manufactured life—high and low—will have been categorized as less than life, as nothing but common chemicals."[21]

The *Diamond* decision has potentially opened the door to the legalization of the remaking of man. Albert Rosenfeld, in *The Second Genesis*, writes with a seeming fascination: "Coming: the control of life. With man at the controls . . . a new Genesis—The Second Genesis. The creator, this time around—man. The creation—again, man. But a new man. In a new image. A whole series of new images. What will the new images be?"[22]

New genetic knowledge could be used in a beneficial way. However, once the uniqueness of people has been removed, mankind is viewed as only one of the gene patterns. As Schaeffer and Koop note:

> [T]here is no reason not to treat people as things to be experimented on and to make over the whole of humanity according to the decisions of a relatively few individuals. If people are not unique, as made in the image of God, the barrier is gone. Once this barrier is gone there is no reason not to experiment genetically with humanity to make it what someone thinks to be an improvement socially and economically. The cost here is overwhelming. Should the genetic changes once be made in the individual, these changes will be passed down to his or her children, and they cannot ever be reversed.[23]

The *Diamond* decision is the application of cold, steely sociological law. There is no concern for values or ethics.

A disturbing aspect of *Diamond* is that the Supreme Court, without question, gave the future control of genetic engineering to industry and business concerns. The giant technological corporations will be controlling the destiny of genetics in terms of the cruel world of economics. As demonstrated in the past, "to make a fast buck" the American business community will literally stop at nothing. There will be no moral considerations—only technological and economical growth. Moreover, what will the scruples be of medical personnel who earned $250,000 a year killing the unborn when they are given the opportunity to earn an extra $1,000,000 a year by some genetic tinkering on the side? Will the Court defend anyone? I think not, given the precedent set in *Roe* v. *Wade*.

We are thus at the disposal of sheer economic greed in terms of future life. And mankind is in danger of being made over arbitrarily into an

"...mama...dada..."

image of what some people think mankind ought to be. However, to the humanist—who has failed in his attempt to manage the affairs of human beings in their present state—this is something to look forward to.[24]

Where Do We Go from Here?

It is obvious that the ideas of humanism have had a devastating impact. In calling for the abolition of man as an individual, B. F. Skinner proclaims: "His abolition has long been overdue. Autonomous man is a device used to explain what we cannot explain in any other way. He has been constructed from our ignorance, and as our understanding increases, the very stuff of which he is composed vanishes. . . . To man *qua* man we readily say good riddance."[25] Skinner proposes that man, the spiritless and materialistic machine, be placed in a highly manipulative and regulated environment in order to control him.[26]

Humanism posits that man is no more than a machine or used "junk," which can be aborted when it is deemed desirable.

Francis Schaeffer notes the position in which modern man has placed himself: "[T]he concept [of man's dignity] is gone. We are in the post-Christian world. Man is junk, and man can be treated as junk. If the embryo is in the way, ditch it. If the old person is in the way, ditch him. If you're in the way . . . and that's what lies before us."[27]

The danger created by the pervasive influence of humanism is apparent. Judicial relativism deposits "raw power" in the hands of state institutions and, in particular, the courts. Then, the courts are free to establish law and effectuate control as they see fit. "In these circumstances," law professor Jacques Ellul states, "the order of society and the established human rights are in no way protected against arbitrary power, and there is no reason why the discernment of right and wrong should not be given over to an all-powerful State charged with making its own criteria."[28]

The possibility of an imposed order becoming a reality in the modern state is imminent. Imposed order, if it comes, will find its justification in the nondignity of man. It can be stemmed by recovering the value of man as posited by Christian theism. The future of freedom, therefore, is as always dependent upon how we apply the truths of the past—truths founded upon the Bible.

Chapter Thirteen

The Christian Response

We are at an important crossroads in time and history. Any man can take one of two ways. But Christ made it very clear that one cannot serve a pagan ideology and Christian truth at the same time. If you mix humanism with Christian truths, the basic message of Christianity is destroyed. The vitality of the Christian faith is lost, and the church is unable to respond effectively to the forces of humanism.

It is time to shed the naive idea that the modern humanistic state exists to perpetuate good government. It is there to perpetuate itself at all costs. It is also time to discard the idea that Christians can simply go about their business, neither looking to the left nor to the right. Every true Christian is in some way on an eventual collision course with the modern technological state, and he should be prepared for it. The technological state has no need for an active church. Indeed, it requires a silent church. There is no room for God in such a state.

A prime example is the Nazi state erected by Adolf Hitler. Hitler believed in neither God nor conscience, which he called "a Jewish invention, a blemish like circumcision." Man's hope was in scientific reason. Alan Bullock in *Hitler: A Study in Tyranny* quotes Hitler in the midst of World War II saying:

> The dogma of Christianity gets worn away before the advances of science. . . . Gradually the myths crumble. All that is left is to prove that in nature there is no frontier between the organic and the inorganic. When understanding of the universe has become widespread, when the majority of men know that the stars are not sources of light, but worlds, perhaps inhabited worlds like ours, then the Christian doctrine will be convicted of absurdity. . . . The man who lives in communion with nature necessarily finds himself in opposition to the Churches, and that's why they're heading for ruin—for science is bound to win. . . . Thousands of excursionists will make a pilgrimage there every Sunday. . . . It will be our way of giving man a religious spirit.[1]

Hitler did not see the state as secular. To him it was a religious institution intent on saving man in terms of its technology.

Christianity is at war even in a world of peace. Christ said he came not to bring peace but a sword. Much too often the modern church has sought peace and compromise with the world. As a consequence, the church has allowed the tide of humanism to roll over society and encompass it. Nowhere has this been more true than in the Christian community's silence and acquiescence to the ever growing power and unconstitutionality of the federal government.

The church must realize that personal evangelism is not enough. Christians have a responsibility for society at large and for the abuses of power in that society. It is up to the Christian community, because we know that the state is not absolute, to stop them.

All too often the Christian community has compromised while laboring under the naive impression that in this way "the church could reach more people." As such, it is not the non-Christian who is most to blame for the cruelty we see today. It is the silent church.

Hail, Caesar!

The religious fervor of the gladiators' salute, "Hail, Caesar!" has its counterpart today. Candidates in modern election campaigns present themselves as heroes whose election will mark the advent of a new world. "This is the man, the one who has been promised again and again." Maybe this is why two- and three-term presidents have become a historical oddity. We realize halfway through the first term that this man is not the savior of our modern world.

Yet as Christians have become more involved with the right or the left in the political arena, the candidate has all too often been characterized as

the hope for a new America. The danger in this lies in the fact that Christ is the only hope. Modern paganism's religious hope has been placed in politics because pagan ideology posits the state as the ultimate order. For the Christian it is not, and cannot be. Consequently, the church as an institution must avoid becoming too closely aligned with the state in an official capacity. As Alan Johnson notes in *The Freedom Letter:* "A Christianity tied too closely to the civil authorities soon finds itself being used as a tool to sanction the particular policies and acts of a government which uses the church to win citizen approval."[2]

Conflict between Christ and Caesar is not inevitable. Jesus specifically commanded his disciples to "render . . . unto Caesar the things which are Caesar's'' (Matt. 22:21). It becomes inevitable when the secular authority—Caesar—demands for himself honors that belong only to God. Church and state can never be entirely separated, for each is interested in a wide range of human concerns, and their interests inevitably overlap. However, as long as the state does not claim absolute authority and autonomy, it can exercise a lawful role in establishing order and civil justice. In this capacity, the state is called the servant of God (Rom. 13:4).

The Roman Empire claimed such absolute and autonomous authority for centuries, until the conversion of the Emperor Constantine in A.D. 313 brought a fundamental change. Still, during the centuries from Constantine to the French Revolution, there were tremendous conflicts between church and state, between God and the various Caesars. But on the whole the state always accepted the theory that it was subordinate to God and to his Word, the Bible. Now, in what many historians term the "post-Constantinian age," the state has come to assert total autonomy and absolute authority once again.

In modern America, the state does not claim divine worship, as pagan Rome did. It permits churches to carry on their worship as before. But it seems to be seeking to make itself the center of all human loyalties, the goal of all human aspirations, the source of all human values, and the final arbiter of all human destiny. Without using the language of religion, it is claiming to be divine, and is creating a potentially devastating conflict with the church.

A president may declare himself to be born again and take an active role in congregational worship, but that is no guarantee that the state that he heads will not continue and even intensify its struggle against Christianity and the churches. Indeed it was under a professing Christian president, Jimmy Carter, that the federal bureaucracy made some of its most threatening inroads into areas of Christian concern, and that the Supreme Court banned the Ten Commandments from the nation's public schoolrooms.

The Bible and Christian Resistance

When confronted by the state, the silent church often presents a weak protest, and if pushed, wilts. This stance was not the position of early Christianity or the position of the biblical writers.

As Francis Schaeffer writes in *A Christian Manifesto:*

> The early Christians died because they would not obey the state in a civil matter. People often say to us that the early church did not show any civil disobedience. They do not know church history. Why were the Christians in the Roman Empire thrown to the lions? From the Christian's viewpoint it was for a religious reason. But

from the viewpoint of the Roman State they were in civil disobedience, they were civil rebels. The Roman State did not care what anybody believed religiously; you could believe anything, or you could be an atheist. But you had to worship Caesar as a sign of your loyalty to the state. The Christians said they would not worship Caesar, anybody, or anything, but the living God. Thus to the Roman Empire they were rebels, and it was civil disobedience. That is why they were thrown to the lions.[3]

We must not forget that at one time the early church was illegal in the Roman Empire. To survive, the church had to go underground—literally—into the catacombs. In doing this the church was violating the law. It was considered rebellion.

The battle for Christian existence may be upon us. As the state becomes increasingly pagan, it will continue to exert and expand its claims to total jurisdiction and power over all areas, including the church. Inasmuch as only those who hold to Judeo-Christian absolutes have a reference point outside the state, it will take Christian rebels to stem the tide of the humanistic state—rebels in the sense that they will resist, challenge, or protest all institutions and thought forms that are at variance with the Bible.

Strong biblical grounds serve as a foundation for Christian resistance to state paganism. The basic text for such resistance is found in the thirteenth chapter of Romans. It is interesting that this chapter is often used by those who claim the state has authority to mandate anything that Christians must blindly follow. This argument can be advanced only if Romans 13 is used improperly.

In Romans 13 the Bible instructs that the state (or state official) is a "minister of God to thee for good. But if thou do that which is evil, be afraid; for he beareth not the sword in vain: for he is the minister of God, a revenger to execute wrath upon him that doeth evil" (v. 4).

The Greek noun for the word *minister* in Romans 13 is *diakonos,* which means a servant, attendant, or deacon. *Diakonos* is used by Christ in Mark 10 when he states, "whosoever will be great among you, shall be your minister" (v. 43) or servant. It is used by Paul in 1 Timothy 4 to refer to "a good minister of Jesus Christ" (v. 6). In 1 Thessalonians 3 Paul refers to Timothy as a "minister of God" (v. 2), and in Ephesians 6 to Tychicus as "a beloved brother and faithful minister in the Lord" (v. 21).

Later in Romans 13 (v. 6) Paul again uses the term *minister* to describe a state official. The Greek word used in this verse, however, is *leitourgous,* which describes earthly rulers, who though they may not act consciously as servants of God discharge functions that are the ordinance of God as he so wills.

These particular Greek words are used in the Bible for a specific reason. It is God's way of telling us that legitimate state officials or civil rulers are to be servants under God, not lords or sovereigns. "For there is no power but of God" (Rom. 13:1). When the civil authorities divorce themselves from God and the Bible, they become self-styled lords and lawless as well. As St. Augustine of Hippo pointed out, godless civil rulers are no more than bands of robbers. Moreover, being lawless in relation to God, they are lawless and predatory in relation to men.

In Chapter 13 of Romans the apostle Paul describes the authority but also the limits of civil government. God has appointed civil magistrates to perform a twofold function (which reflects the general purpose of the state). *First,* the state must not destroy or subvert the good of society but protect and promote it. *Second,* the civil government must deter crime and bring to punishment those who foster evil in society.

Paul states very clearly in Romans 13:1 that all government is ordained and established by God. In the Bible, parents, pastors, civil authorities, employers, and others are said to have received their authority to govern from God. This authority, however, is delegated authority. It is not to be exercised independent of God's Word. For the courts, the Internal Revenue Service, and other civil agencies to speak of their authority as being over all areas of life and as being derived from the state is blasphemy.

In general, whenever the state is discussed in the New Testament, the scope and limits of its authority are defined. For example, in 1 Timothy 2 Paul writes:

> I exhort therefore, that, first of all, supplications, prayers, inter-
> cessions, and giving of thanks, be made for all men; For kings, and
> for all that are in authority; that we may lead a quiet and peaceable
> life in all godliness and honesty. For this is good and acceptable in
> the sight of God our Saviour; Who will have all men to be saved,
> and to come unto the knowledge of the truth (vv. 1-4).

Paul makes it clear that as part of the state's task of protecting the good, it is to create an atmosphere where men can be saved and come to the knowledge of the truth. Paul links this idea to our prayers and our attitude toward the state.

If the state is established by God to be a "minister of God to thee for good," then the question is: What about a civil government that acts diametrically opposed to the principles of the Bible? Does God also ordain such a government? If the answer is in the affirmative, then it can logically be argued that God was in support of Hitler's and Stalin's regimes.

Christians through the centuries have fallen into two fundamental errors with regard to the state. The first (that of the Anabaptists and some other enthusiasts) is to claim that the civil government represents the "god of this world" and is totally illegitimate. Christians are to have nothing to do with it.

The second (sometimes called Caesaropapism or Erastianism) holds that the state is divinely ordained in all respects, and that Christians owe it absolute obedience. Romans 13 refutes both errors: The state is a legitimate institution, ordained in principle by God, and intended to act as his servant to promote justice in the civil and social realm.

But its legitimacy is conditioned on its promotion of justice. If the state becomes totally hostile to the ends for which God has ordained it, then it becomes lawless.

However, what is to be done when the state does that which violates its legitimate function? If it commands that which is contrary to the Word of God, then, as Dr. Schaeffer says, "There is not only the right, but the duty, to disobey the state."[4]

Alan Johnson writes in his study of Romans that "the proper role of government is in promoting good and punishing evil. . . . It can be assumed that if either of these conditions are not met there is ground for resistance or even disobedience. That state is not absolute in its demands over us, nor is it infallible or always on the side of justice.''[5]

A popular myth invoked by Christians and non-Christians alike to justify their refusal to stand against immoral state acts has been the assertion that Jesus and the apostles were pacifists. This is not true. The question of pacifism did not arise, but Jesus was certainly not silent. He felt free to criticize not only the Jewish civil leaders (John 8:18-23), but also the Roman-appointed ruler Herod Antipas in referring to him as a ''fox'' (Luke 13:32). Jesus whipped the money changers and chased them out of the temple (John 2:13-17). And Christ is ultimately portrayed in the Book of Revelation as exercising righteous vengeance on the secular humanistic state.

Paul likewise accused one of the members of a grand jury, who commanded him to be hit on the mouth, of being a ''whitewashed wall,'' although he apologized when he learned that the man who issued the order was the high priest (Acts 23:1-5). Moreover, we must not forget that the majority of Paul's epistles in the New Testament were written from jail cells. Certainly he wasn't in prison for being a model citizen. He was in jail because he was considered a perpetrator of civil disobedience.

Peter's resistance in Acts 5 is a classic example of standing for the faith against the illegitimate acts of the state. Peter and others were thrown in jail for preaching. God himself defied the local authorities, and an angel opened the doors of the prison, freeing them. This was highly illegal.

God, however, identified with the men who defied the state. He takes Peter out of the prison, and then instructs the apostles to go and stand in the temple and preach. Again, this was in contradiction to the mandates of the state, and the apostles were brought before the Sadducees (or religious leaders) to answer for their ''crime.''

In response to the charges of preaching in Jesus' name, Peter replied: ''We must obey God rather than men'' (Acts 5:29, NAS). The apostles were then beaten and commanded not to preach Jesus. However, in Acts 5:42 we learn that ''daily in the temple, and in every house they ceased not to teach and preach Jesus Christ.'' Nothing could stop them. They were too intent on turning the world upside down for Christ (Acts 17:6).

It is not foreign to Christianity to protest the illegitimate acts of civil government. Total silence by the church is received as an endorsement of all the state does. But it is viewed as an act of treason by God. In fact, the Bible proclaims: ''A righteous man falling down before the wicked is as a troubled fountain, and a corrupt spring'' (Prov. 25:26).

Lex, Rex, and Resistance

Today most Christians naively accept a kind of Caesaropapism. The consensus is that civil government belongs in the realm of God's providential rule. While we may enjoy the right to representation and remonstration, we feel that Christians are obliged to obey the degrees of state authority. This is diametrically opposed to the principles set forth by Samuel Rutherford in *Lex, Rex*.

Acts of the state that do not have a clear reference point in the Bible are considered to be illegitimate and acts of tyranny (ruling without the

"This manuscript is great. . . . It should make the top ten of every book-burning list in the country!"

sanction of God), Rutherford argued. He held that a tyrannical government is always immoral, a work of Satan. "A power ethical, politic, or moral, to oppress, is not from God, and is not a power, but a licentious deviation of a power; and is no more from God, but from sinful nature and the old serpent, than a license to sin."[6]

Some might argue that tyranny would be legitimate if a people contracted or agreed to be governed by a tyrant. Not so, argues Rutherford, for the people can never enter into a valid contractual obligation with a ruler when the terms of the contract are outside the Law of God.

The trust relationship arises from a covenant (or a contract, a constitution) between the ruler (or state) and the people, in which the state agrees to rule the people according to God's Word. The ruler also has a covenant with God to obey his Word. The people agree to obey the state as long as the state functions on biblical principles.

"We give you a Throne," says Rutherford, "upon condition you swear by him who made heaven and earth, that you will govern us according to God's law."[7] If the state fails to rule according to the Word of God, Rutherford argues that the people are "loosed from the contract."[8] The implications of Rutherford's thesis are important, for it makes the vast majority of governments in the world today illegitimate.*

Rutherford presents several arguments to establish the right and duty of resistance to unlawful government. *First,* since tyranny is satanic, not to resist it is to resist God. The converse is also true: To resist tyranny is to honor God. *Second,* since the ruler is granted power conditionally, it follows that the people have the power to withdraw their sanction if the conditions are not fulfilled. The civil magistrate is a fiduciary figure (he holds his authority in trust for the people).[9] Violation of that trust gives the people a legitimate base for resistance.

Citizens have a *moral* obligation to resist unjust and tyrannical government. Unfortunately, this has long been overlooked in churches as a whole. While we must always be subject to the office of the magistrate, we are not to be subject to the man in that office, if his commands are contrary to the Bible. Rutherford wrote that "to obey God rather than man, as all the martyrs did, shall receive to themselves salvation."[10] It is an article of Christianity to resist injustice in all walks of life, including civil government.

Rutherford offered suggestions concerning illegitimate acts of the state. A ruler, he wrote, should not be deposed merely because he commits a singular breach of the compact he has with the people. Only when the magistrate acts in such a way that the governing structure of the country is being destroyed (when he is attacking the fundamental constitution or cove-

---

*Another book that influenced the American Revolution also discusses Christian resistance: *Vindiciae Contra Tyrranos* (or *Vindication Against Tyrants*), which John Adams held to be one of the most influential books of his time. *Vindiciae Contra Tyrranos* put forth four basic doctrines.

First, any ruler who commands anything contrary to the law of God thereby forfeits his rule. Second, we are rebelling against God when we obey a ruler who commands that which is against God's law. We are to obey God, not man. Third, since God's law is the fundamental law—and the only true source of law (neither king nor subject is exempt from it)—war is sometimes required in order to defend God's law against the ruler. Fourth, legal rebellion requires the leadership of lesser magistrates who can oppose the state. All these doctrines were basic to the colonial cause and were best expressed by Rutherford's *Lex, Rex.*

nant of society) is he to be relieved of his power and authority.[11] This is an application of God's grace and mercy to man through man.

The Appropriate Level of Resistance

Any discussion of civil disobedience is a very serious and frightening matter. This is more so because of the great number of mentally and ideologically imbalanced people who live in the world today. Any concept or proposed action can, and most likely will, be taken to its illogical conse-

"Here comes Congressman Blotts with more silly suggestions!"

quences by someone. Martin Luther and the other Reformers faced this problem. In a fallen world, this is to be expected. Such a fact, however, should not deter us from looking at the appropriate levels of resistance as outlined by Samuel Rutherford in *Lex, Rex*. The fact that we may be facing a totalitarian state compels consideration of these principles.

Rutherford was not an anarchist. In *Lex, Rex* he does not propose armed revolution as a solution. Instead, he sets forth three levels of resistance in which a private person may engage. First, he must defend himself by protest (in contemporary society this would usually be by legal action). Second, he must flee if at all possible; and, third, he may use force, if absolutely necessary, to defend himself. But a person should not employ force if he may save himself by flight. Nor should one employ flight if he can defend himself by protest and the employment of constitutional means of redress.[12] Rutherford illustrated this pattern of resistance from the life of David.[13]

When the state commits deliberate illegitimate acts against a corporate body such as a duly constituted state, or local body, or even a church, then flight is often an impractical and unrealistic means of resistance.[14] For a corporate group or community, there are two levels of resistance: remonstration (or protest) and then, if absolutely necessary, force is employed in self-defense. In this respect, Rutherford cautioned that a distinction must be made between a lawless uprising and lawful resistance.

When illegitimate state acts are perpetrated upon a community, resistance must be under the aegis of the duly constituted authorities: in particular, it must be under the rule of the lesser magistrates or local officials. Rutherford urged that local officials are just as much immediate vicars of God as the highest state official. They all respect God, and they are all bound to follow the Bible.

For example, if one believed he was being treated unfairly by some governmental agency he could contact his congressman and file a protest. The congressman could then represent him by going directly to the federal agency involved and correcting the matter. Rutherford stresses the need for representation by a duly appointed official; the Bible does not authorize anyone taking the law into his own hands.

The colonists followed Rutherford's model in the American Revolution. They elected representatives from every state who by way of the Declaration of Independence protested the acts of Great Britain. Failing that, they defended themselves by force.

Christian resistance does not mean that Christians should take to the streets and mount an armed revolution. There is no example in the Bible of any man of God who set out with the design to overthrow his government by violence. The emphasis in Scripture (as illustrated by Peter and Paul) is that by fulfilling the law of God without regard for the consequences, a true cultural revolution will occur.

Nor is Rutherford's suggestion of flight an option for the Christian in today's society. Due to the immense power of the modern state, there probably will be no place to flee to. The Pilgrims could escape tyranny by fleeing to America. But we live in a shrinking world. The so-called safety zones, such as Switzerland, are fading. Besides, the church has been taking flight spiritually for the last one hundred years. It is time for the church to get its head out of the sand and take a stand to fight the slide toward totalitarianism.

Protest is our most viable alternative at this time in history. The freedom yet exists for us to utilize our democratic right of protest to the maximum. However, we must realize that protest can be a form of force. When Peter was ordered not to preach Jesus in the temple, he ignored such illegitimate commands and reentered the temple to preach salvation to the Jews. This is force or compelling others to listen to something they do not want to hear.

A contemporary situation can serve to illustrate the principle of resistance. In the decision of *Stone* v. *Graham,* the Supreme Court, as I have mentioned before, ruled unconstitutional a Kentucky law that required the

"I admire Kranston . . . does all he can to keep an optimistic outlook!"

posting of the Ten Commandments in the public school classrooms of that state. Did the state of Kentucky have to follow the dictate of the Court in that instance?

This question can first be answered by determining if the Court's decision was nonbiblical. Does God want children to know the Ten Commandments? Jesus Christ himself said: "If ye love me, keep my commandments." There are numerous other biblical references concerning the instruction of children in the Commandments of God.

Second, did the Supreme Court, in making this decision, break the federal government's covenant with the people as well as that required by God? If Rutherford's analysis is used, then the answer must be, "Yes."

God's definition of good and proper government is one where there is a free flow of the Gospel into society. Not allowing schoolchildren to realize the vital importance of the Ten Commandments is an attack on this principle.

If the Court's action is indeed nonbiblical, and thus an illegitimate act of authority, then determining the proper mode of resistance would be the next step. In this case, the local school officials, based upon solid biblical grounds, could simply have refused to remove the Ten Commandments from the schoolhouse walls. Some local school districts in Kentucky did exactly that.

The Supreme Court cannot execute its own decisions. The entire system depends on people following what the Court says. The time may have come when a local community or a state may have to disobey the Supreme Court or other federal and state agencies that act contrary to the principles of the Bible. In light of Rutherford's arguments, this would not be inappropriate.

There does come a time when force, even physical force, is appropriate. When all avenues to flight and protest have closed, force in the *defensive posture* is appropriate. This was the situation of the American Revolution. The colonists used force to defend themselves. Great Britain, because of its tyranny, was a foreign power invading America. Note that the colonists did not cross the Atlantic Ocean and mount a physical attack against Great Britain itself. They defended their homeland. As such, the American Revolution was a conservative counterrevolution. The colonists saw the British as revolutionaries trying to overthrow the colonial governments. If not seen in this light, the American Revolution does not make sense.

Modern Christians face a more powerful foe than ever faced by the church before. If the totalitarian regime ever assumes complete control, the opportunities for use of force will present themselves. And we must act accordingly. We must always, no matter the circumstances, protect and defend God's people.

For instance, a true Christian in Hitler's Germany should have defied the state and hidden his Jewish neighbors from the SS Troops. Christians in the Soviet Union should do everything in their power to undermine the atheistic Communist regime. This should be true of all Communist regimes. Christ has proclaimed that all the earth is his and that his disciples are to preach to all nations. No government has any authority to restrict the free flow of God's Word. When they do, they should be resisted.

Call to Action

In Matthew 5 Christ states that the church is to be the salt or preservative in society. If not, Christ said, then the church is "good for nothing, but to be cast out, and to be trodden under foot of men'' (v. 13). The discussion of resistance only comes when the church has failed to be the preservative influence in society. When the church is silent, then there is a need for Christian rebels. With the humanistic consensus gaining a stronger foothold each day, it is not a farfetched notion to envision a time when we will see the church trodden under the feet of the humanists.

The unthinkables of yesterday—abortion, infanticide, euthanasia, and rational suicide—are here. The church must resist what is happening now to ensure that more ''unthinkables'' do not become ''thinkables.'' The church

"Do you realize you're the only one on this block that doesn't keep a gun in the house for protection!"

cannot be a spectator in the war that is raging. It must take a stand or there is no hope for a return to a society that cherishes life and seeks meaning.

We as Christians must once again commit ourselves to the whole view of Christianity. We must influence all areas of life including law and politics. We can leave nothing untouched by the Bible. We must begin anew to study all intellectual disciplines and apply the Bible to them. We must prepare to be the warriors we should be.

Whether we want to acknowledge it or not, the church is at war. The battle lines are drawn between humanism and Christianity. It is time to stop deluding ourselves by believing that things will somehow ''work out.'' Christians in all walks of life need to turn the tide and fight back against the inhuman trends that surround us. Moreover, Christians must unite to reenter the whole of society in all walks of life, especially law and government, and reclaim the world for Christ.

We need to remember God's warning in the First Commandment:

> Thou shalt not bow down thyself to them [other gods, such as humanism], nor serve them: for I the Lord thy God am a jealous God, visiting the iniquity of the fathers upon the children unto the third and fourth generation (Exod. 20:5).

If we do not heed the warnings of the Bible, if we do not remember that God judges the compromising church along with the country it inhabits, we are faced with but one alternative: to capitulate in the face of the totalitarian state. In effect, to say to the new fuhrer, "Hail, Caesar. We who are about to die salute you."

Chapter Fourteen

Plan
For
Action

Prophets of doom surround us. Many believe that the current political and social order is crumbling. The humanistic foundation that undergirds the West cannot stand the tensions of contemporary society. Instead of making the Christian fret, this should cause him to rejoice. It means that Christians can do something to effect change. The Christian can speak with clarity in the midst of the chaos. And, although things may grow worse—the collapse of the economy, threats of war, and such—the Christian must take Romans 8 seriously: "And we know that all things work together for good to them that love God, to them who are the called according to his purpose" (v. 28).

The Christian who sees no hope is not living consistently with the teachings of the Bible. We should view the world through the mind of Christ, because he is working for *all* things to come together for the good of the true church. It is the humanist who should have no hope. For him there is no God; only a cold grave awaits him.

We must, however, realize that things have steadily declined for the worse. It is difficult to find much truth on any subject in the media or even the law. Issues are not what they seem. The humanists have succeeded in rewriting and rewording most forms of communication—including the Bible. This is so people won't know what the truth is.

Such censorship was the focus of Ray Bradbury's novel, *Fahrenheit 451,* where a futuristic state burned all books in order to hide the truth from the people. As Bradbury wrote in an afterword to a later edition of the book: "Fire-Captain Beatty, in my novel *Fahrenheit 451,* described how the books were burned first by minorities, each ripping a page or a paragraph from this book, until the day came when the books were empty and the minds shut and the libraries closed forever." The Christian community, therefore, must realize that the humanists, like the firemen in Bradbury's tale, are slowly whittling away at the substance of truth in our world.

Recovering the Externality Idea

Philosophy is important. A person's philosophy dictates how he will act. If Christians continue to take the position that they are impotent in the face of the crises we face, then we will continue to have little effect on the culture.

Once, after I spoke on the obvious peril in the coming years, a lady told me that although the church may be persecuted, "Christians can go to the lions singing." Indeed, but we have a responsibility to try and stop the downward spiral before we get to the lions!

Often people come up and tell me they will be praying for me. I appreciate the power of prayer; I have seen its effectiveness in my own life. However, such a mentality can be a cop-out. It is easy to say, "I'll pray for you," and then go home and sink into an easy chair and watch television. If people who assume this position really mean it, they will act on their prayers. The apostle James tells us that faith is dead without works.

The church is holding "the truth in unrighteousness" when the church remains silent on the issues and fails to act as the Bible requires. Christians literally stagnate in churches that have no external political, legal, or moral impact upon the world. Truth cannot be bottled up and be effective.

The church must learn to externalize the principles of its faith as practiced by Christians during the Reformation and in early America. The truths of the Bible must flow from the mind into the world. A false pietism, a false "spirituality," and all the exclusively internal activities that so often make up the contemporary church neither bring revival nor reformation. The light must be taken from beneath the basket and placed on the hill.

Remembering the Cultural Mandate

The church has a mandate from the Creator to be a dominant influence on the whole culture, as I have mentioned before. In Matthew 5 Christ mandates or requires the church to be "salt" to the culture: "You are the salt of the earth; but if the salt has become tasteless, how will it be made salty again?" (v. 13, NAS). Salt not only preserves meats; salt makes one thirsty. If the church is

"OK, it's settled then. Heads we'll kill 'Thou shall not steal,' or tails 'Thou shall not commit adultery'!"

fulfilling its proper role, the culture should be thirsty for the knowledge of biblical truth.

Salt, if placed on metal and dampened with water, will slowly eat through steel. The church, which holds truth, should be able to penetrate and defeat the arguments and actions of paganism. Any Christian who believes he cannot effectively answer the secularist's arguments either doesn't really know his Bible or has not taken the time to study how to apply what he believes.

There is a strong emphasis in some sections of the church today on personal evangelism. That is admirable, but it is only one part of being "salt" to the world. It cannot be the only emphasis. The church has to touch and influence the entire community. Christians are not simply witnessing machines. We are a *whole people,* and we live in a *whole world.* To give a large section of the world over to paganism without a fight is to cheat God.

As theologian J. Gresham Machen pointed out in 1912: "We may preach with all the fervour of a reformer and yet succeed only in winning a straggler here and there, if we permit the whole collective thought of the nation . . . to be controlled by ideas which, by the resistless force of logic, prevent Christianity from being regarded as anything more than a harmless delusion."

Clearly, if Christ's mandate to be the salt is denied by the church (and it is a voluntary refusal to follow Christ's orders), then Christ sees the church as good for nothing but to be trampled under the feet of men. The consequence is persecution. It is a form of judgment, but it is also a way of forcing the church to respond to the cultural mandate.

But when the church refuses to act as salt, it also brings judgment upon the culture surrounding it. Not only must the church suffer but also the non-Christian culture. And when the final judgment comes, the blood of those who have never heard the consistent Christian message and die without Christ is on the hands of the church. It is a terrible burden to bear.

Pluralism

The church must beware of the concept of "pluralism" as it is advocated today. I am not saying that we should be opposed to the fact that cultures and races are different, and they should be respected for what they are. This was the old concept of pluralism. But the new form is different. It says that a Christian should not seek to force his or her religious beliefs on another. Unfortunately this has led to a consensus within society that anything is acceptable. Nothing is right or wrong; it is only a matter of preference.

To say this runs contrary to the mandates of the Bible. There is truth and untruth. There is good and evil. Christianity is truth. In the Great Commission Christ charged the church to conquer alien belief systems and to convert the individuals holding them. The pluralistic concept promulgated by modern society is a way of keeping the church from fulfilling the cultural mandate. The Christian is to "make disciples" of individuals, institutions, and cultures, not cower before alternative belief systems.

The church, it seems, has learned, as a successful Volkswagen commercial once put it, "to think small." This idea must be reversed or it stands to reason that we face perilous days ahead. To put it bluntly, as a man "thinketh in his heart, so is he." If the church really takes the Bible seriously, it can think like God. His plan ends in victory for the church, not defeat.

What Can We Do?
The first step is to recognize the problems within the Christian community itself. We must remove the beam from our own eye by putting God and the Bible first and recognizing that Christ is Lord over all areas of life. Then we are ready for action. Politics, the legal profession, social commentary, the press, all the fields of communication and academia are open to the Christian.

By sheer number the individual Christian, can effect great change. We must be aware of the need to be educated on the issues and, once educated, wary of compromise. Many fine books have been written that deal with aspects of the topics discussed in this book. Here is a representative sample:

- Schaeffer, Francis. *A Christian Manifesto*. Westchester, Illinois: Crossway Books, 1981.
- Schaeffer, Francis. *How Shall We Then Live?* Old Tappan, New Jersey: Fleming H. Revell Co., 1976.
- Schaeffer, Francis, and Koop, C. Everett. *Whatever Happened to the Human Race?* Old Tappan, New Jersey: Fleming H. Revell Co., 1979.
- Rushdoony, R. J. *This Independent Republic*. Fairfax, Virginia: Thoburn Press, 1964.
- Brown, Harold O. J. *The Reconstruction of the Republic*. New Rochelle, New York: Arlington House, 1977.
- Schaeffer, Franky. *Addicted to Mediocrity*. Westchester, Illinois: Crossway Books, 1981.
- Peters, Charles. *How Washington Really Works*. Reading, Massachusetts: Addison-Wesley Publishing Co., 1980.
- Jackson, Jeremy C. *No Other Foundation*. Westchester, Illinois: Crossway Books, 1980.

These books, plus those cited within the text, will give you a good start.

We live in a visual age, and the electronic media have great impact. It would be a good idea to purchase or rent the films *How Should We Then Live?* and *Whatever Happened to the Human Race?* and show them to community groups and individuals, as well as *The Second American Revolution,* the film counterpart to this book.

Once you have developed a knowledge of the issues, keep informed on current legislation. If you are involved in Christian broadcasting or publishing, begin a radio spot or a column that will feature issues that affect our religious liberty. If you are a lay person, suggest such a program to your Christian network or favorite magazine.

The most important contribution the individual can make is to become actively involved in local community affairs, politics, and legal battles. If America is going to be revitalized or reformed in a Christian sense, it will be done at the local level. America was meant to be primarily a system of local governments. The giant federal machine we have today in Washington, D.C., was never intended by the framers and must eventually be dismantled piece by piece.

Getting involved in local politics will eventually mean Christians running for office. This will include attending and eventually taking control of party conventions where grass-roots decisions are made. But you must begin right now by becoming involved in various political committees, thereby getting your name before party leaders as well as the electorate. We simply cannot expect a consistent Christian response to issues from non-Christian officials.

At the local level committed Christians, who understand the lordship of Christ over all of life, can have a tremendous impact. I have seen instances where one Christian sitting on a public board composed of seven members tipped the balance on the most crucial issues. Public school boards are probably one of the most important and influential organizations at the local level. They determine which books and educational materials go into the schools as well as the curriculum teachers teach. The potential for influencing the education of young minds is staggering.

Short of running for office, your contact with your local, state, and public officials is vital. In my involvement on the federal level with senators and congressmen, it has always amazed me how little input these men and women receive from the Christian community before voting on legislation. Many of the problems churches and Christian schools face with state intervention and interference today would never have arisen if the church and individual Christian had done their homework.

Letter writing is very important—not form letters, but handwritten letters voicing objection or approval concerning a piece of legislation. Christians within the various churches can form local political groups to coordinate letter writing. This means getting organized. These groups can also make sure that your representatives receive personal visits from people in the community. These are the tactics used by the proponents of legislation designed to destroy the Christian way of life. If done with honest and sincere motives, there is nothing wrong with telling your representative how you feel on an issue. In fact, your letter may tip the scale on how he votes.

The most powerful tool available to the individual, and individuals as organized in a group, is the ballot box. If your representative does not heed your advice on the central issues, then unseat him. This may involve running your own candidate.

Where possible seek out lawyers and judges who are sympathetic to your cause and push hard for their appointment to judgeships. Moreover, by placing pressure on your elected representatives, try to stop the appointment of anti-Christian judges. Something must be done to balance the courts. Forcing your representative to appoint judges who are sympathetic to the Judeo-Christian world view could very well impede the activism of the courts.

The Moral Majority has proven that grass-roots efforts can have a

tremendous impact on the national level. No matter what else can be said about the Moral Majority, it has used the freedom we still have in the political arena to stand against the state. The ordinary citizen can affect the political process.

Humanistic Influences

We also need to be constantly questioning the influences that surround us. Much of the humanistic indoctrination of society is being carried on by agencies that appear to be independent private groups but, because of their funding by the federal government are, in reality, arms of the state. An example of such an organization is the Public Broadcasting Service (PBS), which, although providing some good program content, consistently airs programs that favor unbiblical choices. Besides the program "Choosing Suicide," which I mentioned earlier, PBS has aired other programs like "Guess Who's Pregnant Now?" Forty-five minutes of this one-hour special was given to directors of Planned Parenthood and others who advocated liberal sex education in the public schools. In contrast a few minutes of a film clip from a Southern pastor's sermon represented the Christian stand. Throughout the program Christians were depicted as being against all sex education, as expecting their children to blindly follow the Seventh Commandment. Actually Christian groups are objecting to the promiscuity and amoral standards taught in some sex education programs, not sex education itself. The commentator's denouncing of the Christian stand as ignorant and irrelevant was veiled but insidious.

Public Broadcasting Service also aired a six-part program "Hard Choices," which discussed without moral comment such issues as genetic screening and amniocentesis, the inserting of a hollow needle through the uterus to determine fetus sex, and the subsequent abortion of unborn children because they are not the sex parents desire.

An organization, which is responsible directly or indirectly for much of the proabortion propaganda that has been infiltrated throughout the United States, is Planned Parenthood Federation of America. Amazingly enough, Planned Parenthood and its over one hundred affiliates have received over $100 million by direct grants and reimbursements from the federal government to promote, in effect, genocide.

Through such groups the federal government has placed itself in the position of advocating a prodeath position. Moreover, the federal state is using taxpayer's money to do it. Your representatives in Congress should be encouraged to remove the government funding for these projects. It is certainly not a province of the government to urge such policies. If your representatives do not respond, then it is time to institute legal action to stop this abuse. Don't let the false political dictum of separation of church and state stop you from getting involved.

After all is said and done, the basic change in our country will come through the truly Christian family. In view of the fact that the present humanistic culture is tenaciously attacking the institution of the family, Christians must take a hard look at what they are doing in their own families.

The family should be the center of Christian life. No other institution (including the church) or activities should get in the way of family life. Parents must develop relationships with their children, and this means spending time with them. There is nothing more spiritual than this.

Christian parents must counter the influence of the brainwashing of public schools, television (all media), and literature. Most television turns every home into a classroom where basically humanistic principles are taught. Allowing your children to watch very little television is an excellent idea. In fact, eliminating television entirely would bring more gain than loss. Television is a violent invasion of the privacy of the family. It not only consumes valuable time, but it is also stealing your children's minds.

As Christian parents, you must make sure that your children are being raised as complete Christians. This will involve instructing them in the

realities of the culture we are living in as well as the Bible. For example, are you teaching your children that Christianity is a system of thought that applies to all of life? Are they being educated to be a generation that will vigorously resist humanistic values and infringement on their rights? Are you guiding your children to help them understand twentieth-century problems so the coming generation will know how to attack the desperate crises we face from a Christian perspective?

Finally, in the context of the family, it is important to note that the cultural mandate given in Genesis 1: 26-28, "Let us make man . . . to be the master of all life upon the earth and in the skies and in the seas" (Living Bible), was bestowed upon Adam and Eve collectively as a potential family.

Intimately connected to the cultural mandate is the command to have children in verse 28: ''Be fruitful and multiply.'' God expects us to disciple the children he has entrusted to us.

The Law Student

Those planning to attend law school and those presently involved in law school can have a great impact on the systems of law and civil government. Much of what is taught in law school today is directly opposed to the teachings of the Bible. It is a humanistic system in need of a Christian orientation.

In my third and final year of law school, one of my law professors began his class by making this statement: ''Always remember that you are never in the courtroom to get justice, but to win!'' This is the legal mentality that is passed on to thousands of law students yearly. It is a survival-of-the-fittest mentality. When it is applied to the criminal justice system and legislation, we can see why we are facing a trauma in law today.

The apostle Paul in 1 Timothy 1 spoke about those who teach the law without biblical content:

> Now the end of the commandment is charity out of a pure heart, and of a good conscience, and of a faith unfeigned: From which some having swerved have turned aside unto vain jangling; Desiring to be teachers of the law; understanding neither what they say, nor whereof they affirm. But we know that the law is good, if a man use it lawfully (vv. 5-8).

A number of those in legal education today teach a legality without the content of true law. The Christian student cannot sit in class and allow this to happen. A vocal Christian law student can be an effective witness of the truth. Christian students must challenge professors who urge an immoral, pagan base to law. Law professors need to be reminded that much of law is still based on the Bible.

Christian law students should propose a course on William Blackstone or the common law, if their school does not have one. This can be done through the various student-faculty committees. Most contemporary law schools attempt to cover all the historical bases of law in one three-hour course called jurisprudence. It is not sufficient.

If the school refuses to alter the curriculum to study the Christian foundation of law, then Christian law students and those concerned should start their own extracurricular study group. Make it an honor society with prestige. More could be learned in one of these groups than in many courses taken in the current legal education system.

Many Christians believe and accept the fact that they are second-class citizens. Too often it is true that they are. However, this should not be the case. The Christian law student should be an example to the rest of the students. He or she should excel, if possible. If you are a serious law student, you can do well. Be the best.

Eventually, I believe more Christian law schools will come into existence. There are several in operation at this time. As this occurs more Christians will go to these schools. Until that happens, however, the Christian

"Harry 'Mad Dog' McDumm, I sentence you to the first available vacancy in the state penitentiary!"

must be prepared to enter the humanistic schools of law and thrust Christian ideas into the system. Moreover, as Christian law schools open, they must, if they are to serve any viable purpose beyond adding to the present pietistic jargon, teach law in a way that will lead to Christian activism by their graduates on all the frontiers of the justice system.

The lawyers who graduate from these schools should have a firm knowledge of Christian philosophy and of the true legal roots of American society. They should have studied the works of those writers cited in this book thoroughly and should leave with a sense that their practice of law is not as much a livelihood as a vocation to take society by the horns and turn it around.

The Lawyer

We who are Christian lawyers have reason to be ashamed. We, who supposedly have a working knowledge of God, have often lagged behind in dedication to the truth. Christian attorneys have simply failed to use their profession effectively.

In Matthew 13 Christ says: "Therefore every scribe [or lawyer] which is instructed unto the kingdom of heaven is like unto a man that is an householder, which bringeth forth out of his treasure things new and old" (v. 52). The lawyer who is learned in biblical law and applies it in the external world will produce much good fruit.

The role of the lawyer in modern society cannot be exaggerated. The entire American system is structured upon law. If the lawyer who professes Christ so desires, he or she can have a major influence in the direction of the culture. However, many attorneys believe their professions are somehow separate from their Christian calling. They compartmentalize their faith and practice.

The person who becomes a lawyer must see that he has taken on a high calling and, as such, must be a steward of what God has given him. One cannot be a lawyer from the hours of nine to five during the working week and thereafter act as a Christian. His Christian faith and his legal practice must be integrated.

The attorney who is a Christian must see the practice of his profession as a vocation, not a business. This may, and often does, mean that not all he does will be profitable financially. However, Christians have not been placed on this planet solely to make money but to communicate the consistent Christian message to the whole culture and change history.

At one time in the profession, attorneys were routinely called "counselors at law." That is an important term, which indicated that attorneys were advisers not only in legal and technical matters but consolers and counselors in the biblical sense. Proverbs 11 instructs: "Where no counsel is, the people fall: but in the multitude of counsellors there is safety" (v. 14).

We need fewer legal technicians and more attorneys who can counsel their clients on matters of divorce, abortion, child abuse, and other areas of moral concern. The Christian attorney's first prerogative should be to help people solve their problems.

Christian attorneys need to become aggressively and actively involved in local community affairs and politics. Most people will listen when an attorney speaks. The problem has always been in getting the Christian attorney to become involved in something other than church activities. The world needs the counsel of the godly lawyer.

Christian lawyers need to organize in local attorney groups not only to fellowship but to strategize on how they can influence their community. Imagine a strong local Christian lawyers' group threatening legal action against abortion clinics or upholding the right of a Christian teacher to talk about Christ in the public school classroom.

An involvement in local, statewide, and national bar association functions is important. Most of these groups have degenerated into social outlets. With proper guidance, they could become vocal on the issues and an excellent educational tool for both lawyers and society at large. Attorneys, however, must realize that their first loyalty is not to a bar association (or to keeping peace with their colleagues) but to Christ himself. In that spirit these lawyers should be willing to shoulder the burden of creating controversy locally and nationally in the cause of Christian absolutes.

We are all aware of the downward plight of the legal profession—that in and of itself should be the motivation for change. However, change in the Christian sense will not come unless those attorneys who profess Christ become visible in their profession. The legal system should be flooded with Christian lawyers dedicated to bringing change and fighting the evil that now pervades the courts and the whole enterprise of law. In this way, there is hope for a troubled profession. The challenge to the Christian attorney is to be a vocal, dynamic spokesman for the true legal profession—the one with Christ at its center—and to stop at nothing less than reclaiming the whole system.

The Church

Most of the books of the New Testament, as well as Christ's references in the Book of Revelation, are letters written to local churches. I believe this is because God first desires action to be taken there. Failing this, God works through organizations and individuals outside the local church. Those pastors who have voiced their dismay at the numerous evangelical groups who have organized outside the local church have only themselves to blame. Those groups are in essence a judgment on local churches and on the institutional church as a whole, a church that has not fulfilled the requirements God has set forth for it. These words are not written merely to be critical but in the hope that they will be heard. Tragically, the church has been apathetic to much of what has been going on outside its four walls.

Sermons, seminars, lectures, and books are all geared by the church for the individual Christian within the congregation. The same ideas are always being presented to the same people. Christ broke with the Pharisees on a similar issue. Jesus ate with sinners because he came to give a Christian message to them. Christ thus taught that the Christian message is an external thing. It has to flow out into the world, not be entombed within the church building.

The grave problems in the courts, in the law, and in civil government are the consequence of a century of church teaching that involvement in church activities is more important than involvement in the affairs and institutions of the world. Christian pastors must define church activities in such a way to recapture the biblical emphasis that involvement in all areas of the culture is a necessary part of true spirituality. In this way the church will thrive, instead of having to fight for its very existence as it is today.

The true church, by its very nature, is a political institution—political from the standpoint that, as Christ's exclusive preserve, the state has no legitimate authority over it. The true church says "hands off" to Caesar. This is a political statement—a delineation of the authority of the state. When this principle is aggressively upheld by the church, a balance is maintained between church and state.

An excellent program for churches to sponsor would be a free legal aid clinic to the poor and the helpless, which is now sadly lacking. As James states: "Pure religion and undefiled before God and the Father is this, To visit the fatherless and widows in their affliction, and to keep himself unspotted from the world" (James 1:27).

Local churches, as missions, could sponsor young people who want to go to law school. Churches should encourage their young people to study law and encourage Christian lawyers to reexamine ways to apply their faith to their profession. The church, if it took its task seriously, could flood the law schools with Christian law students who would eventually influence the legal and governmental systems. If any institutions need missionaries, it is the law schools. It is a mission field ripe for harvest.

Most importantly, the local church, as the pillar and the ground for truth, should instruct all its people in the laws and mandates of God. Instead of the numerous conferences on how to feel good spiritually, seminars on biblical law and the political system would be profitable. The people could be educated and given the tools to exercise the cultural mandate. The local church should be a teaching institution, not just a fellowship group. Through the teaching church a generation of Christians who know the issues and dare to speak out will be born. It was with twelve men like this that Jesus changed the world.

Summary of Action

I would like to summarize the immediate objectives of Christian action for everyone—the individual, the law student, the lawyer, and the church.

First, the power of the federal government must eventually be broken down to its constitutional limit, returning much of the power of the federal bureaucracy to the state and local governments. This is the federalistic principle upon which the American government was originally founded. This would entail curbing and, if necessary, eliminating the massive federal bureaucratic agencies such as the Internal Revenue Service. It will also mean a severe delimiting of the authority of the federal courts.

These objectives can be obtained in several ways. An initial effort must be made to influence Congress to act against these agencies and their

"Blast it, Hawkins, I didn't say make the new tax forms harder. . . . I said make them impossible!"

programs. Congress can effectively curtail the power of the federal government and its agencies by withdrawing funds to them or by eliminating certain agencies in their entirety.

As for the courts, Article III of the Constitution of the United States affords Congress the authority to restrict the Supreme Court's and the lower federal courts' power to hear most cases. Although it has been seldom used, under this constitutional provision Congress could virtually eliminate the federal courts. Certainly Congress could use this provision to limit the number of federal courts that are established, which would curtail the awesome power now claimed by the courts.

If Congress fails or refuses to respond to efforts to curtail the federal bureaucracy, then possible legal actions could be instituted to attack various acts and programs carried on by the federal agencies. There is a problem, however, in petitioning the courts to limit a federal bureaucracy of which they themselves are an integral part.

Ultimately, the people themselves will have to take control of their own affairs and refuse assistance from and control by the federal government. States, towns, and communities are often taken over by the federal government, in effect, if not in fact, because they accept funds from federal agencies. Many local governmental entities have become more or less addicted to the federal purse. When and if they decide to disobey some agency, the federal government threatens to withdraw its funds. It's like getting hooked on heroin. The pusher knows he can control the addict by threatening to hold back on selling the drug.

The pusher also pushes the price higher and higher. Writing in *U.S. News & World Report,* Gerald Thompson, who was serving as the secretary of the Washington State Department of Social and Health Services at the time said: "And the addiction is progressive. As we rely more on government agencies to handle our problems, we become less effective in dealing with them ourselves, as individuals, in families, in communities. We lose skills. We forget how to do certain things, and if the process goes on long enough, we may even forget that there was ever another way." Moreover, whatever the federal government funds, it usually controls. Loss of freedom is a heavy price to pay. (This is true not only of local governmental entities but of Christian institutions as well.)

Second, situations will arise when the Christian community, either through groups or individuals, will be forced to pursue legal action. At some point all avenues to alternative action may be closed. If legal action becomes feasible, it should be pursued aggressively. Humanist groups such as the American Civil Liberties Union (ACLU) have taken the offensive in pushing their version of social change onto society through the courts and with great success.

It is emphasized that court battles cannot be won, as a whole, from a defensive posture. The Supreme Court cases removing Judeo-Christian practices from the public schools serve as a good example of this principle. In every one of those cases, the local school boards or governmental entities were the defendants. They had been sued for establishing Bible reading, prayer, or what have you in the schools. Moreover, no Christian groups intervened or attempted in any way to join in the lawsuits and in no way supported the school boards in those cases. The defensive posture is clearly a losing situation.

There is an advantage to suing before being sued. The principal advantage is that the entity suing chooses the court in which the case will be heard, and, by suing, frames the issues and arguments from his point of view. There are other advantages, but they can be summed up by saying that the first man out of the chute has the jump on the others involved in the race. It is a matter of strategy and planning.

An example of aggressiveness in handling a court action was epitomized in the case of *Walker* v. *First Orthodox Presbyterian Church of San Francisco*. I acted as lead attorney for the church, and was assisted by two

"Well, all wasn't lost. . . . I got him to sign my gun control petition!"

other attorneys (Tom Neuberger of Wilmington, Delaware, and Susan Paulus of San Francisco). In that case the church was sued by a practicing homosexual who had been dismissed from his position of church organist after his homosexuality had been discovered and the pastor of the church had talked with him without result. The man alleged employment discrimination based upon a San Francisco gay rights law.

Note that the church was sued. However, due to careful planning and strategy, we filed a motion for summary judgment several months later, asking the court to decide the case on the Constitution (because there was no dispute among the parties on the facts). By doing this, a lengthy trial analyzing the discrimination charge was avoided. Instead of staying on the defensive, we put the church on the offense; the homosexual (and the homosexual legal organization backing him) were placed in the position of having to defend their position. In April 1980, the court ruled that the gay rights ordinance was unconstitutional as applied to the church. An entirely different outcome could have resulted if we had gone on the defensive.

Third, the public education system, which includes the entire educational structure up through the university level, must be reinstilled with Judeo-Christian theism. The education system is of primary importance because it trains the citizens of tomorrow. At present, the system is producing wave after wave of graduates who have little or no knowledge of Christianity and who, in most instances, are actively anti-Christian. The secularizing of the public schools has effectively been carried out through decisions removing the Judeo-Christian base from education. Humanist Paul Blanshard writing in *The Humanist* in an article entitled "Three Cheers for Our Secular State" said:

> I think that the most important factor moving us toward a secular society has been the educational factor. Our schools may not teach Johnny to read properly, but the fact that Johnny is in school until he is sixteen tends to lead toward the elimination of religious superstition. The average American child now acquires a high-school education, and this militates against Adam and Eve and all other myths of alleged history. . . . When I was one of the editors of *The Nation* in the twenties, I wrote an editorial explaining that golf and intelligence were the two primary reasons that men did not attend church. Perhaps I would now say golf and a high-school diploma.

If there is little hope of revamping public education—and this is more than a probability—then Christians must remove their financial support from the system. In most states, the highly suspect real estate tax is used to support the public educational system.* Legislation should be passed exempting those opposed to the materialistic world view taught in these schools from having to support them. If the legislature fails to act, then the people can, by referendum, place such a measure on the ballot and, in effect, pass their own law.

Christians should establish their own institutions while fighting the decay of the public education system. Already Christian schools are flourish-

*The troubling aspects of the real estate tax are discussed in the Appendix, Essay III.

ing and growing at a rapid rate. We must take care, however, that these institutions produce children who know how to affect the world they live in for Jesus Christ. If not, Christian schools will simply be the "religious" counterparts of the secular school system.

Fourth, the massive federal government we have today is by and large the result of a church that has not taken its duty seriously and provided for the education and welfare needs of the people. It is a function of Christ's church to care for the sick and needy. The reason many non-Christians see no value in the church today is because the church does little to meet the physical

"Psst . . . I don't want the American Civil Liberties Union to hear me, but I bring you good tidings of great joy. For unto you is born this day in the city of David . . ."

needs of the people. The church should be a servant church, one designed to provide health, education, and welfare. If the people could be served in this way, the need for welfare would be nonexistent. All it takes is the church serving its proper function: externalizing the faith.

Taking a Stand

The church cannot be timid in the face of crises. One strong local church can demand respect from the entire community. The world is looking for someone or something that will take a stand. Moreover, the bolder the church becomes, the stronger Christians in general become. The church is not to have a spirit of timidity but of power: the power of God, which is at the church's disposal.

As we face the massive machine of government, we are at a very similar position to that of the colonists who congregated to declare their independence from Great Britain in 1776. They brought about a revolution. It is now time for another revolution, a revolution in the reformative sense. It should not be a revolution designed to kill people or to tear down and physically destroy society, but a revolution in the minds and the souls of human beings—a revolution promulgated to be a total assault on the humanistic culture. A Second American Revolution founded upon the Bible in its totality. In this, and only this, is there hope for the future.

Inquiries may be sent to:
John Whitehead
P.O. 510
Manassas, VA 22110

Essay I

Law and Nature

Supreme Court Justice Hugo Black in a 1970 case referred to the "natural law due process notion by which this Court frees itself from the limits of a written Constitution."[1] This concept of natural law, as used by the Supreme Court, would play a major role three years later in the Court's decision that unborn children do not have a right to live.

The concept of natural law is one of the most confused ideas in the history of Western thought. It has played a prominent role in the formulation of both law and governments. Because of their Christian faith or background, many have assumed that natural law means that, because God created the world, God's laws are basic to the constitution of all created being. Indeed, this is one aspect of the natural law tradition.

Men, however, use the same words to mean different things. Because of their fallen nature, men fail to understand one another, not only when they speak alien tongues but also when they speak the same language. They use the same words but with diverse meanings. For example, Christians and humanists speak of "law" but with little identity in meaning.

Words have meaning only in terms of their reference point. If, for instance, the reference point in ideas and language is the Bible, then there is an absolute common ground in the meaning of words. If, however, the reference point is in a relativistic ideology of some sort, then a word can mean what the speaker wants it to mean. The reference point, then, will determine the meaning of a particular word. So it is with the concept of natural law.

The Laws of Nature

Men not only speak in words but also speak in the language of history. Their words must be heard in the context and meaning of their time and place. It was the language of American colonial history that was written into the founding documents. John Burnham in *Congress and the American Tradition* (1959) has noted that the colonists in shaping the American system made reference "not only to Locke, Montesquieu, but Aristotle and Cicero and Plutarch, Hobbes, Burlamaqui, Milton, Hooker, Bolinbroke, Blackstone, Burke, Shaftesbury and a score of collateral branches."[2] However, as Burnham comments: "The Fathers were the masters, not the victims, of these inherited ideas, and sometimes it is the rhetoric more than the ideas that is taken over."[3] Their common Christian base provided a foundation from which they could sift through the myriad of ideas without being dominated by them.

The framers' reference to "the Laws of Nature and of Nature's God" in the Declaration of Independence has caused some misunderstanding of their intentions respecting the ultimate basis of law and government. They were not endorsing Aristotelian or Thomistic "natural law." William Blackstone, the probable source of the phrase, uses the phrase "the laws of nature" in a distinctive and significant way in his *Commentaries* (1765-1770). Blackstone states very clearly that all law must be seen in terms of the revealed law, the Bible. Moreover, in the *Commentaries,* after affirming the Bible as the source of law, he states: "Yet undoubtedly the revealed law has infinitely more authenticity than the moral system which is framed by ethical writers, and denominated the natural law; because one is the law of nature, expressly declared so to be by God himself; the other is only what, by the assistance of human reason, we imagine to be that law."[4] Thus, the "laws of nature" as part of the higher law are not seen as something clearly evident from nature but understandable and valid only in terms of the absolute reference point. The laws of nature can be seen to some extent through reason but lack compelling authority until they are "expressly declared . . . by God himself."

The Greeks and the Natural Law

The concept of natural law is essentially Greek in origin. René Wormser in *The Story of the Law* (1962) credits Aristotle (384-322 B.C.) with propounding, in its modern sense, the theory of natural law, which "continues to have enormous influence upon the law and legal processes."[5] Actually, it was an ancient Hellenic idea that the universe was an ordered and orderly system governed by a type of cosmic law. Whereas the Hebrew people came to their understanding that there is only one true God from the promulgation of his law, which applied everywhere to all people, the Greeks approached the same insight from a different perspective. Lacking access to special revelation (the Bible), the pagan Greeks were able to discern the unity and coherence of the universe and thus came to a kind of monotheistic conclusion: the universe has a sole author. Plato spoke of a creation, Aristotle somewhat more ambiguously of a prime mover, but in one way or another pre-Christian Greek philosophy did postulate a kind of monotheism and an orderly universe with laws that could be discerned by human reason.[6]

There is a fascinating similarity between the insights of natural man into the laws of God and the Bible itself. St. Paul speaks of the pagan Romans as "knowing the judgment of God" (Rom 1.32). At the same time, because man is fallen, his reason and judgment are clouded; he quickly begins, as Paul writes, to "suppress the truth in unrighteousness" (Rom. 1:18).

The concept of natural law should tell us of such things as the sanctity of human life, but because it is subject to fallen human reason it frequently does not do so effectively. Aristotle, usually cited as the originator of natural law theory, was a student of Plato (428-347 B.C.). Plato himself had already developed a theory of natural law. In fact, Plato's *Republic* was intended as a statement of what constitutes pure reason in the application of natural law for man and the state.

Like most Utopian writings, Plato's *Republic* is totalitarian in its implications, and Plato was thus the first totalitarian philosopher. In his ideal state there were three classes of citizens: the common people, the army, and the "guardians." The common people did all the work. The army was the protector of the state against external enemies, but it was also the police force. Here, Plato appears to have foreseen the police-state pattern with which we have become all too familiar in our own era. The guardians were the elect. They were an especially trained and educated class, an aristocracy of brains and ability. This elite, the philosopher-kings, was to be the voice of the natural law. The law was thus to be what they declared it to be—although, in theory at least, they were bound to make their declarations in harmony with nature.

In Plato's ideal society the children were to be reared by the state. They were to be taken away from their parents at birth, and the close relationship of family life was to be unknown. Every male of a previous generation was to be addressed as "father" and every female as "mother." Every male of the same generation was to be called "brother" and every female "sister." Both man and child were to be creatures of the state. That's how quickly the mind of man can change a natural structure into an unnatural one, all in the name of reason and natural law.

In Plato's scheme justice in the true sense exists in the state when everybody does his job and no one interferes with anyone else. The state was to determine each man's job.

Although Plato later modified the structure of the state as set forth in the *Republic* when he wrote his *Laws,* a more moderate work, his concept of the ideal state as formed in the *Republic* has had ongoing consequences. Once ideas are placed into the flow of history, they will continue to have results. In actuality, Plato drew the presuppositional blueprint for a Communist society, all in the name of natural law.

However, it was Aristotle who probably had the greatest influence on the European thought that led to the character of the modern state. Aristotle distinguished between "man-made" laws and natural law. Man-made laws could be adjudged as good or bad by the extent to which they happened to conform to a set of absolute laws, which were to be found in nature. It was the duty of society to organize itself to live in an ideal state where the natural laws could exercise full play. In essence, the theory of natural law posits that there is a form of higher law in nature, which man's reason can discover. This higher law, which is in and of nature, is the true law by which men and nations must be governed. Thus Aristotle, at least in principle, opposed autonomy: man's reason is not a law unto itself.

Aristotle associated natural law with matter, not mind—with existing reality, not with a theoretical ideal. The expression of the material world is the state, and man is a political animal. The life of the state is law, and law expresses nature (and justice) when it gives every man his due. Aristotle thus exalted the state and, in his *Politics,* advocated slavery. Slavery, according to Aristotle, is a natural institution: Some people are born to be slaves, others free. He posited that there are superior races and inferior races. All this is highly reminiscent of the Nazi theories of race and is also material for segregationists.

From this we can see both the value and the danger of natural law thinking. The law of nature should teach us the dignity of man. But our minds are sufficiently blinded by our sinful nature to permit us to make illegitimate distinctions between various races and classes of people. Only the revealed law of God in the Bible can curb natural law and prevent it from degenerating into something resembling the "survival of the fittest."

Aristotle contributed syllogistic reasoning (a deductive scheme of formal argument consisting of a major and a minor premise and a conclusion) to the arena of ideas. It remains a reasoning tool of both judges and lawyers today. Aristotle, using the syllogism, reduced reasoning to simple formulas, which are as self-evident as the simple propositions of geometry. Using Aristotle's syllogism, this reasoning is consistent:

> Major premise: All men are animals.
> Minor premise: I am a man.
> Conclusion: I am an animal.

The following is an unsound syllogism:

> Major premise: All men are animals.
> Minor premise: A horse is an animal.
> Conclusion: Therefore, I am a horse.

To get at the truth of reasoning, it is merely necessary to determine whether a minor premise is properly related to a major premise, and whether the conclusion naturally follows from that relationship. Of course, the premises must be correct to begin with. If an autonomous state starts with a false major premise—"All men are devils," or, "All men are gods"—and is unchecked by a higher authority, the state can wreak havoc.

From a Christian perspective there are severe problems with the theory of natural law. To begin with, nature is posed as being normative. The difficulty lies in the fact that Christian theism teaches that nature is fallen, just as man is. To construct a system of law based upon nature is not valid, because nature is cruel as well as noncruel.

Second, the natural law theory is based on the presupposition that man, through reason alone, can discover the existence of the natural laws. Man has the capacity, without reference to any special revelation, to comprehend the principles of natural law and to place them into force. However, man's intellect is also fallen. He misunderstands, distorts, and misapplies principles.

Even if man can treat the so-called natural laws as absolutes for society and government, the consequence is cruelty to man. Without the reference point in the Bible, there is no basis to judge which laws of nature are applicable to government and man. Depending upon the man or elitist group in power, many different things can be perpetrated and be justified on the basis of natural law.

The Church and Natural Law

Thomas Aquinas (1225-1274) was one of the first major Christian theorists who attempted to integrate Christian theology and Aristotelian philosophy.[7]

Aquinas conceived of natural law as ordained by God. Natural law exists because man, a rational creature, "has a share of the Eternal Reason, whereby it [the rational creature] has a natural inclination to its proper act and end; and this participation of the eternal law in the rational creature is called the natural. . . . It is . . . evident that the natural law is nothing else than the rational creature's participation of the Eternal law."[8] Therefore, Aquinas postulated that the natural law is a rule of reason, promulgated by God in man's nature whereby man can discover how he should act.

The flaw in Aquinas's natural law theory was his denial of the whole Fall of man. As discussed earlier, Aquinas did not fully accept the fact that man's intellect had fallen. The harmony between will and intellect was disturbed, but the intellect remained. Man was thus cut loose to discover the law as revealed in nature.

What this really means is that man's reason, not nature, is normative. However, man's reason cannot be normative because it is flawed. Without the Bible as a reference point, reason can compound errors and, ultimately, anything goes.

According to Aquinas, "natural" is the state of affairs that usually happens or is expected to happen. What is expected to happen can be discovered by the exercise of reason. Those who follow Aquinas and other natural law theorists err by falling into the naturalistic fallacy. Just because something is a certain way does not establish that it ought to be that way. Simply put, you cannot reason from the *is* to the *ought* on autonomous grounds, especially in a fallen world.

In terms of Christian theism, nature taken alone cannot be normative. The Christian cannot say, as the moral anarchist says, that a thing is good because it is "natural"—because it occurs in nature. Crimes, murder, thefts, perversion, and all manner of evils occur in nature. Such crimes are "against nature," the natural law proponents would say, although they occur in nature.

But it is nearly impossible to draw the line. According to comedian-philosopher Lenny Bruce, "Truth is 'what is.'" In other words, every kind of activity—criminal or not—is equally as true. The *lie* then becomes that which tries to impose a standard of right and wrong over nature, thus "contradicting" what is. The imposition of such a standard, however, is precisely what the law of God does in a fallen world. This is the position that the church must take. Even fallen nature is under the law of God, and it is the law of God that is the true norm.

Aquinas's theory of natural law was once predominant in the church but was significantly shaken during the Reformation. However, it still has vitality within the Roman Catholic Church. It was vehemently attacked by Karl Barth (1886-1968) but is enjoying a certain revival among some Christian jurists and ethicists. Like natural theology, natural law becomes wild and uncontrollable once cut off from a definite reference point in revealed law.

Rousseau

There have been many proponents of natural law. French philosopher Jean-Jacques Rousseau (1712-1778) has had a marked influence on modern thought through his modification of traditional natural law theory. He rethought the concept of natural law, making it dependent on the expression of the general will, rather than man's clear understanding. The Enlightenment, of which Rousseau was a part, was characterized by a questioning of traditional doctrines and values with an emphasis on the idea of human progress by free use of reason. It broke with the past by emphasizing the autonomy of human reason rather than the duty of reason to seek out and submit to a providential order in nature.

Rousseau denied the Fall in its entirety. He viewed primitive man, "the noble savage," as superior to civilized man. He wrote that "if man is good by nature, as I believe to have shown him to be, it follows that he stays that as long as nothing foreign to him corrupts him." Therefore, in a state of nature, man is free and unfettered. It is society that corrupts that perfect state by imposing restraints on man.

For Rousseau, nature meant spontaneity, rather than order. Rousseau could proclaim: "Man was born free, but everywhere he is in chains." If man in the state of nature was good, then the obvious consequence was for Rousseau to argue for autonomous freedom for man—freedom from any restraint or law, including any supposed ordering of nature by God. The result was that natural law, seen not as rational order but as autonomy, became the source of the theory of natural rights, which are inherent to man and in man without reference to the Creator. Rights established apart from the Creator, however, are relative and arbitrary in character, not unalienable, and are subject to limitation and even liquidation as well as to creation by the state, as we see all too well in our own day.

For Rousseau, individual freedom would be perfectly reflected in a new concept, the "general will" through the social contract. In *The Social Contract* (1762), he argued that in "order that the social contract may not be an empty formula, it tacitly includes the understanding, which alone can give force to the rest, that whoever refuses to obey the general will shall be compelled to do so by the whole body. This means nothing less than that he will be forced to be free." Thus, the greatest crime in society is antisocial behavior.

The standard is not really the order of nature, but society's orders. Differentiation, delineation, or differences of any kind that cause inequality among men must be rejected. In their place the "unity of equality" is inserted. Rousseau said: "Anything that breaks social unity is worthless; all institutions which set a man in conflict with himself are worthless." In this respect, Rousseau urged that Christianity was contrary to the social spirit because it was "so far from attaching the hearts of all citizens to the state. . . . It detaches them from it, as from all earthly things."

Christianity thus was an exhibition of antisocial behavior—an echo of the anti-Christian charges of Roman paganism.

The evident danger of Rousseau's philosophy is the fact that it centralizes power in the state—a state that has the objective to force men to be "free." Freedom to Rousseau thus means conformity to the general will, and right is established by might to achieve what the state views the natural law to be.

In a modern context, the Supreme Court's attempts to read the "collective conscience" of the people before making decisions read like a page out of Rousseau's *Social Contract*. However, as Rousseau's general will postulate must degenerate into despotic rule by an elite, so has the Court's reading of the collective conscience—with the Court setting itself up as the elite.

The logical conclusion of Rousseau's philosophy appeared in the French Revolution. The Revolution and its regime demonstrated the triumph—and failure—of natural law and the rights of man. What began as an appeal to nature ended as the assertion of arbitrary power. In the Declaration of the Rights of Man and of Citizen, by the National Assembly of France, it was proclaimed: "The nation is essentially the source of all sovereignty; nor can any individual, or any body of men, be entitled to any authority which is not expressly derived from it."

The "rights of man" were to be measured only in terms of the state; and so-called "Right Reason" was proclaimed as the revolutionary regime, and natural law was nothing more or less than whatever the state declared it to be. The atrocities of the French Revolution hardly need to be recounted here. They do demonstrate the fact that without the biblical reference point anything goes. Law is what man says it is, and even murder can be committed in the name of the law.

Clearly, the ghosts of the French Revolution are still with us today in acts carried out by "revolutionary justice" across the world. On a daily basis, in the name of liberation and freedom, atrocities are committed in various countries, which are nothing less than savage murders of whole classes of people. The South American breed of leftist revolution, the revolution in Iran, and the continuing class struggle and purges by the left in Eastern Europe, China, and elsewhere all attest to the fact that the dangerous perversion of the philosophy of natural law as interpreted by the leaders of the French Revolution did not die with them. It is alive and well and flourishing. It continues to produce a string of brutal murders in the name of progress. It is also a true example of the semantic game in which language is used to change the way people view something that otherwise would be repulsive. Revolutionary justice sounds much better than torture, rape, murder, and pillage.

The Darwinian Influence

Darwinism dealt the traditional concept of natural law a second, disastrous blow. It undermines the entire concept even more effectively than Rousseau's autonomous general will. If the theory of evolution is true; then nature—instead of representing a perfect, stable, and absolute law order—is a blind, lawless force working its way upward and establishing its own rules by blind, unconscious experience. In a society that will not use the Bible as its reference point, law eventually must be the product of the arbitrary will of man. There is no longer even any natural law. In reality, Darwin's theory shattered all confidence in any form of orderly law, including the system based on Christian absolutes. Random chance became lord of the universe. As a result, man has been placed in a desperate situation: Failure to compete successfully means literal extinction—the survival of the fittest.

Justice Holmes noted, "The life of the law has not been logic: it has been experience." Holmes quickly recognized that the acceptance of Darwinism inevitably undermined the concept of natural law. Law must be an *intelligent* experience, and an intelligent reflected experience is known only to man, not to inanimate nature. Experience is used by man to formulate law. In contemporary society, therefore, law is *positive law* (that is, man-made law), not a transcendent or higher law. Law is the experience of society as embodied in the statutes written by the state; it is the expression of the general will.

Based on experience and in a framework of evolution, law must be a changing, developing process. Instead of being bound by a higher law or a past constitution, human statutes must reflect the constant flow of experience and changing reality. A constitution is fixed; it reflects the past or dead experience, whereas man's present life is governed by living experience. Even legislative enactments are too inflexible. It is up to the courts, therefore, to reflect the growing experiences of society intelligently and conscientiously. Only the courts can ascertain the direction and form of these experiences. There is no absolute law for a reference point. Law is what the courts say it is.

If the Bible is rejected as the reference point, then the state is left with either natural law or positive law. But if evolution is true, natural law as the expression of normative justice is hopelessly dead. Some natural law thinkers, however, refuse to wilt even in the face of the contradiction of their views—many exercise *double think* in holding to a belief in both the absoluteness of natural law and simultaneously to evolution. They refuse to face realistically the unpalatable implications of Darwinism for any fixed standard of natural law. Thus a tension is created. The courts, in choosing between the two positions of natural standards and evolutionary change, have simply kept up with the times.

Intellectually, the Supreme Court justices have been sensitive to the philosophical currents of the day, and they have reflected with consistency what most people believe without consistency. In fact, it would not be too much to say that the Supreme Court has now descended to the level of a popular poll-taking agency, reacting to the whims of the many or to the pressures of the few. It certainly can no longer be regarded as a court of justice—divine, natural, or constitutional.

In a unique sense, evolutionary thought has been superimposed upon the natural law concept and has transformed it. Man, evolving with nature, becomes more aware of his status as he develops and becomes more enlightened. But all the while he is being directed by the forces of nature within and without him. Unfortunately, nature no longer bears any loyalty to "Nature's God."

Thus, man can arrive at a "natural" justice, but it is meted out by the state by way of the courts and does not correspond to any higher law. In the tradition of Christopher Langdell, this philosophy is being promulgated through the legal education system. An example is offered by the ideas of Harvard law professor Laurence Tribe, a respected authority on constitutional law. In *American Constitutional Law* (1978), Professor Tribe endorses this philosophy of evolving natural justice. He states that "the Constitution is an intentionally incomplete, often deliberately indeterminate structure for the participatory evolution of political ideals and governmental practices."[9] It does not reflect any eternal law, biblical or natural.

Tribe goes on to write that "the highest mission of the Supreme Court, in my view, is not to conserve judicial credibility, but in the Constitution's own phrase, 'to form a more perfect union' between right and rights within that charter's necessarily evolutionary design."[10] What the framers viewed as setting limits to man's autonomy, Tribe transmutes into *carte blanche* for arbitrary innovation.

Professor Tribe, however, notes the tension created by the attempt to merge a natural law concept with evolution:

> Society alters; some say evolves. Values change. Majorities grow more complacent; factions rigidify. Locked into frozen configurations, legislators may ignore sound opportunities for progress, or opt for novelty without adequate thought of consequences. An unchecked spiral of change ultimately entails the same danger threatened by the most stubborn opposition to change. Either possibility can impart a teleology to positivist lawgiving which may equal legislated perpetual conformity.[11]

This is typical of the inconsistent way the "principles" of law are taught in law schools today.

Evolution demands perpetual change, but the natural law concept (based upon a static nature or absolute) is resistant to change. This is why in Rousseau's theory the asocial individual (or the one aspiring to change) had to be rooted out of the system. Thus we have a paradox: Conformity is the key, but conformity is impossible in the constant change brought on by evolution. This tension necessarily demands an all-encompassing, all-directing totalitarian state. Conformity to transitory standards replaces liberty under God's laws. Logically, the philosophy of law taught in the law schools demands an all-powerful state to keep the people in line with the developing law. No one may change too rapidly or too slowly.

This fact points up the glaring philosophical inconsistencies and irrational approach of modern humanism, which, having rejected a sound basis for understanding reality in terms of Judeo-Christian principles, is now manifesting itself in harsh and inhuman ways. Philosophically, the humanists have failed to develop a coherent system. When applied in the external world, humanistic logic fails and brute force becomes necessary for the system to function. Thus, having begun by extolling autonomous man and his freedom, society slides more and more toward a totalitarian state system which, because of its sheer strength, does not have to explain itself or even to make sense.

The Higher Law

In repudiating natural law in favor of a written constitution, the framers and early jurists were not doing away with the concept of higher law. They were, however, fearful of any principle that gave total discretion to any agency of the state. That was the danger inherent in a natural law concept.

The framers knew very well that the higher law with its reference point in the Bible provided advantages beyond what was called natural justice. *First,* through the higher law an explicit, non-question-begging standard of absolute justice is provided. *Second,* the biblically revealed higher law offers the only reliable guide to personal and national health (and thus to the preservation of individual and corporate life). George Washington's remarks in his farewell address are apropos: "Whatever may be conceded to the influence of refined education . . . reason and experience forbid us to expect that national morality can prevail in exclusion of religious principle."

Third, the higher law imparts biblical principles to society and culture, which in turn should lead men to an understanding of the Bible. *Fourth,* if the biblical higher law undergirds a law system, it provides a tangible standard whereby justice can be obtained. The law system that has its reference point in the Bible works because it conforms to truth and the way in which the world really functions. The early American judicial system is a good example of a system that worked because of the Christian absolutes that undergirded it.[12] Even though there will be shortcomings as a result of man's fallen nature, the biblical higher law provides a range of freedom within which man can operate without state control.

As we see the humanistic state bog down, we must remember that if it appeared to work at one time, this was for the simple reason that, by sheer inertia, the past Christian memory provided a base. However, the humanistic system destroys the past while drawing upon it. It becomes harsher and more intolerant in order to safeguard its power while, at the same time, it has nothing to offer for the future.

Disposable Man

With the rise of natural law and the assertion of man's autonomy, the higher law, as revealed in the Bible, has lost its influence. The destruction of the Bible had its roots in the eighteenth century. Aquinas had earlier opened the door to the argument that finally significant truth could be discovered outside the Bible. Luther spoke vehemently against the autonomy of reason, which he called a harlot, but by the eighteenth century it was argued (as did Thomas Paine in *Age of Reason,* 1794-1795) that truth is at the disposal of man's reason alone. Biblical absolutes themselves were called into question. G. E. Lessing (1729-1781) accepted them as a preliminary stage in human development, superseded as the race matures.

In the nineteenth century God himself was called into question. In the first intimations of the "death of God" movement, Friedrich Nietzsche (1844-1900) in

Thus Spake Zarathustra (1891) could proclaim: "I teach you the Superman. Man is something that is to be surpassed."[13] The autonomy of man has been the consequence and, as Nietzsche noted, "the autonomous man knows but one law; and that law is his own law, the law of his own force, the law which is at once its own sanction and its own delimitation."[14] Nietzsche sounded extreme in 1891, but his principles have in large part come to prevail. John Warwick Montgomery in *The Law Above the Law* (1975) summarized the consequences of the death of God movement by stating that "the loss of God leaves man at the naked mercy of his fellows, where might makes right."[15] But where "God is dead," man also dies—he becomes a disposable object.

Finally, in the twentieth century the call has been for the death of man as the all-encompassing state has assumed the power to control all aspects of life, including man and nature. C. S. Lewis in *The Abolition of Man* (1947) wrote that when man attempts to control nature, with nature regarded as a means to human ends, "Nature turns out to be a power exercised by some men over other men with Nature as its instrument."[16] When the power is realized, "Man is as much the patient or subject as the possessor, since he is the target both for bombs and for propaganda."[17] If man is seen as nothing more than a product of evolutionary natural forces, then the means by which nature is controlled must simultaneously pose a threat to the freedom of other men. Men seek power over nature in order to assert their freedom from nature's caprices—to harness nature, so to speak. In doing so, however, they see their own freedom from other men and state institutions slipping away. This is the nature-freedom dichotomy that has plagued modern man. Lewis writes:

> Man's conquest of Nature, if the dreams of some scientific planners are realized, means the rule of a few hundreds of men over billions upon billions of men. There neither is nor can be any simple increase of power on Man's side. Each new power won *by* man is a power *over* man as well. Each advance leaves him weaker as well as stronger. In every victory, besides being the general who triumphs, he is also the prisoner who follows the triumphal car.[18]

If man, as he has done, gives up the Judeo-Christian base to law in favor of a law based on the autonomy of nature, the consequence is that man becomes the means to a cruel end. As Lewis noted: "Nature, untrammelled by values, rules the Conditioners and, through them, all humanity. Man's conquest of Nature turns out, in the moment of its consummation, to be Nature's conquest of Man."[19]

Only in this atmosphere could Harvard behaviorist B. F. Skinner in *Beyond Freedom and Dignity* (1971) say that man's "abolition has long been overdue. Autonomous man is a device used to explain what we cannot in any other way. He has been constructed from our ignorance, and as our understanding increases, the very stuff of which he is composed vanishes. . . . To man *qua* man we readily say good riddance."[20] Man is junk. He is a throwaway—disposable. (Note that Skinner means "responsibility" by his expression "autonomy." Man is not only not a law unto himself, but does not even have any responsibility for his conduct.)

The eventual consequence of the loss of the higher law and the rise of a perverted, autonomous natural justice is that the state, developing as the expression of a manipulative elite, dictates law. This is legal positivism, and it produces the volumes of laws we see emanating from the federal and state governments today. Aleksandr Solzhenitsyn has said, with much insight, that if people give away the absolutes of right and wrong as found in the laws of God, there is nothing left but to manipulate one another. As such, it is therefore logical for Joseph Stalin to say that in order to create his omelet he would have to break some eggs. As a result of this reasoning, millions have died in Soviet concentration camps. This was natural justice to Stalin. It is the sad irony of humanism. In the end, the consequence of natural law severed from the Creator's revelation in the Bible logically leads to totalitarianism in one form or another. And no matter how it may be disguised to make it acceptable, it is still tyranny.

Essay II

The Law of the People

John Wycliffe's belief that the Bible is for the government of the people, by the people, and for the people led to his English translation of the Bible. In believing this, he and his Lollard followers were articulating a commonly granted assumption in his day: that law should be based on the Bible.

What was startling was Wycliffe's contention that the people themselves should read and know the law of the Bible (hitherto the province of the clergy) and that they should in some sense govern as well as be governed by it. From this thesis (which has historical roots as far back as Moses) emerged a set of principles based upon the Bible and applied by the courts that came to be known as the common law or the law of the people.

The common law became established in the English courts, and when the Constitution was being drafted, it was incorporated as part of that document. However, with the rise of sociological law the importance of the common law has declined and with it freedom and liberty.

Justice Holmes and the Common Law

Oliver Wendell Holmes, Jr., in *The Common Law* (1881) laid the basis for the undermining of the common law. In his treatise Holmes saw the common law as basically governed by the motive of revenge. Lawrence Friedman, a professor of law at Stanford University, in *A History of American Law* (1973), has called this treatise "The most important 19th-century book, from the 20th-century viewpoint."[1]

In Holmes's theory—summed up in the expression that the law is not logic but experience—law was the product of man's opinion, supported by the absolute rights of the majority. Thus, the principles of the common law, which had guided courts and governments for centuries before America was settled, were to be left in the dust of history for the concept of evolving law. As a consequence common law is virtually ignored in legal education today. Very few attorneys even have an understanding of what the common law is.

This is unfortunate since the remnants of the common law that still exist in American law continue to affect the operation of the legal system. This is evidenced by the fact that the Supreme Court in various decisions, including *Roe* v. *Wade,* has made reference to the common law in the process of deciding cases.

The Law of the People

The comon law, so-called because it was a law common to the people universally, is an age-old doctrine that had a profound effect on European and, specifically, English law. To some extent, the common law has been present with us ever since the teachings of Moses, in that common law is essentially biblical principles adapted to local usage. It was an application of biblical principles—essentially the Ten Commandments—to the problems of everyday life. Eugen Rosenstock-Huessy commented in *Out of Revolution* (1938) that the common law "was the product of a union between universal Christian laws and local customs."[2]

Likewise, John C. H. Wu, professor at law at Seton Hall University, has said: "Whatever you may say of its defects, which are incidental to all human institutions, there can be no denying that the common law has one advantage over the legal system of any country: it was Christian from the very beginning of its history."[3] He further notes: "No doubt there are many causes for this superiority; but in my humble opinion, the most important is that, while Roman law was a deathbed convert to Christianity, the common law was a cradle Christian."[4]

As Rosenstock-Huessy pointed out, the common law was the mainstay of the people: "Common Law was the good law which could not be deprecated by the King's arbitrary power. It did not claim a national origin, but was the dowry of Christian baptism."[5]

The customs and traditions of the people, as based upon biblical principles, were thus seen as a check on arbitrary statist power. This was true because the common law represented the higher law to which even the king or the state was responsible. Thus supremacy of the law meant that neither the king, state, nor any agency of the state was above the law. The people had a law apart from the state's written law to appeal to in the courts. As a consequence the courts, by virtue of common law, were themselves independent of the state. They were not the coercive arm of the state as the courts have become today.

So important was the common law in determining the theory of jurists and government leaders that much time was devoted to considering it. As early as Augustine (354-430), the principle of the common law was expressed. He wrote: "The usages of God's people and the institutes of our forefathers are to be held for law."[6] Thomas Aquinas stated that to "set aside the customs of a whole people is impracticable," even if attempted in accordance with law of the state.[7]

Interestingly enough, the common law has its origin in the church. Wu writes: "It may be said that canon law was the nurse and tutor of the common law."[8] The very term *common law* was derived from the *jus commune* of the canonists of the Roman Catholic Church. It was not until the twelfth century that the name began to be generally used by lawyers.

Wu cites Sir Frederick Pollock and Frederick William Maitland in support of the proposition that the canon law sprang forth from the church. In quoting their book, *History of English Law,* Wu states:

English law was administered by the ablest, the best educated men in the realm; nor only that, it was administered by the selfsame men who were "the judges ordinary" of the church's courts, men who were bound to be, at least in some measure, learned in the canon law.[9]

Thus, the modern legal system owes a debt to the church and the canon for building a basic structure for the law.

Stare Decisis

Over a period of several hundred years the English judges decided countless cases using the common law. From these decisions came *precedents,* which are cases that set the mode for the way future cases are to be decided. This developed the doctrine of *stare decisis,* which in the Latin means "to abide by or adhere to decisions." With reference to the law, it means that once a logical principle is decided it should apply to all future cases where the facts are substantially the same. Thus, it should not be disturbed except in extenuating circumstances.

In speaking of the law of contracts and the common law, Justice Holmes stated that "judges do and must legislate, but they can do so interstitially; they are confined from molar to molecular motions. A common law judge could not say, 'I think the doctrine of consideration a bit of historical nonsense and shall not enforce it.'"[10] Holmes recognized that the common law restricted the ability of judges to fabricate law. The restraint of arbitrary state power was the intrinsic value of following precedent law.

The doctrine of *stare decisis* is clearly based upon biblical principles. Russell Kirk in *The Roots of American Order* (1974) writes:

> The purpose of *stare decisis* is to ensure that evenhanded justice will be administered from one year to another, one decade to another, one century to another; that judges will not be permitted to create laws or to decide cases arbitrarily, or to favor particular persons in particular circumstances. They must abide by the accumulated experiences of legal custom, so that the law will be no respecter of persons, and so that people may be able to act in the certitude that the law does not alter capriciously.[11]

Again, power is restrained because the absolutes of the higher law do not change, although they may bring varying results as applied to different circumstances or different cases.

The law of the courts under common law was thus considered a law of precedents. This precedent of precedents was based upon Judeo-Christian principles as they had been expressed in judicial decisions. Past decisions provided a ground for deciding present cases because past decisions were developments of the implications of the basic principle that was based on biblical absolutes. Common law rules then were conceived as founded in principles that were permanent, uniform, and universal. Consequently, the judges at common law conceived their roles as merely that of discovering and applying preexisting rules, derived from the rule of strict precedent. Standards of the common law underlying the precedents could be discoverable by the judge through reference to the Bible as applied in the community. It followed then that "judicial innovation itself was regarded as an impermissible exercise of will."[12]

This does not mean that case precedents are inviolable. Fallen men do make mistakes in their decisions. And when this was discovered to be true, even under *stare decisis,* a precedent could be changed. The absolutes of the higher law, however, were not seen as changing; merely there were instances where the higher law was improperly applied.

Although precedent law has remained to a great degree in the American legal system, it has subsided in a perverted form. The contemporary court system has used precedent law to restructure the legal and political system. With the passing away of the common law, the concept of *stare decisis* has in large part fallen by the wayside. Nothing is settled in modern law because there is no final answer within which to work, and the system of absolutes found in the common law is deliberately ignored.

It was a significant aspect of the common law that it was not statute law—that is, it was not based upon written law enacted by an agency of the state. The judge could base his decision concerning a particular situation with reference to the Bible. Attorney J. W. Erlich in *The Holy Bible and the Law* (1962) cites an 1836 New Hampshire case where a judge decided a case in terms of the Bible, because the common law made such a procedure not only legitimate but basic. If a crime were committed, it was not necessary to find a specific written law to cover the situation. The case was already covered by a basic principle of justice: Christian principles as adapted to local usage. R. J. Rushdoony in *Law and Liberty* (1971) notes that this afforded an advantage to the common law. He states that as "a result, the common law had a great deal of flexibility, whereas statute law is very rigid; statute law is governed by the letter of the law rather than by the principle of justice, and legal appeal becomes more an exercise in legal phariseeism than justice."[13]

The rise of legal positivism—unknown in early American law—through statute law has resulted in a decline in American liberties. Justice itself has become a remote concept, which is the esoteric concern of a group of legal technicians and professionals who codify the concerns of almost every area of life in some form of statute or bureaucratic regulation. As a consequence, the people are governed by a myriad of impersonal rules, which, in many instances, have no true relation to real life.

The Common Law in America

Although there was some aversion in colonial America to the common law—mainly because it was considered by Americans to carry with it British influence—it soon became a mainstay in the laws of colonial and postcolonial America. The Supreme Court in *Roe* v. *Wade* recognized this fact: "In this country, the law in effect in all but a few states until mid-19th century was the pre-existing English common law."[14]

Moreover, most states, as they began the codification process by way of reception statutes received the common law into their laws by reference. Of course, the entire common law of England was not brought to America verbatim, because some of it was peculiar to the English system. However, it was, in its Christian form, substantially implanted in the American legal system.

Early American jurists had great reverence for the common law. Chancellor James Kent was so deferential to "the general oracles of the common law" that it was reported he would listen to them "with delight and instruction."[15] Kent published his *Commentaries on American Law* in four volumes between 1826 and 1830. Kent's *Commentaries* were considered the most towering achievement of American law up to that date. They were thoroughly infused with the principles and precedents of the common law.

Kent not only wrote about common law theory, but he applied the common law in the decisions of his court. For example, in 1811 there came an appeal from a lower New York court to Chancellor Kent in the case of *People* v. *Ruggles*. After partaking heavily in a local tavern, Mr. Ruggles had been accused of standing before its door and in a loud voice blaspheming God, Christ, and the Holy Spirit. Kent upheld the stiff fine that had been levied on Ruggles, citing William Blackstone's statement that open blasphemy is an offense at common law.

Kent reasoned that the "people of this State, in common with the people of this country, profess the general doctrines of Christianity" so that publicly "to scandalize the author of these doctrines . . . is a gross violation of decency and good order." Kent noted that the New York Constitution guaranteed "the free, equal and undisturbed enjoyment of religious opinion, and the free and decent discussion on any religious subject." But to revile with contempt "the religion professed by almost the whole community" was to commit an offense "inconsistent with the peace and safety of the State," which was to "strike at the root of moral obligation and weaken the security of the social ties."[16] To construe religious liberty as breaking down the common law protections of Christianity, concluded Kent, would be a perversion of its meaning.

Noting the biblical base to the common law, Supreme Court Justice Joseph Story, in his inaugural address as professor of law at Harvard in 1829, remarked: "There never has been a period of history, in which the Common Law did not recognize Christianity as lying at its foundation."[17] And Story wrote to an English judge in 1840: "What nobler triumph has England achieved, or can she achieve, than the proud fact that her Common Law exerts a universal sway over this country, by free suffrage of all its citizens? That every lawyer feels that Westminster Hall is in some sort his own?"[18]

The Constitution, the Common Law, and Trial by Jury

Common law definitions of the terms used in the Constitution "are necessarily included as much as if they stood in the text" of the Constitution, Justice Story stated in a case in 1820.[19] Supreme Court Chief Justice John Marshall gave expression to this view in an early case by stating that "for the meaning of *habeas corpus* resort may unquestionably be had to the common law."[20] Moreover, Marshall looked to the common law in defining the scope of the treason clause in the Constitution.[21] And Justice Holmes in an obvious reference to the common law remarked that the "provisions of the Constitution . . . are organic living institutions transplanted from English soil. Their significance is to be gathered not simply by taking the words and a dictionary but by considering their origin and the line of their growth."[22] Thus, in considering the meaning of the Constitution the common law was a reference point.

The Seventh Amendment is an example of common law usage found in the Constitution itself. This amendment's mention of the common law is explicit: "In Suits at common law, where the value in controversy shall exceed twenty dollars, the right of trial by jury shall be preserved, and no fact tried by a jury, shall be otherwise reexamined in any Court of the United States, than according to the rules of the common law." An important aspect of the common law is its provision of trial by jury. This was so basic that the founders believed it necessary to incorporate both the right to trial by jury and the common law into the Bill of Rights.

Trial by jury at common law thus had a very significant purpose. Today the law and court decisions are the creature of the legal technicians. However, at common law administration of justice was given into the hands of amateurs. Justice, as administered by the jury, was based not on technical knowledge of statute law but on Christian principles. A jury made of laymen from the community do not possess the lawyer's knowledge of the law. Obviously, they will be ignorant of the multitude of technicalities, which complicate contemporary law. The jury simply acted on Christian principles and the legal tradition of the community in meting out justice.

In recent years, the common law jury system has come under attack by the legal positivists because trial by a lay jury is a contradiction to a system designed to function on the technicalities of written statute law. When a vast body of laws, regulations, and court decisions govern the details of a particular case, the law is governed by procedural technicalities and not common law principles developed from the community at large. Instead, in contemporary society numerous violations of the statute law occur and go unpunished because the technicalities of the procedural aspects of the statute law prevent successful prosecution of crime. In fact, the statute law becomes progressively more unwieldly and less enforceable.

Evidence that the jury system is under strong attack is exhibited in the Supreme Court's 1970 decision in *Williams* v. *Florida*.[23] In that case the Court reversed strong precedent and held that a six-man jury satisfied the requirement of trial by jury. However, in delivering the opinion for the Court, Justice Byron White acknowledged that a twelve-man jury has been the invariable common law practice since "sometime in the 14th century"—for 600 years. Previously, the Supreme

Court had held in 1930 that "it is not open to question . . . that the jury should consist of twelve men, neither more nor less."[24] Because Justice White believed that history furnished no concrete explanation of why the number twelve was chosen, he dismissed it as "an historical accident."[25]

Adherence to a practice for 600 years can hardly be rendered accidental. Especially when Lord Edward Coke, the noted English jurist and strong advocate of the common law, has held that "usage and ancient course maketh law."[26] This is all the more so when the usage is embodied in the Constitution's Seventh Amendment, which dictates that trial by jury is to be administered "according to the rules of the common law."

Harvard law professor Raoul Berger has written that from "Chief Justice Marshall onward the meaning of the common law terms or institutions, which had a fixed content at the time they were incorporated into the Constitution, is to be ascertained by resort to that content."[27] Justice White, however, rejected that meaning as representing "mystical, or superstitious insights into the significance of '12'."[28] This statement was an obvious reference to Lord Coke's remark that "it seemth to me, that the law in this case delighteth herselfe in the number 12; for there must not onely be 12 *jurors* for the tryall of all matters of fact but 12 judges of ancient time for tryall of matters of law *in the Exchequer* Chamber . . . And that *number of twelve* is much respected in *holy writ,* as in 12 apostles."[29] Again, the common law, as based on Christian principles, most likely derived its numerical makeup of juries from the Bible.

Trial by jury was a central pillar for the early American colonists in erecting their government. For centuries it had served as a cherished buffer against oppressive prosecutors and judges. The door is opened now to the eradication of the system in its entirety. When will the jury number be reduced to three? To one? To none? Then the people are at the mercy of the legal technicians. With the rise of technological law, the day may not be too far off when the only hearing a citizen receives will be before a computer possessed with the ability to decide the legality of actions.

Roe v. Wade and the Common Law

The decision in *Roe* v. *Wade* is another example of how the legal profession has strayed from its common law moorings. In deciding this case, the Supreme Court took a brief look at the common law's position on abortion, among other considerations. After a brief study of various views on the common law status of abortion, the Court said it now appears "doubtful that abortion was ever firmly established as a common-law crime even with respect to the destruction of a quick fetus."[30] The entire subject of the common law and its position on abortion was discussed in only four pages.

A basic error of the activist Supreme Court, or any activist court, is that it reads history from the present to the past. If seventeenth-century history is viewed from twentieth-century eyes, and thus outside its historical context, then nearly any result can be obtained. Moreover, if, as the Supreme Court did in *Roe* v. *Wade,* the common law is considered without reference to the biblical principles, then it will make little sense.

First of all, at common law, abortion, as an intentional act, was extremely rare. So much so that the Court strained to find any historical facts concerning abortion and the common law. Second, those who formulated and argued the common law did not have the scientific evidence available to the contemporary jurists, most of which points clearly to the fact that a human being exists in the womb. This was the basis for Bernard Nathanson altering his position from a strong proabortion stance to an avid antiabortion stance in his book *Aborting America* (1979). And although up to a certain point the unborn child is unable to live apart from the womb—just as many born children are unable to live outside the womb—he or she is nevertheless a creature made in the image of God.

The Court also discussed the renowned English jurist Lord Edward Coke (1552-1634) and his view that abortion was a crime. To discredit this view, however, the Court cited a study, which indicated that Coke had, himself, participated as an advocate in an abortion case. The Court implied that Coke's strong feelings against abortion, coupled with his determination to assert common-law jurisdiction ''to assess penalties for an offense that traditionally had been an exclusively ecclesiastical or common-law crime,''[31] made him biased against abortion. Thus, his views were dismissed by the Court.

The Court seems to imply that had the common law clearly held abortion a crime, then it might have affected the outcome of *Roe* v. *Wade*. However, in all likelihood, this is not true. The Court rejected the Judeo-Christian view of abortion in the decision, and Christianity and the common law are inseparable. It could have as easily rejected any common law right to life. These facts point very clearly to the Court's awesome power to do what it wishes. If a result is desired, there is nothing that will stand in the way of the judges, including the Constitution.

Legality

The common law rights received into the Constitution and the various state laws are indeed too numerous to be enumerated here. Suffice it to say that as they have been sifted out of the Constitution, justice has been replaced with legality—whatever the state says is law is legal and right. For example, *Roe* v. *Wade* was the federal state's expression of what was right. Abortion-on-demand was pronounced by the Supreme Court to be legal. This is legality in one of its worst forms. It is the making of what has always been a heinous crime—murder—legal.

Although early American justice was sometimes rough and wide, in most instances it stood for basically Christian principles. The court and the judge had a certain flexibility to meet a crisis and develop a particular case in light of biblical principles. However, with the rise of legal positivism and sociological law, the flexibility once reserved to the common law judge is given over to the legal technician—or to the modern judge who sits without the Bible as his guide and who, in fact, is often openly hostile to the Bible and Christian principles.

Essay III

The Fading Constitution

Ronald Reagan, speaking to an American Farm Bureau Federation Convention in 1979, cited English historian and political theorist Lord John Acton (1834-1902) as saying that the framers of the American Constitution had solved with amazing ease the most perplexing problem of political philosophy throughout the ages: how to endow a government with enough power to preserve public order and govern effectively, while at the same time restraining that government from unduly infringing upon the liberties of its citizens. And Lord Acton was right—the basic theme of the Constitution is the distribution and limitation of powers and liberties.

Why was the American experience different from that of the French during that same period? A principal difference between the American Revolution and the French Revolution was this: The American revolutionaries in general held a biblical view of man and his bent toward sin; while the French revolutionaries in general attempted to substitute for the biblical understanding an opportunistic doctrine of human goodness advanced by the philosophes of the rationalistic Enlightenment. As Russell Kirk says, the "American view led to the Constitution of 1787; the French view, to the Terror and to a new autocracy. The American Constitution is a practical secular covenant drawn up by men who (with few exceptions) believed in a sacred Covenant, designed to restrain the human tendencies toward violence and fraud; the American Constitution is a fundamental law deliberately meant to place checks upon will and appetite."[1]

Kirk goes on to say: " 'In God we trust,' the motto of the United States, is a reaffirmation of the Covenants made with Noah and Abraham and Moses and the Children of Israel, down to the last days of prophecy."[2]

Thus, the Constitution (our covenant) was drawn up to restrict the fallen nature of man from gaining too much power in restricting the freedom of others. The Constitution, then, arose from the Judeo-Christian base. Without such a base, there may have never been a Constitution.

The Liberty of Conscience

There were many philosophical contributions that were considered by the framers in drafting the Constitution. Essentially, however, the Constitution was a product of Reformation thinking. Without knowing it, two men laid the foundation for both the American revolution and the Constitution. These men were Martin Luther (1483-

1546) and John Calvin (1509-1564).

Like all the Reformers, Martin Luther stressed that the final authority in all matters was the Bible. Just as important was Luther's attack on the church of Rome. In attacking its authority as an institution, he necessarily had to attack the infallibility of the pope: "It is not the pope alone who is always in the right if the article of the Creed is correct: 'I believe one holy Christian church,' otherwise the prayer must run: 'I believe in the pope at Rome,' and so reduce the Christian church to one man—which would be nothing else than a devilish error."[3] In concluding his attack on the institutional church, Luther evoked the powerful image of the priesthood of all believers:

> Since we are all priests and all have one faith, one gospel, and one sacrament, why then should we not have the authority to test and determine what is right in the faith? Abraham had to listen to Sarah who was more subject than we are to anyone on earth, and Balaam's ass was wiser than the prophet himself. If then God could speak through an ass against a prophet, then can he not speak through a godly man against the pope? . . . Therefore it behooves every Christian to espouse the cause of the faith, to understand and defend it, and to rebuke all errors.[4]

The revolutionary ideas posed by Luther were that both the church and civil authorities were under the Bible—the law. Moreover, it is up to each believer to decide what the Bible actually requires. Thus, there was a *liberty of conscience* for each man to decide what the Bible actually says. Consequently, no authority—church or state—had the power to dictate matters of conscience.

Luther's questioning of church authority cannot be seen as merely an attack on the church. It was an attack on all authority that acted contrary to the Bible. Thus the deinstitutionalization of authority had volatile implications for the existing political structures. It meant that citizens could exercise a certain liberty of conscience in challenging what were considered invalid acts by the state. John Calvin in his *Institutes of the Christian Religion* (1536) magnified this concept. He argued that rather than obey a law that is contrary to God's moral law the Christian subject ought rather to "spit in the face of the magistrate."[5]

The point emphasized by Calvin was that man owes obedience to God first and to man's institutions secondarily. Moreover, Calvin argued that the "law of God, which we call the moral law, must alone be the scope, and rule, and end, of all laws."[6] Calvin gave enormous importance to "the law" as found in the Old Testament. If the civil government transgressed the divine law, the Christian was at liberty to disobey. Therefore, although there was an authoritarian political structure, it was under law and not above it.

The liberty of conscience, with its roots in Luther, Calvin, and others, was expressed through the English theologian William Perkins (1558-1602) who penned an extended treatise on conscience in which he wrote, "God hath now in the New

Testament given a liberty to the conscience."[7] In reflecting Calvin and Luther, Perkins wrote: "If it should fall out that man's laws be made of things evil, and forbidden by God, then there is no bond of conscience at all: but contrariwise men are bound in conscience not to obey."[8]

Two centuries later, as the United States Congress met for the first time, James Madison (1751-1836), a major contributor to the framing of the Constitution, argued that the First Amendment to the Constitution should include liberty of conscience, "the rights of conscience" being a subject about "which the people of America are most alarmed."[9] During the two centuries that separated Perkins from Madison, many people spoke of their concern for conscience, including such persons as James I (1567-1625), Roger Williams (1604-1683), John Milton (1608-1674), Oliver Cromwell (1599-1658), and John Locke (1632-1704). Moreover, many important religious and political documents specifically commented on conscience, among them the Westminster Confession of Faith, the charters of most seventeenth-century American colonies, and all the new state constitutions created at the time of the American Revolution.[10] Historian L. John Van Til in *Liberty of Conscience* (1972) has written that in "a broad perspective it became obvious that the concern for conscience expressed by James Madison at the time of the American Revolution was part of a tradition of liberty of conscience that was directly related to the views of William Perkins."[11] Perkins, in turn, was essentially relating the ideas of Luther, Calvin, and other Reformers. These ideas lay at the base of the Constitution.

It must not be forgotten that Catholic churchmen laid ideas that were drawn upon by the Protestants during the Reformation, particularly in the writing of the Magna Charta, which opens by stating:

> Know that We by divine impulse, and for the salvation of Our soul, and of the souls of Our ancestors, and of Our heirs, and for the honor of God, and the exaltation of Holy Church, and the amendment of Our kingdom,. . . .

The Magna Charta led to the liberty enjoyed by Englishmen, which was later translated into the American Constitution. The Reformation did not build on itself. It built on the truth established by the Catholic church.

Calvin and Luther were also products of an earlier Christian era, one characterized by civil disobedience and persecution. Although the Jews had rebelled against Roman authorities, the early Christian resistance against Rome was different. Early Christians were gentiles who resisted their own government; they were Roman citizens. In refusing to violate God's law, the early Christians went to the lions. This resistance eventually led to many of the rights we now enjoy. As Harvard professor Harold Berman has said:

> Thus, the first principle of Christian jurisprudence, established by historical experience, was the principle of civil disobedience: laws that

conflict with Christian faith are not binding in conscience. . . . [T]he Christian era began with the assertion of a moral right—indeed, a duty—to violate a law that conflicts with God's will. This right and duty, reasserted in our time by such men as Martin Luther King and the Berrigan brothers, is one of the foundations of our constitutional law of freedom of speech."[12]

Constitutionalism itself is a product of the Christian thinkers. It is defined as limited government under rule of law. The idea of limited civil government, as opposed to arbitrary government power, has its basis in a recognition of the fallen nature of man. However, civil government is also limited by the liberty of conscience over against laws contrary to the Bible. The rule of law also places a restraint on arbitrary power, and it places man and civil government *under* law. In terms of early American constitutionalism, the rule of law was seen through the grid of Christian theism. The reference point was the Bible.

Controlling the Future of Freedom

The Constitutional Convention held in Philadelphia in 1787 and its product, the United States Constitution, was a landmark historical event. James Wilson (1742-1798), a prominent Pennsylvania attorney and delegate to the convention, summed up its significance by saying: "America now presents the first instance of a people assembled to weigh directly and calmly and to decide leisurely and peaceably upon the form of government by which they will bind themselves and their posterity."[13]

The framers thus assembled to draft a legal document that would not only guarantee their freedoms but also the freedom of those who would follow them. In fact, the general rule is that the authors of a legal document are trying to control the future. The framers were thus writing a constitution that they hoped would keep form and order to America in the future.

The concept perpetrated today in constitutional law that the Constitution is an evolving document was a foreign concept to the framers. Such an idea could only mean tyranny. Therefore, the Constitution was seen as a fixed standard alterable only by amendment. Change in the basic structure of government and law would be a slow process. Witness to this fact is the arduous time proponents of the Equal Rights Amendment have had in gaining ratification.

But American government has become radically different today when the Supreme Court can decide an issue, have it apply as a universal, and knock down years of tradition and precedent.

The Idea of Federalism

The Constitution was drafted with an extreme distrust toward fallen men as exercising authority through civil government. Therefore, a system of checks and balances was built into the Consitution. The framers saw very clearly that if man was to be restrained in the exercise of arbitrary power it would have to be under the authority of a written instrument. Thomas Jefferson summed up the philosophy of the framers when he said: "It is jealousy and not confidence which prescribes limited constitutions to bind down those whom are obliged to trust with power . . . In questions of power, then, let no more be heard of confidence in man, but bind him down from mischief by the chains of the Constitution."[14] This distrust in man led to the establishment of a *federal republic*.

The Constitution erects a federal system of civil government. *Federalism* is the concept that civil government is composed of a conglomerate of civil governing bodies each with its own sphere of authority. The genius of federalism consists in the fact that it balances units of government one against the other. Federalism thus demands diversity within a framework of orderly association. It is unity, not union, within diversity. The consequence of federalism is that government power is decentralized in and through various levels of government. The claim of total sovereignty by the huge federal machine that exists in Washington, D.C., today would have been considered a totalitarian horror by the framers.

On April 30, 1839, on "The Jubilee of the Constitution" John Quincy Adams (1767-1848) declared: "There is the Declaration of Independence, and there is the Constitution of the United States—let them speak for themselves. The grossly immoral and dishonest doctrine of despotic state sovereignty, the exclusive judge of its own obligations, and responsible to no power on heaven or in earth, for the violation of them, is not there. The Declaration says it is not in me. The Constitution says it is not in me." Centralized power, then, was considered to be the essence of tyranny.

For the modern American who lives in the technological state, it is difficult to realize how loosely connected the states were under the Constitution. We have forgotten the relative isolation of the states in the days of the drafting of the Constitution. It was then a four days' ride from Boston to New York on the best roads in America. "The highways of Pennsylvania were almost impassable, and travel on them was little less than misery. South of the Potomac the roads were still worse; there even the bridges were a luxury."[15]

There were no mass transit or electronic media to bring the people within a global community. "Of the affairs of Georgia," James Madison wrote in 1786, "I know as little as those of Kamskatska."[16]

In colonial times the states were seen as individual governments, not as mere inconvenient extensions of Washington, D.C. There were thirteen sovereignties. When the British government decided to end hostilities, it conceded not to "America" but to the states, calling each of them by name in the Treaty of Paris, which was signed on September 3, 1783. "His Britanic Majesty" noted that they were "to be free, sovereign and independent states; that he treats with them as such." As historian A. V. Dicey in *Law of the Constitution* (1920) notes, "in 1787 a citizen of Virginia or Massachusetts felt a far stronger attachment to Virginia or to Massachusetts than to" the United States.[17] In fact, Thomas Jefferson referred to Virginia as "my country."

Local civil bodies such as counties and towns or cities were the basic governing units of early American federalism. *Localism* is thus stressed in the federal system. Alexis de Tocqueville noted in his *Democracy in America* (1835-1840) that "every village forms a sort of republic accustomed to conduct its own affairs."

Civil government was not viewed as something that was exercised from afar off in a centralized state. Sovereignty was, in general, considered an alien concept in colonial and postcolonial America. It is difficult for modern Americans to understand this position, since we have become accustomed to seeking and receiving gratuities from the American welfare state. Federalism, with its emphasis on various spheres of civil authority, naturally delimited statism.

Federalism was a mainstay in the American political process up to the time of the Civil War. Standard usage in speaking of the federal government was "the United States *are*." After the war a change in political structure occurred. The expression the United States became a singular noun: "the United States *is*." Samuel Morrison and Henry Commager in *The Growth of the American Republic* (1950) write that the "Union had been preserved but only in the narrow sense of territorial integrity had the old Union been restored. The original Federal Union has disappeared, and in its place arose a strong national state, federal chiefly in administrative machinery."[18] Thereafter, a shift in thinking occurred in terms of civil government.

Today the humanistic consensus uses the coincidental association of "state rights" with the slave problem in the past history of the United States to bottle up any in-depth discussion of this important issue. The fact of the matter is that state rights go far beyond this issue and should be reexamined closely if any real change is to be brought about.

The humanist uses state rights and their linguistic identification with racism as an excuse to gloss over the fact that the entire nature of the United States has been radically altered into a centralized authoritarian government. This is the same semantic, manipulative usage of language that is found in the issues of pluralism or church and state. Such concepts are used to stop discussion and expression of ideas before they can get a hearing.

The Republic

The form of government established by the framers in the Constitution was a federal republic. The establishment of the republic, in that it was federalistic in makeup, showed that it could not have been the result of a majoritarian movement rooted in popular will. Historian M. Stanton Evans writing in *The Intercollegiate Review* has remarked: "There can be no adequate appraisal of the American government without recognizing this fact, without understanding that *the states* were the chief agents in founding the republic and maintaining its prolonged prosperity."[19]

Again there was distrust of fallen man, especially in the form of the majority as rooted in popular will. So much so that Alexander Hamilton (1755-1804), an influential framer, referred to the majority as "the Beast." In fact, a basic requirement of a republic is that governmental power is exercised in a representative capacity. Representatives act as buffers between the concerns of the people and the state. People have access to government only through their representatives, thus preventing mob-type actions against the state.

There were several fundamental reasons for establishing a republic under the Constitution. *First,* the individual state governments were already republican in nature. Thus the Constitution adopted the form of government already in being in the United States. *Second,* the Judeo-Christian base, especially as expressed through Presbyterianism and the related movement of Congregationalism, gave impetus to the republican form. This fact has been ignored in the great majority of the modern historical texts. Presbyterianism had a strong influence in early America through such men as John Witherspoon (1723-1794), who was a follower of John Calvin and applied his theology to the political process.

Calvin held that the church under God was a "spiritual republic," so the Presbyterian church was republican in its church government from the start. Presbyterianism can be summed up as placing the legitimate source of power in the people as properly delegated to the clergy but with the stipulation that both the clergy and the laity are entitled to an equal and coordinate authority. As Francis Schaeffer has written in *How Should We Then Live?* (1976):

> The constitutionalist model, implicit in Presbyterian church government, was not just an example but an education in the principle of political limitation. And where, as in England, Presbyterianism as such did not triumph, its political ideas were communicated through the many complex groups which made up the Puritan element in English public life and played a creative role in trimming the power of the English kings. As a result, the ordinary citizen discovered a freedom from arbitrary governmental power in an age when in other countries the advance toward absolutist political options was restricting liberty of expression.[20]

The framers felt so strongly about the republican form of civil government that in the Constitution itself they drafted a provision guaranteeing to the states such a structure of government.

The Covenant

The Constitution is a *covenant* between the people (collectively in and through the individual states) and the federal government. The covenant concept of civil government adopted by the framers was also a product of the Reformation. It found its influence in America through *Lex, Rex* and men such as John Witherspoon.

A covenant is a contract. The Constitution was intended to be a contract between two parties. The states, in consideration for delegating some of their authority to the federal government, received in turn certain benefits. The new federal government was to provide for the common defense of the states as well as assist in regulating business and trade. (This was meant to alleviate boundary disputes as well as conflicts in the conduct of commerce between the states.)

However, it is a mainstay in contract law that if a dispute arises as to the meaning of the contract—the Constitution—the court or arbitrator must analyze the intent of the parties who made the contract. The Constitution in providing for posterity was meant to be viewed in this light. As Chief Justice John Marshall stated, the words of the Constitution are not to be "extended to objects not . . . contemplated by its framers."[21] Contemporary jurisprudence, however, has either directly or by implication denounced this principle because the Constitution is seen as evolving with court decisions.

The breakdown of the *covenant* basis of the Constitution has a very serious implication. It affords the federal government, and its agencies, an almost free reign to do as they please. If, however, the people, through Congress, could gain enough momentum to reassert their contract rights under the original governing document, then much could be regained. Unfortunately, the contemporary Congress often acts as if it represents the federal machine instead of the people.

The Limited Government
The Constitution is a document of *enumerated powers*. It established a limited federal government, which possessed only the powers enumerated (or specifically listed) in the Constitution itself. The powers it possessed were delegated to it by the states. This principle was stressed throughout the *Federalist Papers*—a group of essays written by James Madison, Alexander Hamilton, and John Jay (1745-1829) that explained and opted for ratification of the Constitution by the states. For example, in *Federalist Papers* No. 45 James Madison gave the classic formulation of these principles:

> The powers delegated by the proposed Constitution to the federal government are *few and defined*. Those which remain in the state governments are *numerous and indefinite* [emphasis added]. The former will be principally external objects, as war, peace, negotiation, and foreign commerce; with which last the power of taxation will, for the most part, be connected. The powers reserved to the states will extend to all objects which, in the ordinary course of affairs, concern the lives, liberties, and properties of the people, and the internal order, improvement, and prosperity of the state.[22]

The states were considered by the framers to be the vital element in the operation of the new government. A major role of the state governments was the preservation of life, liberty, and property. It was not contemplated that the federal courts or any federal bureaucracy would be deciding the liberty of citizens. That was a state province. The framers foresaw that if the federal government could decide issues of life, liberty, and property on a national scale, then the power in the federal government would be ultimate and unlimited. Therefore, it was made plain that the *new* federal government would be one of severely limited powers. Its authority would extend only to matters given it in the Constitution, and would be barred from all matters not so designated.

With the accumulation of power by the modern federal machine, the doctrine of enumerated powers has been contravened. It should be a mainstay in constitutional law and history. However, few Americans are even aware of its existence due to the failure of modern education.

Another of the checks and balances built into the Constitution is the concept of the *separation of powers*. The new federal government was divided into three coequal branches—judicial, legislative, and executive—to prevent a concentration of power. This, too, was a product of the Judeo-Christian world view. As James Madison wrote in *Federalist Papers* No. 51:

> It may be a reflection on human nature, that such devices should be necessary to control the abuses of government. But what is government itself, but the greatest of all reflections on human nature? If all men were angels, no government would be necessary. If angels were to govern men, neither external nor internal controls on government would be necessary. In framing a government which is to be administered by men over men, the great difficulty lies in this: you must first enable the government to control the governed; and in the next place oblige it to control itself. A dependence on the people is, no doubt, the primary control on government; but experience has taught mankind the necessity of auxiliary precautions.[23]

Thus, in Madison's view the government had to be limited because of man's fallen nature, which tends toward abuse of power.

One fundamental aspect in guaranteeing a limited government was the emphasis placed on private property by the framers. When writing in *Federalist Papers* No. 10, James Madison argued that the protection of private property "is the first object of Government." Private property is essential to freedom because if private property truly exists it means that there is an area that the state cannot control.

Private property has suffered greatly in the United States through two basic statist measures: zoning laws and real estate taxes. Although zoning laws place severe restrictions on the use of private property, in many instances real estate taxes are even more dangerous. Virtually unknown in early America, real estate taxes are nearly universal in contemporary America. In reality, real estate taxes are a form of rent to the state for use of the property. Even if one "owns" his home, he can lose the land if he does not pay his property taxes. There is no true private property when the state can exercise this power. The state owns everything and its authority is ultimate.

The Beast

The framers did not see the federal government or any governing body in a majoritarian sense. In the Virginia convention to ratify the Constitution James Madison said the parties to the Constitution would be "the people—but not the people composing one great body; but the people as composing thirteen sovereignties."[24] The modern concept of a majoritarian democracy was an abhorrent concept to the framers. This was in part a reaction to the problems that were brewing in France at the time, which eventually ended in the Reign of Terror and 40,000 deaths.

As late as 1815 John Adams proclaimed that democracy "has never been and never can be so desirable as aristocracy or monarchy, but while it lasts, is more bloody than either. Remember, democracy never lasts long. It soon wastes, exhausts and murders itself. There never was a democracy that did not commit suicide."[25]

In a day when everything is determined by political polls, the framers' concept of a representative government is waning severely. Instead of government officials leading, they follow public opinion—or at least the opinion of the humanistic elite who often have the ear of the state and the media.

It is probably considered heresy to say that the general populace does not always possess the answer. Instead, with the advent of the monolithic electronic media, the mass man is instructed more than he instructs. Majoritarianism places the reference point in decision making in man alone, and this is a humanistic principle.

Deciding cases, according to Supreme Court Justice Felix Frankfurter, involves a "judgment that reflects deep, even if inarticulate, feelings of our society. Judges must divine that feeling as best they can."[26] This means that judicial decisions are not based on law but on the opinions of the majority.

"Let us remember," Francis Schaeffer notes, "that on the basis of the absoluteness of the 51-percent vote, Hitler was perfectly entitled to do as he wished if he had the popular support. On this basis, law and morals become a matter of averages. And on this basis, if the majority vote supported it, it would become 'right' to kill the old, the incurably ill, the insane—and other groups could be declared non-persons. No voice could be raised against it."[27]

The Bill of Rights

The Constitution as originally submitted to the states for ratification was free of amendments of any kind. But the various state delegations were distrustful of the document as drafted. It was commonly believed that if specific immunities from the federal government were not spelled out, then the states would be in danger of losing their power. Wilson, Madison, and Hamilton all replied that no bill of rights was necessary, because the new government was one of enumerated powers. Incursions by the federal government against freedom of speech, press, religion, and other liberties would be impossible, they argued, because no authority was given to the federal government to interfere with such things. Moreover, a partial enumeration of "rights" could be highly dangerous, because it might create the presumption that rights omitted from the list were not secure from governmental interference.

Hamilton in *Federalist Papers* No. 84 argued that a "bill of rights, in the sense and to the extent which they are contended for, are not only unnecessary, but would even be dangerous. They would contain various exceptions to powers not granted; and, on this very account, would afford a colorable pretext to claim more than were granted. For why declare that things shall not be done which there is no power to do?'' However, the fear of the new federal government was so strong that a bill of rights was demanded and became an eventuality.

In many ways the fears of Hamilton and others have been realized. In *Roe* v. *Wade* the ''rights'' to privacy and abortion (the bases of that decision) were acknowledged not to exist in the Constitution by the Supreme Court itself. However, the Court found the right to privacy in the penumbrae of certain of the amendments. The Court presumed it had the power to declare such a right, because of the existence of these amendments.

The Bill of Rights—the first ten amendments—are essentially a list of immunities from interference by the federal government. Elbridge Gerry (1744-1814) of Massachusetts in the constitutional convention observed: ''This declaration of rights, I take it, is designed to secure the people against the maladministration of the [federal] Government.''[28]

For example, the First Amendment was intended to insure that the federal government would not interfere with the matters of religion, speech, press, assembly, and the like:

> Congress shall make no law respecting an establishment of religion, or prohibiting the free exercise thereof; or abridging the freedom of speech, or of the press; or the right of the people peaceably to assemble, and to petition the Government for a redress of grievances.''

The emphasis in the First Amendment was on ''Congress'' because, if any branch could be tyrannous, it would be Congress. Congress had control over the purse strings and could pass burdensome laws. The framers did not concern themselves in detail with the courts because Congress could control the courts under Article III of the Constitution. What they did not foresee was the breakdown of Judeo-Christian theism, which undergirded and gave a moral strength to Congress. With that gone, Congress has been virtually powerless in dealing with the courts.

The Bill of Rights was essentially a stance against statism—a clear rejection of a centralized federal government. As a result, the Ninth and Tenth Amendments were added to the list of rights. The Ninth Amendment states: ''The enumeration in the Constitution, of certain rights, shall not be construed to deny or disparage others retained by the people.'' In other words, the Bill of Rights should not be used against the American people to destroy what rights they already possess.

Does the Supreme Court, which (and I emphasize) is an arm of the federal government, have the power to rule that schoolchildren cannot pray and read the Bible in the public schools of the individual states? Should the Supreme Court exercise or mold a national law virtually establishing abortion-on-demand, which is binding on all the states? Not under the structure established by the framers.

The Tenth Amendment is just as important. It reads: ''The powers not delegated to the United States by the Constitution, nor prohibited by it to the States, are reserved to the States respectively, or to the people." The Tenth Amendment is a product of federalism—the states were guaranteed a substantial amount of sovereignty to deal with local affairs. It was to be the province of the states to deal with the issues of life, liberty, and property of the people, not the federal government. Government was not to be from afar off but was to be localized. In commenting on the Tenth Amendment, Thomas Jefferson said that to "take a single step beyond the boundaries thus specifically drawn around the powers of Congress is to take possession of a boundless field of power, no longer susceptible of any definition."[29] Jefferson was correct in his conclusion. But his object of concern was misplaced. It would be the courts and not Congress that would eventually wield the undefined power.

The Civil War Amendments

Following the Civil War, the South entered the Reconstruction Era, wherein the southern states were denied their rights as states. In particular, their readmittance to the Union was conditioned on their ratification of the Fourteenth Amendment. Three amendments to the Constitution resulted from the post-Civil War Congress, which, in effect, ruled the entire country during this period of history. The products of what has been termed by various historians as a "radical" Congress were the Thirteenth, Fourteenth, and Fifteenth Amendments. Although these amendments contain much admirable content, the Fourteenth Amendment in particular has been a focal point in transferring power to the federal government. Through Supreme Court interpretation this amendment has transformed the basic nature of American government.

Section one of the Fourteenth Amendment contains four phrases. The second and third are of particular importance: "*No state* shall make or enforce any law which shall abridge the privileges and immunities of citizens of the United States; nor shall any state deprive any person of life, *liberty,* or property, without *due process* of law."

Historically, as affirmed by Harvard law professor Raoul Berger and others, the Fourteenth Amendment was enacted to limit the individual state governments from enforcing laws (termed "Black Codes"), which prohibited black citizens from owning property.[30] This was the intention of the framers of this amendment, but the Supreme Court has taken it far beyond this protection.

It is important to note that the Fourteenth Amendment affirmatively proclaims that "no state" shall enforce or deprive any person of life, liberty, and property. *First,* its implications strongly suggest that federalism is inoperative. *Second,* and related, it transfers immense power to the federal government to restrict the actions of the state governments.

Invocation of the Bill of Rights against the states is of fairly recent origin. In 1833 in *Barron* v. *Baltimore* the Supreme Court held that the Bill of Rights had no application to states.[31] However, in *Gitlow* v. *New York* in 1925 the Supreme Court "assumed" arguendo that the free speech guarantee of the First Amendment is protected by the due process clause of the Fourteenth Amendment—that is to say, the free speech clause applied to the individual states. From there the Bill of Rights in its entirety is now a matter of federal government enforcement against the states.

To understand how a relativistic state agency such as the Supreme Court gains power, one must understand that the distortion of words and ideas is essential—as well as history. This is no more tolerable than the Court's "interpretation" of the Fourteenth Amendment. In particular, the Supreme Court has taken the word *liberty* found in the due process clause to refer to the freedoms of the Bill of Rights. Since the Fourteenth Amendment reads, "No State shall . . . deprive any person of . . . *liberty,*" the Court holds that this alters the meaning of the Bill of Rights so that it now is a prohibition on the states. The significance of such reasoning is that the Bill of Rights, which was once a source of freedom against federal governmental interference, is now a source of intervention by the federal government into the very heart of the state governments. Therefore, the power in what were once local matters is transferred to the centralized bureaucracy.

The transformation of the Fourteenth Amendment has also played a key role in the Supreme Court's removal of the Judeo-Christian base that once under-girded American culture. In particular, the First Amendment (as discussed in chapter eight) has been turned on its head. Instead of guaranteeing Christian freedom it now restricts the input of Christian ideas into the public arena. The result has been the secularization of society. This is even how the humanists understand it. Paul Blan-shard in an article entitled "Three Cheers for Our Secular State" in *The Humanist* (March/April 1976) called the Court's use of the Fourteenth Amendment "the turning point" in secularizing American culture.

Lest one should think that the Supreme Court was unaware of what it has been doing, it is apropos to note a statement by Supreme Court Justice William O. Douglas. He observed: "Due Process, to use the vernacular, is the wild card that can be put to such use as the judges choose."[32] As Professor Berger has noted: "The Fourteenth Amendment is the case study par excellence of what Justice Harlan described as the Supreme Court's 'exercise of the amending power,' its continuing revision of the Constitution under the guise of interpretation."[33] Thus the Fourteenth Amendment can be whatever a judge says it is. The law is totally arbitrary.

The Legal Revolution

A legal revolution has occurred. The fundamental emphases of the framers—the duality of federal, state, and local power and the rule that the central government is denied what is not granted—have been reversed. All authority is ceded to Washington, D.C. The central government's powers are no longer "few and defined" but, as the state governments' powers were intended to be, "numerous and indefinite." As Professor Edward S. Corwin has said: "In general terms, our system has lost its resiliency and what was once vaunted as a Constitution of Rights, both state and private, has been replaced by a Constitution of Powers."[34] It is vital that this sad trend of affairs be reversed, or we may be facing an undefinable statist horror in the future.

Footnotes

CHAPTER 1

1. Ethelbert Stauffer, *Christ and the Caesars*, pp. 81-88.
2. H. G. Wood, *Christianity and Civilization*, p. 2, as quoting Sir Richard Livingstone in *The Future of Education*, p. 109.
3. *Los Angeles Times*, 1 April 1978.
4. Harold J. Berman, *The Interaction of Law and Religion*, p. 21.
5. *Ibid.*
6. David J. Danelski and Joseph S. Tulchin, eds., *The Autobiographical Notes of Charles Evans Hughes*, p. 143.
7. Ernst von Hippel, "The Role of Natural Law in the Legal Decisions of the Federal German Republic," p. 110.
8. Marbury v. Madison, 5 U.S. (1 Cranch) 137, 163 (1803).
9. Max Freedman, ed., *Roosevelt and Frankfurter*, p. 383.
10. Cooper v. Aaron, 358 U.S. 1, 17-19 (1958).
11. Francis A. Schaeffer, *How Should We Then Live?*, p. 80.

CHAPTER 2

1. James W. Sire, *The Universe Next Door*, p. 31.
2. Rousas J. Rushdoony, *This Independent Republic*, p. 3.
3. Richard B. Morris, *Seven Who Shaped Our Destiny* (New York: Harper and Row, 1973), p. 192.
4. Schaeffer, *How Should We Then Live?*, p. 109.
5. *Ibid.*, p. 110.
6. Perry Miller, *The Life of the Mind in America*, p. 115.
7. Daniel Boorstin, *The Mysterious Science of the Law*, p. 3. Although thoroughly accepted in basic espousal of Christian theism, Blackstone, on the eve of the war with Great Britain, was criticized by various American colonial leaders, chief of whom may have been the Virginian, Thomas Jefferson (1743-1826). The criticism stemmed from the sovereignty Blackstone placed in the English Parliament. Shortly before the war, Blackstone remarked: "If the Parliament will positively enact a thing to be done which is unreasonable, I know of no power in the ordinary form of the Constitution that is vested with authority to control of it." Perhaps Blackstone, as a loyal Englishman, in his defense of the British Parliament was only echoing a sentiment of the times. On the other hand, Blackstone may have been saying—which was true—that in the "ordinary" form what Parliament enacted was law. Extraordinarily, if the

enactment were "unreasonable" one might resort to "extraordinary" forms for recourse. This the colonists did. No matter the flaw (if it were indeed a flaw) in his thinking on this subject, Blackstone's real contribution was the foundation he laid for law and government in America; and his contributions were strongly felt up to the mid-nineteenth century.

8. William Blackstone, *Commentaries on the Law of England,* Chitty ed., p. 28.

9. William Blackstone, *Commentaries on the Law of England* (Tucker edition: 1803), p. 39.

10. *Ibid.*

CHAPTER 3

1. C. Gregg Singer, *A Theological Interpretation of American History,* p. 284.

2. Alexis de Tocqueville, *Democracy in America,* p. 291. Moreover, Tocqueville noted: "Unbelievers in Europe attack Christians more as political than as religious enemies; they hate the faith as the opinion of a party much more than as a mistaken belief, and they reject the clergy less because they are the representatives of God than because they are friends of authority." *Ibid.,* p. 300.

3. Ernest Lee Tuveson, *Redeemer Nation,* p. 12.

4. Miller, *Mind in America,* p. 10. ff.

5. Douglas Dewar and H. S. Shelton, *Is Evolution Proved?,* p. 4.

6. Amaury de Reincourt, *The Coming Caesars,* p. 179.

7. Herbert Agar, *The Price of Union,* p. 552.

8. *Ibid.*

9. Ralph Henry Gabriel, *The Course of American Democratic Thought,* p. 183.

10. Harvey Cox, *The Secular City,* p. 18.

11. *Ibid.*

12. Berman, *Interaction of Law and Religion,* pp. 67-68.

13. *Ibid.,* p. 72.

14. Harold O. J. Brown, "The Road to Theocracy?", *National Review,* 31 October 1980, p. 1329.

CHAPTER 4

1. Perry Miller, *The Life of the Mind in America,* p. 109.

2. *Ibid.*

3. Fred Rodell, *Woe Unto You, Lawyers!,* p. 3.

4. Alain Clement, "Judges, Lawyers Are the Ruling Class in U.S. Society," pp. A-25.

5. Julian Huxley, "Evolution and Genetics," *What Is Science?,* pp. 272-78.

6. *Encyclopaedia Britannica,* Vol. 20.

7. Herbert Titus, "God, Evolution, Legal Education, and Law," pp. 11, 12.

8. René Wormser, *The Story of the Law* (1962), p. 484.

9. Roscoe Pound, *Introduction to Philosophy* (1922), p. 31.

10. Wormser, *Story of Law,* p. 485.

11. *Ibid.,* p. 483.

12. Laurence Tribe, *American Constitutional Law,* p. iii.

13. *Ibid.,* p. iv.

14. Wormser, *Story of Law,* p. 484.

15. Francis A. Schaeffer and C. Everett Koop, *Whatever Happened to the Human Race?*, p. 25.

16. Oliver Wendell Holmes, Jr., *The Common Law*, p. 1.

17. G. Edward White, *The American Judicial Tradition*, p. 157.

18. *Ibid.*

19. *See,* Mark Howe, ed., *The Holmes-Pollock Letters: The Correspondence of Mr. Justice Holmes and Sir Frederick Pollock, 1874-1932,* 2 vols., 2:36.

20. Max Lerner, ed., *The Mind and Faith of Justice Holmes: His Speeches, Essays, Letters, and Judicial Commentary,* pp. 377, 389, 336-41.

21. Oliver Wendell Holmes, Jr., "Natural Law," *Harvard Law Review* 32, p. 40.

22. Letter from Oliver Wendell Holmes, Jr., to John C. H. Wu, Aug. 26, 1926, published in Harry C. Shriver, ed., *Justice Oliver Wendell Holmes: His Book Notices and Uncollected Letters and Papers,* p. 187.

23. Richard Hertz, *Chance and Symbol,* p. 107.

24. Morton J. Horowitz, "The Emergence of an Instrumental Conception of American Law, 1780-1820," *Perspectives in American History* 5 (1971), p. 303.

25. Raoul Berger, *Government by Judiciary,* pp. 305-06.

26. Marbury v. Madison 5 U.S. (1 Cranch) 137 (1803).

27. Edward S. Corwin, *Court Over Constitution,* p. 74.

28. *Ibid.*

29. Paul L. Ford, ed., *The Writings of Thomas Jefferson,* 10 vols., 8:310.

30. Dred Scott v. Sanford, 19 How. 393 (1857).

31. James D. Richardson, *Messages and Papers of the Presidents,* 12 vols., 6:9-10.

CHAPTER 5

1. James A. Kidney, "Are Judges Getting Too Powerful?" p. 39.

2. *See,* Jon Barton and John Whitehead, *Schools on Fire* (Wheaton; Tyndale House, 1980).

3. John Ashbrook, "Are Judges Abusing Our Rights?" *Reader's Digest,* August 1981, pp. 77, 78.

4. U.S., Congress, Senate, Committee on the Judiciary, *Selection and Confirmation of Federal Judges,* 96th Cong., 1st sess., 27 February 1979; 29 March 1979; 4, 25 April 1979; 2, 16 May 1979; 17, 18, 25 June 1979; 9, 12 July 1979, pt. 2, p. 141-42. *See also,* Jonathan Kwitney and Jerry Landauer "President Carter's Pick of Fred Gray for Judge in Alabama Draws Fire," p. 1.

5. Edward P. Whelan, "The High and the Mighty," pp. 54-55.

6. Kidney, "Are Judges Getting Too Powerful?" p. 39.

7. Jack Anderson, "Judicial Appointments: An Enduring Legacy," p. A-7.

8. "A Unique U. S. Court," p. 99. The Court of Appeals of the District of Columbia is composed of eleven judges and is of vital importance because the majority of the appeals it hears concern those actions by and against the federal government and its bureaucracy and agencies (such as the Department of Health and Human Services, Department of Education, Internal Revenue Service, and others). These agencies promulgate the rules governing Americans—for example, issues concerning health, food, jobs—and this court decides whether or not these agencies are following their own rules or are indeed invading the lives of the citizenry.

9. Patricia Wald, "Making Sense Out of the Rights of Youth," p. 382.

10. *Ibid.*, pp. 382, 387.

11. *Ibid.*, pp. 383-84.

12. *Ibid.*, p. 386.

13. *Ibid.*

14. *Ibid.*, p. 387.

15. *Ibid.*, p. 386.

16. *Ibid.*, p. 388.

17. *Ibid.*, p. 387.

18. U.S., Congress, Senate, Committee on the Judiciary, pt. 2, "Selection and Confirmation of Federal Judges," pp. 140, 142.

19. There were other humanists whom President Carter appointed to the United States Circuit Court of Appeals for Washington, D.C. One such person was Ruth Bader Ginsburg, former Columbia Law School professor and a general counsel to the American Civil Liberties Union. Ginsburg has been called "the intellectual mentor of many of the feminist lawyers in this country." Robert Dugan, *Washington Insight* (Jan. 1980), p. 3. *See generally* Ruth Bader Ginsburg, "Let's Have E.R.A. As a Signal," *American Bar Association Journal* (Jan. 1977). Concerning Ginsburg, one commentator in his opposition to her appointment noted: "not that evangelicals oppose women's rights. Their feeling, however, is that much of the feminists' drive has anti-family repercussions." Dugan, *op. cit.*

Of particular concern is Ginsburg's vocal antifamily sentiments. In referring to the "pregnancy-problem" she advocates breaking down the "sex-based differentials" between men and women. Ruth Bader Ginsburg, "Women, Equality and Bakke Case," *The Civil Liberties Review* 8 (November/December 1977): 14-15.

In respect to the courts' involvement in this issue, she states: "Not only the sex discrimination cases but the cases on contraception, abortion, and illegitimacy as well, present various faces of a single issue: the roles women are to play in society. Are women to have the opportunity to participate in full partnership with men in the nation's social, political, and economic life? This is a *constitutional* question . . ." Ruth Bader Ginsburg, "Sex Equality and the Constitution: The State of the Art," *Women's Rights Law Reporter* 4 (1978): 143. R. Ginsburg has thus advocated that she favors utilizing the courts to overturn and break down "gender lines" in society. R. Ginsburg, "Sex Equality and the Constitution," *Tulane Law Review* 52 (1978): 45.

In order to "equalize" roles within the family, Ruth Bader Ginsburg urges a taxing policy similar to that imposed in Sweden. Under such a taxing program, individual taxation would be stressed where every person, "married or not," would be taxed on earned income separately. Ruth Bader Ginsburg, "Treatment of Women by the Law: Awakening Consciousness in the Law Schools," 5 Valparaiso Law Review 480, 485-86 (1971).

In order to ensure the availability of women to the work force, Ginsburg urges that one of the "[k]ey items on the feminist agenda [must be] generally available quality child care facilities . . ." If one desires an appropriate model, Ginsburg advocates that "models presently exist in the Soviet Union . . ." Thus, to Ginsburg, in most instances government rearing of children is preferable to that of the traditional family. Ruth Bader Ginsburg, *Women and the Law–A Symposium,* 25 Rutgers Law Review 1, 10 (1970).

After a recent visit to Communist China, in conveying her admiration for the "tremendous vision" of the Chinese, Ginsburg noted: "We can admire the tremendous strides made since

1949 through organizing the P.R.C.'s masses, while appreciating that marked limitations on individual liberties prized in our own country attend that organization." Ruth Bader Ginsburg, "American Bar Association Delegation Visits the People's Republic of China," *American Bar Association Journal* 1525 (Oct. 1978).

Very clearly, Ruth Ginsburg has a penchant for government-imposed humanistic values concerning the family. She would even applaud what has been done in Communist China and the "marked limitations" placed on liberty there. Ruth Ginsburg's nomination was confirmed by the Senate, and she is now a federal court of appeals judge.

Another Carter appointment, who found confirmation with the Senate, was Abner Mikva, a former United States representative. He was also appointed to sit with Patricia Wald and Ruth Ginsburg on the United States Circuit Court of Appeals for Washington, D.C. As a United States congressman, Mikva consistently voted for federal funding for abortion and cosponsored several bills granting civil liberties on the basis of sexual orientation and/or preference. This latter group would include homosexuals, lesbians, and those of like persuasion.

Concerning Mikva, Michael Killian of the *Chicago Tribune* wrote:

"It is worth noting, though, that most gun control nuts, such as Congressman Abner Mikva, are of the liberal ideological persuasion. . . . If we are to get those illegal guns out of circulation, it means nasty things like stop and frisk, midnight no-knock raids, teams of police going door to door through high crime neighborhoods. . . . I spent some time in a place where they do such things, a place with the strongest gun control laws in the Free World. You are not only subject to random street searches there; you are searched every time you cross the downtown streets, or go into a store, a restaurant, or hotel. The place is called Belfast, Northern Ireland, and believe me, they still have guns." U.S., Congress, Senate, "Selection and Confirmation of Federal Judges," p. 415.

A defense attorney who testified in opposition to Mikva stated that, "I am appalled by his apparent endorsement of widened stop-and-frisk procedures based on nothing more than mere suspicion that a firearm may be present." *Ibid.*, p. 443.

20. George Gilder, *Sexual Suicide,* p. 6.
21. *Ibid.*
22. Laurence Tribe, *Childhood, Suspect Classifications, and Conclusive Presumptions,* p. 35.
23. In the conflict between the family and the rights of parents and their children in the midst of statist regulation one is reminded rather chillingly of Aldous Huxley's *Brave New World* (1936). The novel concerned a highly technological, socialized, and controlled society several hundred years in the future in which a state social planner, giving a group of cloned children a "history lesson about the time in which we presently live" tells them: "For you must remember that in those days of gross viviparous reproduction, children were always brought up by their parents and not in State Conditioning Centers."
24. George Orwell, *Nineteen Eighty-Four,* pp. 136-37.
25. Abram Chayes, "The New Judiciary," p. 24.
26. William Ray Forrester, "Are We Ready for Truth in Judging?" p. 1213.
27. "Post-Abortion Fetal Study Stirs Storm," p. 21.
28. Robert Woodward and Scott Armstrong, *The Brethren,* p. 233.
29. Forrester, "Truth in Judging?" pp. 1214-15.
30. *Ibid.*, 1214.
31. *Ibid.*, p. 1216.

32. Alpheus Thomas Mason, "The Burger Court in Historical Perspective," p. 89.

33. Arthur S. Miller and Ronald F. Howell, "The Myth of Neutrality in Constitution Adjudication," p. 689.

34. Griswold v. Connecticut, 381 U.S. 479, 493 (1965).

35. Eugene Rostow, "The Japanese American Cases—A Disaster," Allan R. Bosworth in *America's Concentration Camps* places the number of displaced Japanese citizens at over 100,000 persons.

36. Rostow, *Japanese American Cases*, p. 507.

37. *Ibid.*, p. 490.

38. *Ibid.*

39. *Ibid.*, p. 491.

40. *Ibid.*, p. 532.

41. *Ibid.*, p. 497.

42. Arthur E. Sutherland, "Privacy in Connecticut," p. 283.

43. Archibald Cox, *The Role of the Supreme Court in American Government*, p. 50.

44. Leonard Levy, *The Supreme Court Under Earl Warren*, p. 5.

45. Griswold v. Connecticut, 381 U.S. at 520.

46. Leonard Levy, *Against the Law: The Nixon Court and Criminal Justice*, p. 36.

47. Gaillard Hunt, ed., *Writings of James Madison* 2:185.

48. *The New Yorker*, 28 April 1973, pp. 32-34.

49. Kidney, "Are Judges Getting Too Powerful?" p. 39.

50. *Ibid.*

CHAPTER 6

1. Francis Schaeffer, *A Christian Manifesto*, p. 121.

2. Harold O. J. Brown, *The Reconstruction of the Republic*, p. 19.

3. T. Robert Ingram, *What's Wrong with Human Rights*, p. 51.

4. *Ibid.*, p. 60.

5. Rousas J. Rushdoony, *The Nature of the American System*, p. 45.

6. Ingram, *Human Rights*, p. 61.

7. *Ibid.*, p. 62.

CHAPTER 7

1. Herbert Titus, *Moses, Blackstone and the Law of the Land*, p. 5.

2. William Blackstone, *Commentaries on the Law of England*, Tucker ed., p. 63.

3. *Ibid.*, p. 46-52.

4. *Ibid.*, p. 68.

5. Rousas J. Rushdoony, *The Institutes of Biblical Law*, p. 534.

6. Mao Tse-Tung, *The Foolish Old Man Who Removed Mountains* (Peking: Foreign Language Press, 1966), p. 3.

7. Blake Fleetwood, "The Tax Police: Trampling Citizens' Rights," *Saturday Review*, May 1980, p. 33.

8. *Ibid.*, p. 34.

9. Remarks by Jerome Kurtz, given in New York City before the PLI Seventh Biennial

Conference, *Tax Planning for Foundations: Tax-Exempt Status and Charitable Contributions* on January 9, 1978.

10. Charles Peters, *How Washington Really Works*, p. 35.

11. United States v. Euge, 444 U.S. 707 (1980).

CHAPTER 8

1. Franky Schaeffer V, *Plan For Action: An Action Alternative Handbook for Whatever Happened to the Human Race?* (Old Tappan, N.J.: Revell, 1980), pp. 36, 37.

2. Rousas J. Rushdoony, *This Independent Republic*, p. 97.

3. Carl Bridenbaugh, *Mitre and Sceptre*, p. xiv.

4. Roland Bainton, *The Travail of Religious Liberty*, p. 26.

5. James Kent, *Commentaries on American Law*, 4 vols., 2:35-36.

6. Jonathan Elliot, *The Debates of the Several State Conventions on the Adoption of the Federal Constitution*, 5 vols., 3:45.

7. Engel v. Viatle, 370 U.S. 421, 427-28 (1962).

8. Joseph Story, *Commentaries on the Constitution of the United States*, 2 vols., 2:593-95.

9. John Whitehead, *The Separation Illusion* (Milford, Mich.: Mott Media, 1977), p. 90.

10. Michael J. Malbin, *Religion and Politics*, pp. 21, 22.

11. Reynold v. United States, 98 U.S. 145, 164 (1879).

12. *Regulation of the University of Virginia*, 4 October 1824, chap. 2, sec. 1.

13. J. O. Wilson, *Public Schools of Washington*, vol. 1 (Washington, D.C.: Columbia Historical Society, 1897), p. 5.

14. *Ibid.*, p. 9.

15. Edward S. Corwin, *American Constitutional History*, p. 205.

16. Gaillard Hunt, ed., *Writings of James Madison*, 9 vols., 5:176, 132.

CHAPTER 9

1. Fred Rodell, "It is the Warren Court," *The New York Times Magazine*, 13 March 1966, as quoted by Leonard Levy, *The Supreme Court Under Earl Warren*, pp. 137, 142, 138-39.

2. Leonard Levy, *Supreme Court Under Earl Warren*, pp. 137, 142, 138-39.

3. Richard Morgan, *The Supreme Court and Religion*, pp. 40-44.

4. Reynolds v. United States, 98 U.S. 145, 166-67 (1878).

5. Rousas J. Rushdoony, "The State As an Establishment of Religion"; *Freedom and Education*, p. 39.

6. Davis v. Beason, 133 U.S. 33, 341-42 (1890).

7. *Ibid.* at 342-43. In full the Court held:

> The term "religion" has reference to one's view of his relations to his Creator, and to the obligations they impose for reverence for his being and character, and of obedience to his will. It is often confused with the *cultus* or form of worship of a particular sect, but it is distinguishable from the latter. . . . It was never intended or supposed that the [first] amendment could be invoked as a protection against the legislation for the punishment of acts inimicable to the peace, good order and morals of society. . . . However free the exercise of religion may be, it must be subordinate to the criminal laws of the country

passed with reference to actions regarded by general consent as properly the subjects of punitive legislation. . . . Probably never in the history of this country has it been seriously contended that the whole punitive power of the government for acts, recognized by the general consent of the Christian world in modern times as proper matters for prohibitory legislation, must be suspended in order that the tenets of a religious sect encouraging crime may be carried out without hindrance.

Again the Court was equating "religion" with Christian theism and drawing from theism its absolute monogamy standard. *Davis* provides a very appropriate example of the predominant judicial image of religion. Referring to *Davis*, Harvard law professor Laurence Tribe has written that "at least through the nineteenth century, religion was given a fairly narrow reading . . . 'religion' referred to theistic notions respecting divinity, morality, and worship. . . ." Laurence Tribe, *American Constitutional Law*, p. 826.

8. James Madison, *A Memorial and Remonstrance on the Religious Rights of Man* as cited in Donald Manzullo, *Neither Sacred Nor Profane*, p. 71.

9. United States v. Macintosh, 283 U.S. 605, 633-34 (1931), *overruled*, Girouard v. United States, 328 U.S. 61 (1946).

10. United States v. Kauten, 133 F. 2d 703, 708 (2d Cir. 1943).

11. "Toward a Constitutional Definition of Religion," *Harvard Law Review* 91 (1978):1061.

12. United States v. Ballard, 322 U.S. 78, 86 (1944).

13. United States v. Seeger, 380 U.S. 163 (1965).

14. *Ibid.*, p. 175.

15. Paul Tillich, *Dynamics of Faith*, pp.1-2.

16. Paul Tillich, *The Shaking of the Foundation* (New York: Charles Scribner's Sons, 1972), pp. 63-64.

17. United States v. Seeger, 380 U.S. at 166.

18. *Ibid.*, p. 176.

19. Robert Rabin, "When Is a Religious Belief Religious: *United States* v. *Seeger* and the Scope of Free Exercise," *Cornell Law Quarterly* 51 (1966) :244.

20. Torcaso v. Watkins, 367 U.S. 488, 490 (1961).

21. *Ibid.*, p. 495.

22. School District of Abington Township, Pa. v. Schempp, 374 U.S. 203, 303-04 (1963).

23. The Kentucky legislators had tried to avoid an unfavorable court ruling by having the 16 x 20-inch copies of the Ten Commandments paid for with voluntary, private contributions and by including this notation: "The secular application of the Ten Commandments is clearly seen in its adoption as the fundamental legal code of western civilization and the common law of the United States."

24. 374 U.S. at 225.

25. John Whitehead and John Conlan, "The Establishment of the Religion of Secular Humanism and Its First Amendment Implications," *Texas Tech Law Review* 10 (1978):18.

26. Jacques Ellul, *The Theological Foundation of Law*, p. 18.

27. Whitehead and Conlan, "Religion of Secular Humanism," p. 21.

28. Sir Walter Moberly, *The Crisis in the University*, pp. 55-56.

29. Walz v. Tax Commission, 397 U.S. 664, 669 (1970).

30. Erik von Kuehnelt-Leddihn, *Leftism*, p. 427.

31. Francis A. Schaeffer, *How Should We Then Live?* p. 24.

CHAPTER 10

1. Calder v. Bull, 3 U.S. 305, 307 (1798).

2. *Ibid.*, p. 316.

3. Lockner v. New York, 198 U.S. 45 (1905).

4. Allgeyer v. Louisiana, 165 U.S. 578 (1897).

5. Lockner v. New York, 198 U.S. 75.

6. *Ibid.*, p. 76.

7. In 1923 the Supreme Court had had another chance to apply natural justice to the Constitution. In *Meyer* v. *Nebraska* the Court struck down a Nebraska law, which prohibited the teaching of any language in the first eight grades of public and private schools. The Court concluded that a German teacher's *liberty to teach* was protected by the Fourteenth Amendment. The Court stated: "While this court has not attempted to define with exactness the liberty thus guaranteed, the term has received much consideration." 262 U.S. 390, 399 (1923).

8. Griswold v. Connecticut, 381 U.S. 479, 492 (1965).

9. *Ibid.*, pp. 492-93.

10. *Ibid.*, pp. 518-19. That the courts are looking more to opinion polls and surveys is discussed in "Courts Test Mettle of Public Opinion Surveys," *American Bar Association Journal* 66 (1980) : 1511.

11. *Ibid.*, p. 486.

CHAPTER 11

1. Roe v. Wade, 410 U.S. 113, 152 (1973).

2. *Ibid.*

3. John Hart Ely, "The Wages of Crying Wolf: A Comment on *Roe* v. *Wade*," *Yale Law Journal* 82: 943, 947.

4. *Ibid.*, p. 926.

5. Roe v. Wade, 410 U.S. at 159.

6. C. Everett Koop, *The Right to Live, The Right to Die,* pp. 39-40.

7. Archibald Cox, *The Role of the Supreme Court in American Government,* pp. 113-14.

8. Roe v. Wade, 410 U.S. at 162 (Emphasis supplied).

9. Jerome Lejeune, "The Beginning of Life," p. 4.

10. *Ibid.*, p. 5.

11. Koop, *Right to Live,* p. 38.

12. Roe v. Wade, 410 U.S. at 153.

13. Francis A. Schaeffer, *How Should We Then Live?,* p. 205.

14. On June 30, 1980, in the companion cases of *Harris* v. *McRae,* 48 L.W. 4941 (1980), and *Williams* v. *Zbaraz,* 48 L.W. 4957 (1980), the Supreme Court held in a 5-4 decision that neither the states nor the federal government need fund abortions through programs that subsidize other medical procedure. Justice Potter Stewart, in writing for the majority, stated: "Abortion is inherently different from other medical procedure, because no other procedure involves the purposeful termination of a potential life." *Ibid.* at 48 L.W. at 4949. Stewart was joined in his opinion by Chief Justice Burger and associate justices White, Rehnquist, and Powell. Justices Brennan, Marshall, Blackmun, and Stevens each filed dissents. In specific, the Court in *Harris* v. *McRae* ruled:

1. The Medicaid Act does not oblige states to pay for abortions;
2. The right to choose abortion does not create a right to have abortions paid for with public funds;
3. The Hyde Amendment does not effect an establishment of religion; and
4. The Hyde Amendment does not violate the equal protection clause of the Fifth Amendment.

Harris v. *McRae* is significant in its holding that the so-called "right" to abortion does not carry with it a collateral right to government financing of the exercise of that right. The fact that is not altered by the *McRae* case, however, is the Supreme Court's decision in *Roe* v. *Wade,* which remains to date the most destructive decision any American judicial body has ever made.

It is distressing to note that following the *McRae* case, the Massachusetts Supreme Court on February 18, 1981, in *Moe* v. *Hanley* held that as long as Massachusetts funds childbirth, it must also fund abortion. In the process the court invalidated a state statute, which placed restrictions on the use of funds for payment of Medicaid abortions.

15. Planned Parenthood v. Danforth, 428 U.S. 52 (1976).
16. Carey v. Population Services International, 431 U.S. 678 (1977). Also disturbing is a federal court of appeals decision in *Doe* v. *Irwin,* 428 F. Supp. 1198 (W.D. Mich., 1977). Parents sought to prohibit the distribution of contraceptives to their children without notice to the parents. The court involved held that minors possess a right of privacy, which includes the right to obtain contraceptives without having to consult their parents. Although acknowledging that parents are interested in contraceptives being distributed to their children, the court held there is no duty on the part of a family planning center to notify the parents concerned. The United States Supreme Court refused to hear the appeal from this decision.
17. Belloti v. Baird, 99 S. Ct. 3035 (1979).
18. H. L. v. Matheson, 49 L.W. 4255 (March 23, 1981).
19. Wisconsin v. Yoder, 406 U.S. 205, 242 (1972).
20. *Ibid.,* pp. 230-31.

CHAPTER 12

1. Francis A. Schaeffer and C. Everett Koop, *Whatever Happened to the Human Race?* (1979), p. 16.
2. *Ibid.,* p. 17.
3. Aleksandr Solzhenitsyn, *The Gulag Archipelago 1918-1956,* pp. 13, 58.
4. Marshall McLuhan, *The Social Impact of Cybernetics,* pp. 95, 99.
5. Quoted in Schaeffer and Koop, *Human Race,* p. 73.
6. *Ibid.*
7. *Ibid.,* p. 55.
8. Schaeffer and Koop, *Human Race,* p. 212.
9. *Ibid.*
10. *Ibid.,* p. 85.
11. *Ibid.*
12. James Podgers, " 'Rational Suicide' Raises Patient Rights Issues," p. 1499.
13. *Ibid.,* p. 1500.
14. *Ibid.*

15. Schaeffer and Koop, *Human Race,* p. 72.
16. Koop, *Right to Live,* p. 57.
17. Diamond v. Chakrabarty, 48 L.W. 4714 (1980).
18. James Podgers, "Patent Decision Fuels Genetic Research Debate," p. 943.
19. *Ibid.*
20. *Ibid.,* p. 944.
21. *Ibid.*
22. Albert Rosenfeld, *The Second Genesis,* p. 23.
23. Schaeffer and Koop, *Human Race,* p. 26.
24. Albert Rosenfeld in *The Second Genesis,* pp. 23-24, states:

Imagine a dictator with a subject population—the dictator, a man who is sure he knows what is best for everyone: for himself, absolute power, for his subjects, happiness. He has at his command all the electrochemical techniques necessary for controlling the human brain as well as the most advanced methods for controlling human reproduction. He can have entire populations raised "artificially" without resort to sex or family structure. He can also, if he chooses, have electrodes planted in the brains of his subjects, or begin administering "mind drugs" routinely, at a very early age.

This done, he can maintain his subjects in a state of hard-working subservience—constituting, in fact a slave labor force—and at the same time keep them in a state of constant euphoria by stimulating the pleasure centers of their brains. Practically no one in such a society would have any true freedom of choice in any area of life where we now consider free choice important. But everybody would be happy.

25. B. F. Skinner, *Beyond Freedom and Dignity,* pp. 200-01.
26. *Ibid.*
27. Francis A. Schaeffer, *Back to Freedom and Dignity,* p. 23.
28. Jacques Ellul, *The Theological Foundation of Law,* pp. 8-9.

CHAPTER 13

1. Alan Bullock, *Hitler,* pp. 389.
2. Alan Johnson, *The Freedom Letter,* p. 195.
3. Francis A. Schaeffer, *A Christian Manifesto,* p. 92.
4. *Ibid.,* p. 93.
5. Johnson, *Freedom Letter,* p. 195.
6. Samuel Rutherford, *Lex, Rex, or, the Law and the Prince,* published in *The Presbyterian's Armoury* 3 (1846) : 34. And excellent discussion of Rutherford's life and philosophy is found in an essay written by Richard Flinn "Samuel Rutherford and Puritan Theory," *Journal of Christian Reconstruction* 5 (Winter 1978-1979) : 49-74.
7. Rutherford, *Ibid.,* 107.
8. *Ibid.,* p. 97.
9. *Ibid.,* pp. 35, 38, 69.
10. *Ibid.,* p. 145.
11. *Ibid.,* p. 58.
12. *Ibid.,* p. 160.
13. *Ibid.*
14. *Ibid.*

APPENDIX ESSAY 1

1. In re Winship, 397 U.S. 358, 381 (1970).
2. James Burnham, *Congress and the American Tradition*, p. 24.
3. *Ibid.*
4. William Blackstone, *Commentaries on the Laws of England*, Chitty ed. 2 vols., 1:28. (commonly referred to as "Chitty's Blackstone").
5. René Wormser, *The Story of the Law*, p. 80.
6. *See in general* Victor Monod, *Dieu dans l' Univers Essai sur l'action exercée sur la pensée chretienne par les grands systemes cosmologiques depuis Aristote jusqu'a nos jours*.
7. Anton-Hermann Chroust, *The Philosophy of Law of St. Thomas Aquinas*, 19:23.
8. Charles Rice, *Beyond Abortion*, p. 31.
9. Laurence Tribe, *American Constitutional Law*, p. iii.
10. *Ibid.*, p. iv.
11. *Ibid.*, p. 892.
12. An early statement of natural law by the American judiciary is found in the opinion of Supreme Court Justice Samuel Chase (1741-1811) in the case of *Calder* v. *Bull* in 1798. Taking off from a hypothetical—"a law that takes property from A and gives it to B"—Chase declared that even in the absence of express restraint by the Constitution, "it is against all reason and justice, for a people to entrust a Legislature with such powers. . . . the general principles of law and reason" forbid such acts. 3 U.S. (3 Dall.) 386, 388 (1798). Chase's appeal to natural law was flatly rejected by Justice James Iredell (1750-1799) in his opinion in the same case. Iredell had been a delegate to and an active participant in the constitutional convention a decade earlier. To be sure, "some speculative jurists," Iredell noted, had stated that "a legislative act against natural justice must, in itself, be void"; but given a "constitution which imposed no limits on the legislative power . . . whatever the legislative power chose to enact would be lawfully enacted, and the judicial power would never interpose to declare it void." 3 U.S. at 398. Iredell, without specifically saying it, was concerned with the possibility of the exercise of extraconstitutional power by the courts in the name of natural law.

When Supreme Court Chief Justice John Marshall wrote the famous *Marbury* v. *Madison* decision in 1803, although he ruled that the Supreme Court had authority to review congressional enactments under the Constitution, he aligned himself with Justice Iredell's philosophy. 5 U.S. (1 Cranch) 137 (1803). The limits of power, he held, were to be found in a written constitution and not what a judge thought was natural justice. As Robert Cover in *Justice Accused: Anti-slavery and the Judicial Process* (1975) has written, this was the prevailing view of the judiciary up to the early twentieth century and is evident in the pronouncements of various judges. The courts were simply echoing the philosophy of the framers that the country was to be governed by a written constitution, and that it was not the province of judges to make policy or what is, in effect, an unwritten constitution.

The concept of a natural justice that should be applied to an evolving constitution gained significant ground through the law schools until it has found its expression in the courts. *Roe* v. *Wade* was based upon a sense of natural justice in the autonomy of the personhood of the woman. Thus, *Roe* also had roots in Rousseau. For example, Supreme Court Justice Hugo Black noted very clearly in 1975 in *Griswold* v. *Connecticut* that "any broad unlimited power to hold laws unconstitutional because they offend what this Court conceives to be the 'conscience of our people'. . . was not given by the Framers, but rather has been bestowed on the

Court by the Court.'' 381 U.S. 479, 520 (1960), *dissenting opinion*.

The conscience of the people, or what Rousseau termed the general will, however, is very seldom a product of the people, but as in the case of Supreme Court decisions, imposed order from the top.

13. Friedrich Wilhelm Nietzsche, "Thus Spake Zarathustra." (London: George Allen and Unwin, Ltd., 1967), p. 67.

14. George Burman Foster, *Friedrich Nietzsche*, p. 189.

15. John Warwick Montgomery, *The Law Above the Law*, p. 55.

16. C. S. Lewis, *The Abolition of Man*, p. 69.

17. *Ibid.*, p. 68.

18. *Ibid.*, p. 71.

19. *Ibid.*, p. 80.

20. B. F. Skinner, *Beyond Freedom and Dignity*, pp. 200-01.

ESSAY II

1. Lawrence M. Friedman, *A History of American Law*, p. 545.

2. Eugen Rosenstock-Huessy, *Out of Revolution*, p. 270.

3. John C. H. Wu, *Fountain of Justice*, p. 64.

4. *Ibid.*, p. 65.

5. Eugen Rosenstock-Huessy, *Out of Revolution*, p. 271.

6. T. Robert Ingram, *What's Wrong with Human Rights*, p. 43.

7. *Ibid.*, p. 44.

8. John C. H. Wu, *Fountain of Justice*, p. 65.

9. *Ibid.*, p. 66.

10. Southern Pacific Co. v. Jensen, 244 U.S. 205, 221 (1917), *dissenting opinion*.

11. Russell Kirk, *The Roots of the American Order*, p. 185.

12. Morton J. Horowitz, "The Emergence of an Instrumental Conception of American Law," *Perspectives in American History* 5 (1971): 287, 296, 297, 298.

13. Rousas J. Rushdoony, *Law and Liberty*, p. 87.

14. Roe v. Wade, 410 U.S. 113, 138 (1973).

15. Perry Miller, *The Life of the Mind in America*, pp. 123-24.

16. *Ibid.*, p. 66.

17. *Ibid.*, p. 33.

18. *Ibid.*, p. 125.

19. United States v. Smith, 18 U.S. (5 Wheat.) 153, 160 (1820).

20. Ex Parte Bollman, 8 U.S. (4 Cranch) 75, 93-94 (1807).

21. United States v. Burr, 25 F. Cas. (No. 14, 693) 55, 159 (C.C. Va. 1807).

22. Gompers v. United States, 233 U.S. 604, 610 (1914).

23. Williams v. Florida, 399 U.S. 78 (1970).

24. Patton v. United States, 281 U.S. 276, 288 (1930).

25. Williams v. Florida, 399 U.S. at 89-90.

26. Edward Coke, *Institutes of the Laws of England*, 4 vols., 1:155.

27. Raoul Berger, *Government by Judiciary*, p. 398.

28. Williams v. Florida, 399 U.S. at 88.

29. Coke, *Laws of England*, 4 vols., 1:155.

30. Roe v. Wade, 410 U.S. 113, 136 (1973).

31. *Ibid.*, p. 135.

ESSAY III

1. Russell Kirk, *The Roots of the American Order,* p. 29.

2. *Ibid.,* p. 48.

3. Sanford Levinson, "The Constitution in American Civil Religion," p. 128.

4. *Ibid.*

5. John Calvin, *The Institutes of the Christian Religion,* 2 vols., 2:1519.

6. René Wormser, *Story of the Law,* p. 198.

7. William Perkins, *Works,* 3 vols., 1:529.

8. *Ibid,* p. 530.

9. L. John VanTil, *Liberty of Conscience,* p. 1.

10. *Ibid.*

11. *Ibid.,* p. 2.

12. Harold Berman, *The Interaction of Law and Religion,* pp. 52-53.

13. Julia Kathryn Garrett and Lula Underwood, *Our American Constitution,* p. 15.

14. Jonathan Elliot, *The Debates of the Several State Conventions on the Adoption of the Federal Constitution,* 5 vols., 4:543.

15. Andrew C. McLaughlin, "The Problem of Imperial Organization," *Social and Economic Forces in American History* (1913), p. 150.

16. M. Stanton Evans, "The States and the Constitution," p. 180.

17. A.V. Dicey, *Law of the Constitution,* p. 137.

18. Samuel Eliot Morison and Henry Steele Commager, *The Growth of the American Republic* 2 vols., 2:2.

19. M. Stanton Evans, "States and the Constitution," p. 177.

20. Francis A. Schaeffer, *How Should We Then Live?,* p. 108.

21. Ogden v. Saunders, 25 U.S. (12 Wheat.) 213, 332 (1827).

22. Jacob E. Cooke, ed., *The Federalist,* p. 313 (Emphasis supplied).

23. *Ibid.,* p. 349.

24. Alpheus Thomas Mason, *The States' Rights Debate,* p. 72.

25. Amaury de Riencourt, *The Coming Caesars,* p. 73.

26. Haley v. Ohio, 332 U.S. 596, 603 (1948).

27. Schaeffer, *How Should We Then Live?,* pp. 223-24.

28. Raoul Berger, *Government by Judiciary,* p. 135.

29. Evans, *"States and the Government,"* p. 187.

30. *See in general* Raoul Berger, *Government by Judiciary.*

31. Barron v. Baltimore 32 U.S. (7 Pet.) 243 (1833).

32. William Ray Forrester, *Are We Ready for Truth in Judging?* p. 1212.

33. Berger, *Government by Judiciary,* p. 1.

34. Robert G. McCloskey, ed., *Essays in Constitutional Law* (New York: Vintage Books, 1957), p. 186.

Bibliography

Agar, Herbert. *The Price of Union*. Boston: Houghton Mifflin, 1950.

Anderson, J. N. D. *Morality, Law and Grace*. Downers Grove, Ill.: InterVarsity Press, 1972.

Anderson, Jack. "Judicial Appointments: An Enduring Legacy." *Washington Post,* 6 May 1980, p. A-7.

Anderson, Norman. *A Lawyer Among the Theologians*. Grand Rapids, Mich.: Eerdmans, 1973.

Andrew, Brother. *The Ethics of Smuggling*. Wheaton, Ill.: Tyndale House, 1979.

Andrist, Ralph K., ed. *George Washington: A Biography in His Own Words*. 2 vols. New York: Newsweek, 1972.

Angle, Paul M. *By These Words*. New York: Rand McNally, 1954.

_____, ed. *Abraham Lincoln's Speeches and Letters 1832-1865*. 1907. Reprint. London: J. M. Dent & Sons, 1957.

Aristotle. *Politics*. Cambridge: Harvard University Press, 1932.

Ascherson, Neal, ed. *The French Revolution: Extracts from the Times 1789-1794*. London: Times Books, 1975.

Bailyn, Bernard; Davis, David Brian; Donald, David Herbert; Thomas, John L.; Wiebe, Robert H.; and Wood, Gordon S. *The Great Republic: A History of the American People*. Boston: Little, Brown, 1977.

Bainton, Roland. *The Travail of Religious Liberty*. Hamden, Conn.: Shoe String Press, 1971.

Baker, Leonard. *John Marshall: A Life in the Law*. New York: Macmillan, 1974.

Barber, Noel. *Seven Days of Freedom: The Hungarian Uprising 1956*. New York: Stein & Day, 1974.

Barker, Lucius J., and Barker, Twiley, W., Jr. *Civil Liberties and the Constitution*. Englewood Cliffs, N.J.: Prentice-Hall, 1970.

Bartholomew, Paul C. *Ruling American Constitutional Law*. Totowa, N.J.: Littlefield, Adams, 1970.

Bartlett, Irving H. *Daniel Webster*. New York: W. W. Norton, 1978.

Bass, Archer B. *Protestantism in the United States*. New York: Thomas Y. Crowell, 1929.

Bass, Jack. *Unlikely Heroes*. New York: Simon & Schuster, 1981.

Bates, M. Searle. *Religious Liberty: An Inquiry*. New York: Harper and Brothers, 1945.

Baumer, Franklin L. *Modern European Thought*. New York: Macmillan, 1977.

Becker, Carl. *The Declaration of Independence*. New York: Knopf, 1942.

_____. *The Eve of the Revolution*. New Haven: Yale University Press, 1918.

Bellamy, Francis Rufus. *The Private Life of George Washington*. New York: Thomas Y. Crowell, 1951.

Berger, Raoul. *Government by Judiciary*. Cambridge: Harvard University Press, 1977.

Berman, Harold. *The Interaction of Law and Society.* New York: Abingdon Press, 1974.

Berns, Walter. *The First Amendment and the Future of Democracy.* New York: Basic Books, 1976.

Beveridge, Albert J. *The Life of John Marshall.* 4 vols. Boston: Houghton Mifflin, 1919.

Bickel, Alexander M. *The Supreme Court and the Idea of Progress.* New Haven: Yale University Press, 1978.

Bird, Wendell. "Freedom from Establishment and Unneutrality in Public School Instruction and Religious School Regulation." *Harvard Journal of Law and Social Policy* 2 (1979): 125.

Blackstone, William. *Commentaries on the Laws of England.* 2 vols. Philadelphia: J. D. Lippincott, 1866.

Blakely, William Addison, ed. *American State Papers.* Washington, D.C.: Review and Herald, 1943.

Blamires, Harry. *The Christian Mind.* Ann Arbor: Servant Books, 1963.

Blanshard, Paul. "Three Cheers for Our Secular State." *The Humanist,* March/April 1976.

Boorstin, Daniel. *Image; or, What Happened to the American Dream.* New York: Atheneum, 1962.

_____. *The Americans: The Democratic Experience.* New York: Random House, 1973.

_____. *The Mysterious Science of the Law.* Magnolia, Mass.: Peter Smith, 1958.

Borden, Morton. *Parties and Politics in the Early Republic 1789-1815.* London: Routledge & Kegan Paul, Ltd., 1968.

Borisov, Vadim. "Personality and National Awareness." *From Under the Rubble.* New York: Little, Brown, 1975.

Bosworth, Allan R. *America's Concentration Camps.* New York: Bantam Books, 1968.

Boudin, Louis B. *Government by Judiciary.* New York: William Godwin, 1932.

Bourdeaux, Michael, and Rowe, Michael. *May One Believe–In Russia?* London: Darton, Longman and Todd, 1980.

Bowen, Catherine Drinker. *John Adams and the American Revolution.* Boston: Little, Brown, 1950.

_____. *Miracle at Philadelphia.* Boston: Little, Brown, 1966.

_____. *Yankee from Olympus.* Boston: Little, Brown, 1944.

Bowers, Claude G. *Jefferson in Power.* Boston: Houghton Mifflin, 1936.

Bradbury, Ray. *Fahrenheit 451.* New York: Ballantine Books, 1979.

Bradley, Harold Whitman. *The United States 1492-1877.* New York: Charles Scribner's Sons, 1972.

Brant, Irving. *James Madison: The Father of the Constitution 1787-1800.* Indianapolis: Bobbs-Merrill, 1950.

Bridenbaugh, Carl. *Mitre and Sceptre: Transatlantic Faiths, Ideas, Personalities & Politics 1689-1775.* New York: Oxford University Press, 1962.

Brinston, Crane; Christopher, John; and Wolff, Robert Lee. *A History of Civilization.* Englewood Cliffs, N.J.: Prentice-Hall, 1960.

Brodie, Fawn M. *Thomas Jefferson: An Intimate History.* New York: W. W. Norton, 1974.

Brogan, Hugh. *The American Civil War: Extracts from the Times 1860-1865.* London: Times Books, 1975.

Brown, Harold O. J. *The Reconstruction of the Republic.* New Rochelle, N.Y.: Arlington House, 1977.

Bullock, Alan. *Hitler: A Study in Tyranny.* Rev. ed. New York: Harper & Row, 1962.

Bulman, James M. *It Is Their Right*. Greensboro, N.C.: Gateway Publications, 1975.

Burham, John. *Congress and the American Tradition*. Chicago: Henry Regnery, 1959.

Burke, Edmund, and Paine, Thomas. *Reflections on the Revolution and the Rights of Man*. Garden City, N.Y.: Dolphin Books, 1961.

Burlingame, Roger. *The American Conscience*. New York: Knopf, 1969.

Burnham, James. *Congress and the American Tradition*. Chicago: Henry Regnery, 1965.

Burns, James MacGregor, and Peltason, J. W. *Government by the People*. 3d ed. Englewood Cliffs, N.J.: Prentice-Hall, 1972.

Cahill, Fred. *Judicial Legislation: A Study in American Legal Theory*. New York: Ronald Press, 1952.

Calvin, John. *The Institutes of the Christian Religion*. 2 vols. 1536—1559. Reprint. Philadelphia: Westminster Press, 1960.

Campbell, Norine Dickson. *Patrick Henry: Patriot and Statesman*. Old Greenwich, Conn.: Devin-Adair, 1969.

Carroll, Peter N. *Puritanism and the Wilderness*. New York: Columbia University Press, 1969.

Chabannes, Jacques. *Saint Augustine*. Garden City, N.Y.: Doubleday, 1962.

Chandler, Walter M. *The Trial of Jesus*. Vol. 1. Atlanta: Harrison, 1972.

Chayes, Abram. "The New Judiciary." *Harvard Law School Bulletin* 28 (1976): 23.

Chroust, Anton-Hermann. "The Philosophy of Law of St. Thomas Aquinas: His Fundamental Ideas and Some of His Historical Precursors." *American Journal of Jurisprudence* 19 (1974): 1.

Clark, Kenneth. *Civilization: A Personal View*. New York: Harper and Row, 1969.

Clement, Alain. "Judges, Lawyers Are the Ruling Class in U.S. Society." *Washington Post*, 22 August 1980, p. A-25.

Cohen, Carl. *Civil Disobedience: Conscience, Tactics and the Law*. New York: Columbia University Press, 1971.

Coke, Edward. *Institutes of the Laws of England*. 4 vols. 11th ed. London: Eliz. Nutt and R. Goslang (assigns of E. Sayer), 1719.

Cole, Arthur C. *The Irrepressible Conflict 1850-1865*. Chicago: Quadrangle Books, 1971.

Commager, Henry Steele. *The Empire of Reason*. Garden City, N.Y.: Anchor Press-Doubleday, 1977.

Cooke, Alistair. *Alistair Cooke's America*. New York: Knopf, 1973.

Cooke, Edward F. *A Detailed Analysis of the Constitution*. Totowa, N.J.: Littlefield, Adams, 1974.

Cooke, Jacob C., ed. *The Federalist*, Middletown, Conn.: Wesleyan University Press, 1975.

Cooper, James Charles. *The Recovery of America*. Philadelphia: Westminster Press, 1973.

Cortner, Richard C., and Lytle, Clifford M. *Modern Constitutional Law*. New York: Collier-Macmillan, 1971.

Corwin, Edward S. *American Constitutional History*. New York: Harper Torchbooks, 1965.

————. *Constitutional Revolution*. Westport, Conn.: Greenwood Press, 1977.

————. *The Constitution and What It Means Today*. Revised by Harold W. Chase and Craig R. Ducat. 13th ed. Princeton, N.J.: Princeton University Press, 1975.

————. *Court Over Constitution*. Princeton, N.J.: Princeton University Press, 1938.

————. "The 'Higher Law' Background of American Constitutional Law." *Harvard Law Review* 4 (1928): 149-185; 365-409.

————. *Total War and the Constitution*. New York: Knopf, 1947.

Cotham, Perry C. *Politics, Americanism and Christianity*. Grand Rapids, Mich.: Baker Book House, 1976.

_____. *Obscenity, Pornography, and Censorship*. Grand Rapids, Mich.: Baker Book House, 1973.

Countryman, Vern, ed. *The Douglas Opinions*. New York: Random House, 1977.

"Courts Test Mettle of Public Opinion Surveys." *American Bar Association Journal* 66 (1980): 1511.

Cousins, Norman. *In God We Trust*. New York: Harper & Brothers, 1958.

Cover, Robert. *Justice Accused: Antislavery and the Judicial Process*. New Haven: Yale University Press, 1975.

Cox, Archibald. *The Role of the Supreme Court in American Government*. New York: Oxford University Press, 1976.

Cox, Harvey. *The Secular City*. New York: Macmillan, 1965.

Crick, Francis. *Of Molecules and Men*. Seattle: University of Washington Press, 1967.

Cunliffe, Marcus. *George Washington: Man and Monument*. New York: Mentor Books, 1958.

Cushing, Harry Alonzo, ed. *The Writings of Samuel Adams*. 4 vols. New York: Octagon Books, 1968.

Danelski, David J., and Tulchin, Joseph S., eds. *The Autobiographical Notes of Charles Evans Hughes*. Cambridge: Harvard University Press, 1973.

Darwin, Charles. *The Descent of Man*. Philadelphia: R. West, 1902.

_____. *The Origin of Species by Means of Natural Selection or the Preservation of Favoured Races in the Struggle for Life* 1859. Reprint. New York: Oxford University Press, 1963.

Davidheiser, Bolton. *Evolution and Christian Faith*. Philadelphia: Presbyterian and Reformed, 1969.

Davidson, Marshall B. *Life in America*. 2 vols. Boston: Houghton Mifflin, 1974.

Davies, A. Mervyn. *Foundation of American Freedom*. New York: Abingdon Press, 1955.

Davis, Burke. *George Washington and the American Revolution*. New York: Random House, 1975.

Devlin, Patrick. *Enforcement of Morals*. London: Oxford University Press, 1959.

Dewar, Douglas, and Shelton, H. S. *Is Evolution Proved?* London: Hollis & Carter, 1947.

Dewey, John. *A Common Faith*. New Haven: Yale University Press, 1934.

Dicey, A. V. *Law of the Constitution*. New York: Macmillan, 1920.

Donovan, Frank. *Mr. Madison's Constitution*. New York: Dodd, Mead, 1965.

Dornan, Robert K., and Vedlick, Csaba, Jr. *Judicial Supremacy: The Supreme Court on Trial*. Boston: Norland, 1980.

Dostoevsky, Fyodor. *The Brothers Karamazov*. New York: Bantam Books, 1970.

Douglas, William O. *The Court Years: 1939-1975*. New York: Random House, 1980.

_____. *Freedom of the Mind*. Garden City, N.Y.: Doubleday, 1962.

_____. *Go East, Young Man: The Early Years*. New York: Random House, 1974.

Drew, Donald. *Images of Man*. Downers Grove, Ill.: InterVarsity Press, 1974.

Drinan, Robert F. *Religion, the Courts and Public Policy*. New York: McGraw-Hill, 1963.

Drucker, Peter F. *The Unseen Revolution*. New York: Harper & Row, 1976.

Drummond, Henry. *Natural Law in the Spiritual World*. New York: James Pott, 1887.

Dumbauld, Edward. *The Declaration of Independence and What It Means Today*. Norman, Okla.: University of Oklahoma Press, 1950.

Dunn, Richard S. *The Age of Religious Wars 1559-1689*. New York: W. W. Norton, 1970.

Dunne, Gerald T. *Hugo Black and the Judicial Revolution*. New York: Simon & Schuster, 1977.

Durant, Will. *The Story of Philosophy*. New York: Simon & Schuster, 1961.

Durant, Will and Ariel. *The Lessons of History*. New York: Simon & Schuster, 1968.

_____. *The Story of Civilization*. 11 vols. New York: Simon & Schuster, 1954-1975.

Dworkin, Ronald. *Taking Rights Seriously*. Cambridge: Harvard University Press, 1977.

Easton, Stewart C. *A Brief History of the Western World*. New York: Barnes & Noble, 1962.

Elliott, Edward. *Biographical Story of the Constitution*. New York: G. P. Putnam's Sons, 1910.

Elliott, Jonathan, ed. *Debates of the Several States Conventions on the Adoption of the Federal Constitution*. 5 vols. 2d ed. New York: Burt Franklin, 1888.

Ellul, Jacques. *The Political Illusion*. New York: Vintage Press, 1972.

_____. *The Technological Society*. New York: Knopf, 1964.

_____. *The Theological Foundation of Law*. New York: Seabury Press, 1969.

Ely, John H. "The Wages of Crying Wolf: A Comment on *Roe* v. *Wade*." *Yale Law Journal* 82 (1973): 920.

Emery, Noemie. *Washington: A Biography*. New York: G. P. Putnam's Sons, 1976.

Engelmayer, Sheldon, and Wagman, Robert. *Tax Revolt 1980: A How-To-Guide*. New Rochelle, N.Y.: Arlington House, 1980.

Ericson, Jr., Edward E. *Solzhenitsyn: The Moral Vision*. Grand Rapids, Mich.: Eerdmans, 1980.

Erlich, J. W. *The Holy Bible and the Law*. New York: Oceana Publications, 1962.

Evans, M. Stanton. "The States and the Constitution." *The Intercollegiate Review*, November/December 1965.

Fantel, Hans. *William Penn: Apostle of Dissent*. New York: William Morrow, 1974.

Farrand, Max, ed. *The Records of the Federal Convention of 1787*. 3 vols. New Haven: Yale University Press, 1911.

Fay, Bernard. *Franklin, the Apostle of Modern Times*. Boston: Little, Brown, 1929.

Fehrenbacher, Don E. *The Dred Scott Case*. New York: Oxford University Press, 1978.

Feinberg, Joel, and Gross, Hyman, eds. *Philosophy of Law*. Encino, Calif.: Dickinson, 1975.

Fernbach, David. *Karl Marx: Surveys from Exile*. New York: Vintage Books, 1974.

Ferrero, Guglielmo, and Barbagallo, Corrado. *A Short History of Rome*. 2 vols. New York: Knickerbocker Press, 1919.

Feuer, Kathryn, ed. *Solzhenitsyn: A Collection of Critical Essays*. Englewood Cliffs, N.J.: Prentice-Hall, 1976.

Fisher, Gene, and Chambers, Glen. *The Revolution Myth*. Greenville, S.C.: Bob Jones University Press, 1981.

Fleetwood, Blake. "The Tax Police: Trampling Citizens' Rights." *Saturday Review*, May 1980, p. 33.

Flexner, James Thomas. *George Washington*. 4 vols. Boston: Little, Brown, 1965-1972.

_____. *Washington: The Indispensable Man*. Boston, Little, Brown, 1974.

_____. *The Young Hamilton*. Boston: Little, Brown, 1978.

Flinn, Richard. "Samuel Rutherford and Puritan Political Theory." *Journal of Christian Reconstruction* 5:49.

Fogel, Robert William, and Engerman, Stanley L. *Time on the Cross*. 2 vols. Boston: Little, Brown, 1974.

Foner, Eric. *Tom Paine and Revolutionary America*. New York: Oxford University Press, 1976.

Foner, Phillip S., ed. *Basic Writings of Thomas Jefferson*. Garden City, N.Y.: Halcyon House, 1950.

_____. *The Life and Major Writings of Thomas Paine*. Secaucus, N.J.: Citadel Press, 1974.

Ford, Paul Leicester, ed. *The Writings of Thomas Jefferson*. 10 vols. New York: G. P. Putnam's Sons, 1892-1899.

Forkosch, Morris D. *Constitutional Law*. Mineola, N.Y.: Foundation Press, 1969.

Forrester, William. "Are We Ready for Truth in Judging?" *American Bar Association Journal* 63 (1977): 1212.

Foster, George Burman. *Friedrich Nietzsche*. New York: Macmillan, 1931.

Frankel, Marvin E. *Partisan Justice*. New York: Hill and Wang, 1980.

Freedman, Max, ed. *Roosevelt and Frankfurter: Their Correspondence, 1928-1945*. Boston: Little, Brown, 1967.

Freeman, David Hugh. *A Philosophical Study of Religion*. Nutley, N.J.: Craig Press, 1964.

Freud, Sigmund. *Civilization and Its Discontents*. New York: Doubleday, 1958.

_____. *The Future of an Illusion*. Garden City, N.Y.: Anchor Books, 1964.

_____. *Moses and Monotheism*. New York: Knopf, 1949.

Friedman, Lawrence M. *A History of American Law*. New York: Simon & Schuster, 1973.

Friendly, Henry J. *Federal Jurisdiction: A General View*. New York: Columbia University Press, 1973.

Fuller, Lon L. *The Morality of Law*. New Haven: Yale University Press, 1969.

Funston, Richard Y. *Constitutional Counter Revolution?* Cambridge, Mass.: Schenkman, 1977.

Gabriel, Ralph Henry. *The Course of American Democratic Thought*. 2d ed. New York: John Wiley and Sons, 1956.

Galbraith, John Kenneth. *The Affluent Society*. Boston: Houghlin Mifflin, 1958.

_____. *The Age of Uncertainty*. Boston: Houghlin Mifflin, 1977.

Galbraith, John Kenneth, and Randhawa, M. S. *The New Industrial State*. Boston: Houghton Mifflin, 1967.

Galvin, John R. *Three Men of Boston*. New York: Thomas Y. Crowell, 1976.

Garraty, John A. *The American Nation: A History of the United States*. New York: Harper & Row, 1966.

Garret, Julia, and Underwood, Lula. *Our American Constitution: The Story of a Great Document*. Austin, Tex.: Steck-Vaughn, 1977.

Gaucher, Roland. *Opposition in the U.S.S.R. 1917-1967*. New York: Funk & Wagnalls, 1969.

Gaustad, Edwin Scott. *Historical Atlas of Religion in America*. New York: Harper & Row, 1962.

Gay, Peter, ed. *The Enlightenment*. New York: Simon and Schuster, 1973.

Gibbon, Edward. *The Decline and Fall of the Roman Empire*. 6 vols. 1776-1788. Reprint. New York: Dutton, 1910.

Gilder, George. *Naked Nomads*. New York: Quadrangle-New York Times, 1974.

_____. *Sexual Suicide*. New York: Quadrangle-New York Times, 1973.

_____. *Wealth and Poverty*. New York: Basic Books, 1981.

Gilmore, Grant. *The Ages of American Law*. New Haven, Conn.: Yale University Press, 1977.

Ginsburg, Ruth B. "American Bar Association Delegation Visits the People's Republic of China." *American Bar Association Journal* 64 (1978): 1516.

————. "Let's Have ERA as a Signal." *American Bar Association Journal* 63 (1977): 70.

————. "Sex Equality and the Constitution." *Tulane Law Review* 52 (1978): 45.

————. "Sex Equality and the Constitution: The State of the Art." *Women's Rights Law Reporter* 4 (1978): 143.

————. "Treatment of Women by the Law: Awakening Consciousness in the Law Schools." *Valparaiso Law Review* 5 (1971): 480.

————. "Women and the Law—A Symposium." *Rutgers Law Review* 25 (1970): 1.

————. "Women, Equality and Bakke Case." *The Civil Liberties Review*, November/December 1977, p. 8.

Glahn, Gerhard von. *Law Among Nations*. Toronto: Macmillan, 1965.

Goddard, Donald. *The Last Days of Dietrich Bonhoeffer*. New York: Harper & Row, 1976.

Goebel, Julius, Jr., ed. *The Law Practice of Alexander Hamilton*. New York: Columbia University Press, 1964.

Gordon, Ernest. *Me, Myself and Who?* Plainfield, N.J.: Logos, 1980.

Goulden, Joseph C. *The Benchwarmers: The Private World of the Powerful Federal Judges*. New York: Weybright & Talley, 1974.

————. *The Superlawyers*. New York: Weybright & Talley, 1972.

Grant, Michael. *History of Rome*. New York: Charles Scribner's Sons, 1978.

Grey, Thomas. "Do We Have an Unwritten Constitution?" *Stanford Law Review* 27 (1975): 703.

Grimal, Pierre. *The Civilization of Rome*. New York: Simon & Schuster, 1963.

Griswold, Wesley S. *The Boston Tea Party*. Tunbridge Wells, Kent: Abacus Press, 1972.

Guinness, Os. *The Dust of Death*. Downers Grove, Ill.: InterVarsity Press, 1973.

————. *Violence: A Study of Contemporary Attitudes*. Downers Grove, Ill.: InterVarsity Press, 1974.

Gunther, Gerald, and Dowling, Noel T. *Cases and Materials on Constitutional Law*. New York: Foundation Press, 1970.

Gutman, Herbert G. *The Black Family in Slavery and Freedom 1750-1925*. New York: Pantheon Books, 1976.

Haile, H. G. *Luther: An Experiment in Biography*. New York: Doubleday, 1980.

Haines, Charles Grove. *The American Doctrine of Judicial Supremacy*. New York: Da Capo Press, 1973.

Haldeman, H. R. *The Ends of Power*. New York: Times Books, 1978.

Hall, Thomas Cuming. *The Religious Background of American Culture*. Boston: Little, Brown, 1930.

Hall, Verna N. *The Christian History of the American Revolution*. San Francisco: Foundation for American Christian Education, 1976.

————. *Christian History of the Constitution of the United States of America*. 2 vols. San Francisco: American Constitution Press, 1961.

Harrison, Frank Mott. *John Bunyan*. 1928. Reprint. London: Banner of Truth Trust, 1964.

Haskins, George Lee, and Johnson, Herbert A. *History of the Supreme Court of the United States*. Vol. 2. New York: Macmillan, 1968.

Hatfield, Charles, ed. *The Scientist and Ethical Decision*. Downers Grove, Ill.: InterVarsity Press, 1973.

Haubrich, Vernon F., and Apple, Michael W., eds. *Schooling and the Rights of Children*. Berkeley, Calif.: McCutchan, 1975.

Hazlitt, Henry. *A New Constitution Now*. New Rochelle, N.Y.: Arlington House, 1974.

Hegel, Georg W. F. *The Logic of Hegel*. New York: Oxford University Press, 1892.
————. *Philosophy of Right*. New York: Oxford University Press, 1962.
Heidegger, Martin. *Being and Time*. New York: Harper and Row, 1962.
————. *The Question of Being*. Boston: Twayne, 1958.
Heimert, Alan, and Miller, Perry, eds. *The Great Awakening*. Indianapolis: Bobbs-Merrill, 1967.
Heirich, Max. *The Beginning: Berkeley 1964*. New York: Columbia University Press, 1977.
Herdman, Marie L. *The Story of the United States*. New York: Grossett & Dunlap, 1916.
Hertz, Richard. *Chance and Symbol*. Chicago: University of Chicago Press, 1948.
Higgins, Thomas J. *Judicial Review Unmasked*. West Hanover, Mass.: Christopher, 1981.
Hill, Christopher. *The Century of Revolution 1703-1714*. New York: Nelson, 1961.
————. *Milton and the English Revolution*. New York: Viking Press, 1978.
Hillel, Marc, and Henry, Clarissa. *Of Pure Blood*. New York: McGraw-Hill, 1976.
Hillerbrand, Hans J. *The Protestant Reformation*. New York: Walker, 1968.
Hippel, Ernest von. "The Role of Natural Law in the Legal Decisions of the Federal German Republic." *Natural Law Forum* 4 (1959): 106.
Holmes, Oliver Wendell. *Collected Legal Papers*. New York: Harcourt, Brace and Howe, 1920.
————. *The Common Law*. Boston: Little, Brown, 1938.
————. "Natural Law." *Harvard Law Review* 32 (1918): 40.
Horowitz, Morton J. "The Emergence of an Instrumental Conception of American Law." *Perspectives in American History* 5 (1971): 287.
Howe, Mark DeWolfe, ed. *The Holmes-Laski Letters: The Correspondence of Mr. Justice Holmes and Harold Laski, 1916-1935*. Cambridge: Harvard University Press, 1953.
————, ed. *The Holmes-Pollock Letters: The Correspondence of Mr. Justice Holmes and Sir Frederick Pollock, 1874-1932*. 2 vols. Cambridge: Harvard University Press, 1946.
Howell, Daniel Walker, ed. *The American Whigs*. New York: John Wiley & Sons, 1973.
Hudson, Winthrop S. *Religion in America*. New York: Charles Scribner's Sons, 1973.
Hughes, Phillip. *A History of the Church*. Vol. 2. New York: Sheed and Ward, 1949.
Humphrey, Derek. *Jean's Way*. Boston: Charles River Books, 1978.
Hunt, Gaillard, ed. *Writings of James Madison*. 9 vols. New York: G. P. Putnam's Sons, 1900-1910.
Huntford, Roland. *The New Totalitarians*. New York: Stein & Day, 1972.
Huxley, Aldous. *Brave New World*. New York: Bantam Books, 1968.
————. *The Doors of Perception*. New York: Harper & Row, 1954.
————. *Heaven and Hell*. New York: Harper & Row, 1956.
Huxley, Julian. *Essays of a Humanist*. New York: Harper & Row, 1964.
————. "Evolution and Genetics." *What Is Science?* ed. J. R. Newman. New York: Simon and Schuster, 1955.
————, ed. *The Humanist Frame*. New York: Harper & Row, 1962.
Hyde, Douglas. *Dedication and Leadership*. Notre Dame, Ind.: University of Notre Dame Press, 1966.
Hyman, Harold M. *A More Perfect Union*. Boston: Houghton Mifflin, 1975.
Ingram, Robert. *What's Wrong with Human Rights*. Houston: St. Thomas Press, 1978.
————. *The World Under God's Law: Criminal Aspects of the Welfare State*. Houston: St. Thomas Press, 1962.

Irving, Washington. *George Washington: A Biography*. 5 vols. Garden City, N.Y.: Double-day, 1976.

Jackson, Jeremy. *No Other Foundation*. Westchester, Ill.: Cornerstone Books, 1980.

Jackson, Robert H. *The Supreme Court in the American System of Government*. New York: Harper & Row, 1963.

Jaspers, Karl. *Man in the Modern Age*. New York: Doubleday, 1957.

Jastrow, Robert. *God and the Astronomers*. New York: W. W. Norton, 1978.

————. *Until the Sun Dies*. New York: W. W. Norton, 1977.

Jaworski, Leon. *The Right and the Power*. New York: Reader's Digest, 1976.

Jefferson, Thomas. *The Life and Morals of Jesus of Nazareth*. Cleveland: World, 1942.

Johnson, Alan. *The Freedom Letter*. Chicago: Moody Press, 1974.

Jones, R. Ben. *The French Revolution*. London: Minerva Press, 1967.

Kant, Immanuel. *Critique of Pure Reason*. 1781. Reprint. New York: Willey, 1943.

Kaufmann, Walter, trans. *The Portable Nietzsche*. New York: Viking Press, 1968.

Kauper, Paul G. *Civil Liberties and the Constitution*. Ann Arbor: University of Michigan Press, 1966.

Kelley, Dean M. *Why Churches Should Not Pay Taxes*. New York: Harper & Row, 1977.

Kemp, Jack. *An American Renaissance: A Strategy for the 1980's*. New York: Harper & Row, 1979.

Kent, James. *Commentaries on American Law*. Boston: Little, Brown, 1858.

Keppel, Francis. *The Necessary Revolution in American Education*. New York: Harper & Row, 1966.

Ketcham, Henry. *Makers of American History: Abraham Lincoln*. New York: The University Society, 1905.

Key, Wilson Bryan. *The Clam-Plate Orgy: And Other Subliminal Techniques for Manipulating Your Behavior*. New York: Signet Books, 1981.

————. *Media Sexploitation*. Englewood Cliffs, N.J.: Prentice-Hall, 1976.

————. *Subliminal Seduction*. New York: Signet Books, 1973.

Kidney, James. "Are Judges Getting Too Powerful?" *U.S. News & World Report*, 16 January 1978, p. 39.

Kik, J. Marcellus. *The Supreme Court and Prayer in the Public Schools*. Philadelphia: Presbyterian & Reformed, 1963.

Kilgore, Carrol D. *Judicial Tyranny*. Nashville: Thomas Nelson, 1977.

Kinnaird, Clark. *George Washington: The Pictorial Biography*. New York: Bonanza Books, 1967.

Kirk, Russell. *The Roots of American Order*. LaSalle, Ill.: Open Court, 1974.

Kline, Mary-Jo, ed. *Alexander Hamilton: A Biography in His Own Words*. New York: Newsweek, 1973.

Kluger, Richard. *Simple Justice*. New York: Knopf, 1976.

Koch, G. Adolf. *Religion of the American Enlightenment*. New York: Thomas Y. Crowell, 1968.

Koch, H. W. *Hitler Youth: The Duped Generation*. New York: Ballantine Books, 1972.

Koestler, Arthur. *Darkness at Noon*. New York: Bantam Books, 1968.

————. *The Ghost in the Machine*. New York: Macmillan, 1968.

Kolenda, Konstantin. *Religion Without God*. Buffalo, N.Y.: Prometheus Books, 1976.

Kommers, Donald P., and Wahoske, Michael, J., eds. *Freedom and Education: Pierce v. Society of Sisters Reconsidered*. Notre Dame, Ind.: University of Notre Dame Law School, 1978.

Konefsky, Samuel J. *John Marshall and Alexander Hamilton: Architects of the American Constitution*. New York: Macmillan, 1964.

Koop, C. Everett. *The Right to Live, The Right to Die*. Wheaton, Ill.: Tyndale House, 1976.

Kramnick, Isaac, ed. *Thomas Paine: Common Sense*. New York: Penguin Books, 1976.

Kruse, Clifton J. "The Historical Meaning and Judicial Construction of the Establishment of Religion Clause of the First Amendment." *Washburn Law Journal* 2 (1962): 65.

Kuehnelt-Leddihn, Erik von. *Leftism: From de Sade and Marx to Hitler and Marcuse*. New Rochelle, N.Y.: Arlington House, 1974.

Kutler, Stanley I. *John Marshall*. Englewood Cliffs, N.J.: Prentice-Hall, 1972.

Kwitny, Jonathan, and Landover, Jerry. "President Carter's Pick of Fred Gray for Judge in Alabama Draws Fire." *Wall Street Journal,* 2 April 1980, p. 1.

Kyemba, Henry. *A State of Blood: The Inside Story of Idi Amin*. New York: Grossett & Dunlap, 1977.

LaHaye, Tim. *The Battle for the Mind*. Old Tappan, N.J.: Revell, 1980.

Lamont, Corliss. *The Philosophy of Humanism*. New York: Frederick Ungar, 1972.

Langdell, Christopher. *A Selection of Cases on the Law of Contracts*. Littleton, Colo.: Fred B. Rothman, 1980.

Lash, Joseph P. *From the Diaries of Felix Frankfurter*. New York: W. W. Norton, 1975.

Laski, Harold, ed. *A Defense of Liberty Against Tyrants: A Translation of the "Vindiciae Contra Tyrranos."* Gloucester, Mass.: Peter Smith, 1963.

Leder, Lawrence H., ed. *The Meaning of the American Revolution*. Chicago: Quadrangle Books, 1969.

Lejeune, Jerome; Mathews-Roth, Micheline M.; Gordon, Hymie; and Ratner, Herbert. "The Beginning of Human Life." *Studies in Law and Medicine*. Chicago: Americans United for Life, 1981.

Lerner, Max. *The Mind and Faith of Justice Holmes: His Speeches, Essays, Letters, and Judicial Commentary*. New York: Halcyon House, 1943.

Levinson, Sanford. "The Constitution in American Civil Religion." *The Supreme Court Review* (1979): 123.

Levy, Leonard. *Against the Law: The Nixon Court and Criminal Justice*. New York: Harper & Row, 1974.

————. *The Supreme Court Under Earl Warren*. New York: Quadrangle Books, 1972.

Lewis, C. S. *The Abolition of Man*. New York: Macmillan, 1965.

————. *The Discarded Image*. New York: Cambridge University Press, 1964.

Lewis, Paul. *The Grand Incendiary: A Biography of Samuel Adams*. New York: Dail Press, 1973.

Locke, John. *Essay Concerning Human Understanding*. 1690. Reprint. Gloucester, Mass.: Peter Smith, 1973.

————. *On the Reasonableness of Christianity*. 1695. Reprint. Chicago: Henry Regnery, 1965.

Lodge, Henry Cabot. *The Works of Alexander Hamilton*. 12 vols. New York: G. P. Putnam's Sons, 1904.

Lord Gladwyn, Gladwyn Jebb. *Halfway to 1984*. New York: Columbia University Press, 1966.

Lovelace, Richard F. *Dynamics of Spiritual Life*. Downers Grove, Ill.: InterVarsity Press, 1979.

Lowell, C. Stanley, *Embattled Wall*. Washington, D.C.: Americans United, 1966.

Lygre, David G. *Life Manipulation: From Test-Tube Babies to Aging.* New York: Walker, 1979.

Machiavelli, Niccolo. *The Prince.* 1513. Reprint. New York: Penguin Books, 1961.

MacKenzie, John P. *The Appearance of Justice.* New York: Charles Scribner's Sons, 1974.

Malbin, Michael J. *Religion and Politics: The Intentions of the Authors of the First Amendment.* Washington, D.C.: American Enterprise Institute for Public Policy Research, 1978.

Malone, Dumas. *Jefferson and His Time.* 6 vols. Boston: Little, Brown, 1948-1981.

Malthus, Thomas R. *Population: The First Essay.* 1978. Reprint. Ann Arbor, Mich.: University of Michigan Press, 1959.

Mander, Jerry. *Four Arguments for the Elimination of Television.* New York: William Morrow, 1978.

Mannix, Daniel P. *Those About to Die.* New York: Ballantine Books, 1958.

Manzullo, Donald. *Neither Sacred nor Profane.* Jericho, N.Y.: Exposition Press, 1973.

Marcuse, Herbert. *One Dimensional Man.* Boston: Beacon Press, 1964.

Marius, Richard. *Luther: A Biography.* Philadelphia: J. P. Lippincott, 1974.

Marshall, James. *Intention in Law and Society.* New York: Minerva Press, 1968.

Marshall, John. *The Life of George Washington.* 2 vols. 2d ed. Philadelphia: James Crissy, 1835.

Marshall, Peter, and Manuel, David. *The Light and the Glory.* Old Tappan, N.J.: Revell, 1977.

Marx, Karl, and Engels, Friedrich. *The Manifesto of the Communist Party.* 1848. Reprint. San Francisco: China Books, 1965.

Mason, Alpheus Thomas. "The Burger Court in Historical Perspective." *New York State Bar Journal* 47 (1975): 87.

————. *The States' Rights Debates: Antifederalism and the Constitution.* New York: Oxford University Press, 1972.

————. *The Supreme Court from Taft to Warren.* New York: W. W. Norton, 1958.

May, Henry F. *The Enlightenment in America.* New York: Oxford University Press, 1976.

McCloskey, Robert G. *The American Supreme Court.* Chicago: University of Chicago Press, 1960.

McDonald, Forrest. *E Pluribus Unum: The Formation of the American Republic 1776-1790.* Boston: Houghlin Mifflin, 1965.

McLuhan, Marshall. "Cybernation and Culture." *The Social Impact of Cybernetics.* New York: Simon & Schuster, 1966.

————. *Understanding Media.* New York: Mentor Books, 1964.

McManners, John. *The French Revolution and the Church.* New York: Harper & Row, 1969.

McMaster, John Bach. *The Political Depravity of the Founding Fathers.* New York: Noonday Press, 1964.

Meade, Robert Douthat. *Patrick Henry: Practical Revolutionary.* New York: J. B. Lippincott, 1969.

Menendez, Albert J. *Religion at the Polls.* Philadelphia: Westminster Press, 1977.

Methvin, Eugene H. *The Rise of Radicalism.* New Rochelle, N.Y.: Arlington House, 1973.

Middelmann, Udo. *Pro-Existence,* Downers Grove, Ill.: InterVarsity Press, 1974.

Miller, Arthur S. *Social Change in Fundamental Law.* Westport, Conn.: Greenwood Press, 1979.

Miller, Arthur S., and Howell, Ronald F. "The Myth of Neutrality in Constitutional Adjudication." *University of Chicago Law Review* 27 (1960): 661.

Miller, John C. *Origins of the American Revolution*. Boston: Little, Brown, 1943.

_____. *The Wolf by the Ears: Thomas Jefferson and Slavery*. New York: Free Press, 1977.

Miller, Perry. *The Life of the Mind in America*. London: Victor Gallancz, 1966.

Mises, Ludwig von. *Omnipotent Government: The Rise of the State and Total State*. New Rochelle, N.Y.: Arlington House, 1969.

Mitchell, Basil. *Law, Morality, and Religion in a Secular Society*. New York: Oxford University Press, 1970.

Mitchell, Broadus. *Alexander Hamilton: The Revolutionary Years*. New York: Thomas Y. Crowell, 1970.

Moberly, Sir Walter. *The Crisis in the University*. New York: Macmillan, 1949.

Monod, Victor. *Dieu dans l'Univers. Essai sur l'action exercée sur lon pensée chrétienne par les grands systèmes cosmologiques depuis Aristote jusqu'à nos jours*. Paris: Librairie Fischbacher, 1933.

Monsma, Stephen V. *The Unraveling of America*. Downers Grove, Ill.: InterVarsity Press, 1974.

Montgomery, John Warwick. *The Law Above the Law*. Minneapolis: Dimension Books, 1975.

_____. *Jurisprudence: A Book of Readings*. Strasbourg, France: International Scholarly Publishers, 1974.

_____. *The Shaping of America*. Minneapolis: Bethany Fellowship, 1976.

Moore, Barrington, Jr. *Social Origins of Dictatorship and Democracy*. Boston: Beacon Press, 1966.

Morgan, Richard E. *The Supreme Court and Religion*. New York: Free Press, 1972.

Morison, Samuel; Commanger, Henry; and Lauchtenburg, William. *The Growth of the American Republic*. 2 vols. New York: Oxford University Press, 1980.

Morris, Henry M. *Education for the Real World*. San Diego: Creation-Life, 1977.

Morris, Richard B. *Seven Who Shaped Our Destiny*. New York: Harper & Row, 1973.

_____, ed. *Encyclopedia of American History* (1953). New York: Harper & Row, 1976.

_____. *John Jay: The Making of a Revolutionary*. New York: Harper & Row, 1975.

Muggeridge, Malcolm. *Christ and the Media*. Grand Rapids, Mich.: Eerdmans, 1977.

Myrdal, Gunnar. *Beyond the Welfare State*. New York: Bantam Books, 1967.

Nathanson, Bernard N. *Aborting America*. Garden City, N.Y.: Doubleday, 1979.

Neely, Richard. *How Courts Govern America*. New Haven: Yale University Press, 1981.

Neuberger, Thomas Stephen, and Crumplar, Thomas C. "Tax Exempt Religious Schools Under Attack: Conflicting Goals of Religious Freedom and Racial Integration." *Fordham Law Review 48 (1979): 229*.

Newton, Isaac. *The Mathematical Principles of Natural Philosophy*. 2 vols. 1729 ed. Atlantic Highlands, N.J.: Humanities, 1968.

Nietzsche, Friedrich Wilhelm. "Thus Spake Zarathustra." Vol. 1 *Philosophy of Nietzsche*. New York: Modern Library, 1937.

Noonan, John T., Jr. *A Private Choice: Abortion in America in the Seventies*. New York: Free Press, 1979.

_____. *Persons in Mask of the Law*. New York: Farrar, Straus & Giroux, 1976.

North, Gary. *Marx's Religion of Revolution: The Doctrine of Creative Destruction*. Nutley, N.J.: Craig Press, 1968.

_____. *Unconditional Surrender*. Tyler, Tex.: Geneva Press, 1981.

Norton, Thomas James. *The Constitution of the United States: Its Sources and Its Application*. New York: Committee for Constitutional Government. 1965.

Oliver, Frederick Scott. *Alexander Hamilton: An Essay on American Union*. New York: G. P. Putnam's Sons, 1928.

Orwell, George. *Animal Farm*. New York: New American Library, 1963.

————. *Nineteen Eighty-Four*. New York: Harcourt, Brace & World, 1949.

Padover, Saul K., ed. *The Complete Jefferson*. New York: Duell, Sloan & Pearce, 1943.

————. *The Complete Madison*. New York: Harper & Brothers, 1953.

————. *The World of the Founding Fathers*. New York: Thomas Yoseloff, 1960.

Palmer, William J. *The Court-vs.-the People*. Chicago: Chas. Halberg, 1970.

Parrington, Vernon Louis. *Main Currents in American Thought*. New York: Harcourt, Brace, 1927.

Peabody, James Bishop, ed. *John Adams: A Biography in His Own Words*. New York: Newsweek, 1973.

Percy of Newcastle, Lord. *The Heresy of Democracy*. Chicago: Henry Regnery, 1955.

Perkins, William. *Works*. 3 vols. New York: AMS Press, 1971.

Perry, Lewis. *Radical Abolition: Anarchy and the Government of God in Antislavery Thought*. Ithaca, N.Y.: Cornell University Press, 1973.

Perry, Ralph Barton. *Puritanism and Democracy*. New York: Vanguard Press, 1944.

Peters, Charles. *How Washington Really Works*. Reading, Mass.: Addison-Wesley, 1980.

Peterson, Merrill D., ed. *James Madison: A Biography in His Own Words*. 2 vols. New York: Newsweek, 1974.

Pfeffer, Leo. *God, Caesar, and the Constitution*. Boston: Beacon Press, 1975.

Pit, Jan. *Persecution: It Will Never Happen Here?* Orange, Calif.: Open Doors, 1981.

Plato. *Laws*. New York: Penguin Books, 1970.

————. *Republic*. New York: Basic Books, 1968.

Podgers, James. "Patent Decision Fuels Genetic Research Debate." *American Bar Association Journal* 66 (1980): 943.

————. " 'Rational Suicide' Raises Patient Rights Issues" *American Bar Association Journal* 66 (1980):1499.

Polanyi, Michael. *Personal Knowledge: Towards a Post-Critical Philosophy*. Chicago: University of Chicago Press, 1958.

Pollock, Sir Frederick, and Maitland, Frederick William. *History of English Law Before the Time of Edward First*. 2d ed. New York: Cambridge University Press, 1968.

Pontecorvo, G. *Trends in Genetic Analysis*. New York: Columbia University Press, 1958.

"Post-Abortion Fetal Study Stirs Storm." *Medical World News,* 8 June 1973.

Pound, Roscoe. *Contemporary Juristic Theory*. Claremont, Calif.: Claremont College, 1940.

————. *Introduction to the Philosophy of Law*. New Haven, Conn.: Yale University Press, 1959.

————. *The Spirit of the Common Law*. Francestown, N.H.: Marshall Jones, 1921.

Rabin, Robert. "When Is a Religious Belief Religious: *United States* v. *Seeger* and the Scope of Free Exercise." *Cornell Law Quarterly* 51 (1966): 231.

Rawls, John. *A Theory of Justice*. Cambridge: Harvard University Press, 1971.

Reich, Charles. *The Greening of America*. New York: Bantam Books, 1971.

Restak, Richard M. *Premeditated Man: Bioethics and the Control of Future Human Life*. New York: Viking Press, 1975.

Revel, Jean-Francois. *The Totalitarian Temptation*. Garden City, N.Y.: Doubleday, 1977.

Rice, Charles. *Beyond Abortion: The Theory and Practice of the Secular State*. Chicago: Franciscan Herald, 1979

Rich, John Martin. *Humanistic Foundations of Education*. Worthington, Ohio: Charles A. Jones, 1971.

Richardson, James D., ed. *Messages and Papers of the Presidents*. Washington, D.C.: Bureau of National Literature and Art, 1897.

Reincourt, Amaury de. *The Coming Caesars*. New York: Coward-McCann, 1957.

Rodell, Fred. "It Is the Warren Court." *The New York Times Magazine*, 13 March 1966, p. 136.

_____. *Woe Unto You, Lawyers!* Santa Fe, N. Mex.: Rydal Press, 1939.

_____. *Nine Men*. New York: Random House, 1955.

Rogers, Michael. *Biohazard*. New York: Knopf, 1977.

Rookmaaker, H. R. *Modern Art and the Death of a Culture*. Downers Grove, Ill.: InterVarsity Press, 1970.

Rosenfeld, Albert. *The Second Genesis: The Coming Control of Life*. New York: Vintage Press, 1975.

Rosenstock-Huessy, Eugen. *Out of Revolution*. New York: William Morrow, 1938.

Rosten, Leo, ed. *Religions of America*. New York: Simon & Schuster, 1975.

Rostow, Eugene. "The Japanese American Cases—A Disaster." *Yale Law Journal* 54 (1945): 489.

Rousseau, Jean-Jacques. *The Social Contract*. 1762. Reprint. New York: Oxford University Press, 1972.

Rozwenc, Edwin C. *The Causes of the American Civil War*. Boston: D. C. Heath, 1961.

Rushdoony, Rousas John. *Freud*. Philadelphia: Presbyterian & Reformed, 1975.

_____. *The Institutes of Biblical Law*. Nutley, N.J.: Craig Press, 1973.

_____. *Intellectual Schizophrenia*. Philadelphia: Presbyterian & Reformed, 1961.

_____. *Law and Liberty*. Nutley, N.J.: Craig Press, 1971.

_____. *The Messianic Character of American Education*. Nutley, N.J.: Craig Press, 1972.

_____. *The Nature of the American System*. Nutley, N.J.: Craig Press, 1965.

_____. *The One and the Many*. Nutley, N.J.: Craig Press, 1971.

_____. *Politics of Guilt and Pity*. Nutley, N.J.: Craig Press, 1970.

_____. *The Politics of Pornography*. New Rochelle, N.Y.: Arlington House, 1974.

_____. *This Independent Republic*. Fairfax, Va.: Thoburn Press, 1964.

_____. *The Word of Flux*. Fairfax, Va.: Thoburn Press, 1975.

Russell, Francis. *Adams: An American Dynasty*. New York: American Heritage, 1976.

Rutherford, Samuel. *Lex, Rex; or, the Law and the Prince*. 1644. Reprint. Harrison, Va.: Sprinkle Publications, 1980.

Rutland, Robert Allen. *The Birth of the Bill of Rights 1776-1791*. Chapel Hill: University of North Carolina Press, 1955.

Sagan, Carl. *Cosmos*. New York: Random House, 1980.

_____. *The Dragons of Eden*. New York: Random House, 1977.

Schaeffer, Edith. *What Is a Family?* Old Tappan, N.J.: Revell, 1975.

Schaeffer, Francis A. *A Christian Manifesto*. Westchester, Ill.: Crossway Books, 1981.

_____. *Back to Freedom and Dignity*. Downers Grove, Ill.: InterVarsity Press, 1972.

_____. *Death in the City*. Downers Grove, Ill.: InterVarsity Press, 1973.

_____. *Escape from Reason*. Downers Grove, Ill.: InterVarsity Press, 1968.

_____. *The God Who Is There*. Downers Grove, Ill.: InterVarsity Press, 1968.

_____. *He Is There and He Is Not Silent*. Wheaton, Ill.: Tyndale House, 1972.

_____. *How Should We Then Live?* Old Tappan, N.J.: Revell, 1976.

Schaeffer, Francis, and Koop, C. Everett. *Whatever Happened to the Human Race?* Old Tappan, N.J.: Revell, 1979.

Schaeffer, Francis; Koop, C. Everett; Buchfuehrer, Jim; and Schaeffer, Franky. *Plan for Action: An Action Alternative Handbook for Whatever Happened to the Human Race?* Old Tappan, N.J.: Revell, 1980.

Schaeffer, Franky. *Addicted to Mediocrity*. Westchester, Ill.: Cornerstone Books, 1981.

Schiffer, Walter. *The Legal Community of Mankind*. New York: Columbia University Press, 1954.

Schwartz, Bernard. *The Great Rights of Mankind: A History of the American Bill of Rights*. New York: Oxford University Press, 1977.

_____. *Statutory History of the United States*. 2 vols. New York: Chelsea House, 1970.

Scott, Otto J. *Robespierre: The Voice of Virtue*. New York: Mason & Lipscomb, 1974.

_____. *The Secret Six: John Brown and the Abolitionist Movement*. New York: Times Books, 1979.

Sealey, Raphael. *A History of the Greek City States 700-338 B.C.* Berkeley: University of California Press, 1976.

Shapiro, Martin. *Law and Politics in the Supreme Court*. New York: Free Press, 1964.

Shaw, Peter. *The Character of John Adams*. Chapel Hill: University of North Carolina Press, 1976.

Shriver, Harry C. *Justice Oliver Wendell Holmes: His Book Notices and Uncollected Letters and Papers*. New York: Da Capo Press, 1973.

Silving, Helen. *Sources of Law*. Buffalo, N.Y.: William S. Hein, 1968.

Simon, William E. *A Time for Truth*. New York: McGraw-Hill, 1978.

Singer, C. Gregg. *A Theological Interpretation of American History*. Nutley, N.J.: Craig Press, 1969.

Sire, James W. *The Universe Next Door*. Downers Grove, Ill.: InterVarsity Press, 1976.

Sisson, Daniel. *The American Revolution of 1800*. New York: Knopf, 1974.

Skinner, B. F. *Beyond Freedom and Dignity*. New York: Knopf, 1971.

Smith, A. E. Wilder. *The Creation of Life*. San Diego, Calif.: Creation Life, 1981.

Smith, Page. *The Constitution: A Documentary and Narrative History*. New York: William Morrow, 1978.

_____. *Jefferson: A Revealing Biography*. New York: American Heritage, 1976.

_____. *The Nation Comes of Age: A People's History of the Ante-Bellum Years*. Vol. 4. New York: McGraw-Hill, 1981.

Smith, Preserved, ed. *The Life and Letters of Martin Luther*. Boston: Houghton Mifflin, 1911.

Sobel, Robert. *The Manipulators*. Garden City, N.J.: Anchor Press-Doubleday, 1976.

Solzhenitsyn, Aleksandr I. *August 1914*. New York: Ferrar, Straus & Giroux, 1972.

_____. *The Gulag Archipelago 1918-1956*. New York: Harper and Row, 1973.

_____. *The Gulag Archipelago 1918-1956 (Two)*. New York: Harper and Row, 1975.

_____. *The Gulag Archipelago 1918-1956 (Three)*. New York: Harper & Row, 1978.

_____. *Lenin in Zurich*. New York: Ferrar, Straus & Giroux, 1976.

_____. *Letter to the Soviet Leaders*. New York: Harper & Row, 1974.

_____. *The Oak and the Calf*. New York: Harper & Row, 1980.

Sorauf, Frank J. *The Wall of Separation: The Constitutional Politics of Church and State*. Princeton, N.J.: Princeton University Press, 1976.

Speer, Albert. *Infiltration*. New York: Macmillan, 1981.

_____. *Inside the Third Reich*. New York: Macmillan, 1970.

————. *Spandau: The Secret Diaries*. New York: Macmillan, 1976.

Spencer, Herbert. *Principles of Sociology*. 1880-1897. 3 vols. Westport, Conn.: Greenwood Press, 1974.

Stauffer, Ethelbert. *Christ and the Caesars*. Philadelphia: Westminster Press, 1955.

Story, Joseph. *Commentaries on the Constitution of the United States*. 2d ed. Boston: Little, Brown, 1905.

Stout, Cushing. *The New Heavens and New Earth: Political Religion in America*. New York: Harper & Row, 1974.

Sutherland, Arthur E. "Privacy in Connecticut." *Michigan Law Review* 64 (1965): 283.

Swindler, William F. *Court and Constitution in the Twentieth Century*. 3 vols. Indianapolis: Bobbs-Merrill, 1969.

Symes, Lillian, and Travers, Clement. *Rebel America*. Boston: Beacon Press, 1972.

Tatarkiewiez, Wladyslaw. *Nineteenth Century Philosophy*. Belmont, Calif.: Wadsworth, 1973.

Tielhard de Chardin, Pierre. *The Phenomenon of Man*. New York: Harper & Row, 1959.

Tertullian. *Apology*. Cambridge: Harvard University Press. 1931.

Thompson, Gerald. "Government Services—A Dangerous Addiction." *U.S. News & World Report,* 23 June 1980, p. 76.

Thorsmark, Thora. *George Washington*. Chicago: Scott Foresman, 1931.

Tillich, Paul. *Dynamics of Faith*. New York: Harper & Row, 1957.

————. *Systematic Theology* 3 vols. Chicago: University of Chicago Press, 1967.

Titus, Herbert W. "God, Evolution, Legal Education and Law." *Journal of Christian Jurisprudence*. Tulsa, Okla.: O. W. Coburn School of Law, 1980.

————. "Moses, Blackstone and the Law of the Land." *Christian Legal Society Quarterly* 1 (1980): 5.

Tocqueville, Alexis de. *Democracy in America*. 1835-1840. Reprint. 2 vols. New York: Schocken Books, 1961.

Toffler, Alvin. *The Eco-Spasm Report*. New York: Bantam Books, 1975.

————. *Future Shock*. New York: Random House, 1970.

————. *The Third Wave*. New York: Bantam Books, 1981.

Tomlin, E. W. F. *The Great Philosophers*. New York: A. A. Wyn, 1952.

"Toward a Constitutional Definition of Religion." *Harvard Law Review* 91 (1978): 1056.

Toynbee, Arnold. *A Study of History*. 12 vols. New York: McGraw-Hill, 1972.

Tresolini, Rocco J. *Justice and the Supreme Court*. Philadelphia: J. B. Lippincott, 1963.

Tribe, Lawrence. *American Constitutional Law*. Mineola, N.Y.: Foundations, 1978.

————. "Childhood, Suspect Classification, and Conclusive Presumptions: Three Linked Riddles." *Law and Contemporary Problems* 37 (1975): 8.

Trinklein, Frederick E. *The God of Science*. Grand Rapids, Mich.: Eerdmans, 1971.

Tucker, Robert C., ed. *The Marx-Engels Reader*. New York: W. W. Norton, 1978.

Tuveson, Ernest. *Redeemer Nation: The Idea of America's Millennial Role*. Chicago: University of Chicago Press, 1968.

Unger, Irwin, and Reimers, David, eds. *The Slavery Experience in the United States*. New York: Holt, Rinehart & Winston, 1970.

"Unique U.S. Court, A." *Newsweek,* 17 December 1979, p. 99.

Upshur, Abel P. *The Federal Government: Its True Nature and Character*. New York: Van Evrie, Horton. 1868.

U.S., Congress, Senate, Committee on the Judiciary, *Selection and Confirmation of Federal*

Judges, 96th Cong., 1st sess., 27 February 1979; 29 March 1979; 4, 25 April 1979; 2, 16 May 1979; 17, 18, 25 June 1979; 9, 12 July 1979, pts. 1 & 2, 1979.

VanDoren, Carl. *Benjamin Franklin.* 1938. Reprint. New York: Viking Press, 1980.

VanTil, L. John. *Liberty of Conscience: The History of a Puritan Idea.* Nutley, N.J.: Craig Press, 1972.

Verduin, Leonard. *The Anatomy of a Hybrid.* Grand Rapids, Mich.: Eerdmans, 1976.

VerSteeg, Clarence L, and Hofstadter, Richard, eds. *Great Issues in American History: From Settlement to Revolution. 1584-1776.* New York: Vintage Books, 1969.

Viorst, Milton. *Fire in the Streets: America in the 1960s.* New York: Simon & Schuster, 1979.

Vitz, Paul C. *Psychology as Religion: The Cult of Self-Worship.* Grand Rapids, Mich.: Eerdmans, 1977.

Voltaire, Francois Marie Arovet de. *Letters Concerning the English Nation.* 1733. Reprint. New York: Burt Franklin, 1974.

Wald, George. "The Evolution of Life and the Law." *Case Western Reserve Law Review* 19 (1967): 17.

Wald, Patricia. "Making Sense Out of the Rights of Youth." *Journal of the Child Welfare League of America* 55 (1976): 380.

Walton, Rus. *One Nation Under God.* Old Tappan, N.J.: Fleming H. Revell, 1975.

Warren, Earl. *A Republic, If You Can Keep It.* New York: Quadrangle Books, 1972.

Weiss, Benjamin. *God in American History.* Pasadena, Calif.: Geddes Press, 1966.

Wells, H. G. *The Outline of History.* Garden City, N.Y.: Doubleday, 1971.

Wertenbaker, Thomas J. *The First Americans 1607-1690.* Chicago: Quadrangle Books, 1971.

Whelan, Edward. "The High and the Mighty." *Cleveland Magazine,* May 1980, p. 53.

Whipple, Leon. *The Story of Civil Liberty in the United States.* Westport, Conn.: Greenwood Press, 1927.

White, G. Edward. *The American Judicial Tradition.* New York: Oxford University Press, 1976.

————. "Reflections on the Role of the Supreme Court: The Contemporary Debate and the 'Lessons of History.' " *Judicature* 63 (1979): 162.

White, George Abbott, and Newman, Charles, eds. *Literature in Revolution.* New York: Holt, Rinehart & Winston, 1972.

Whitehead, Alfred North. *Adventures of Ideas.* New York: Macmillan, 1933.

Wiedmann, Franz, trans. *Hegel.* New York: Western, 1968.

Wilkinson, J. Harvie III. *From Brown to Bakke.* New York: Oxford University Press, 1979.

Willison, George F. *Saints and Strangers.* New York: Reynal & Hitchcock, 1945.

Wills, Garry. *Inventing America.* Garden City, N.Y.: Doubleday, 1978.

Wilson, Charles Morrow. *The Dred Scott Decision.* Philadelphia: Auerbach, 1973.

Wilson, Edmund. *Patriotic Gore.* New York: Oxford University Press, 1962.

Wilson, J. O. *Public Schools of Washington.* Vol. 1. Records of the Columbia Historical Society. Washington, D.C.: Columbia Historical Society, 1897, p. 5.

Wilson, Woodrow. *George Washington.* 1896. Reprint. New York: Schocken Books, 1969.

Winegarten, Renee. *Writers and Revolution: The Fatal Lure of Action.* New York: New Viewpoints, 1974.

Wish, Harvey. *Society and Thought in Early America.* Vol. 1. New York: Longmans, Green, 1950.

Witherspoon, Joseph P. "Father's Rights in the Abortion Decision." *Texas Tech Law Review* 6 (1975): 1075.

Wolff, Robert Paul, ed. *The Rule of Law*. New York: Simon & Schuster, 1971.

Wood, H. G. *Christianity and Civilization*. New York: Octagon Books, 1973.

Woods, David Walker. *John Witherspoon*. Old Tappan, N.J.: Revell, 1906.

Woodward, Bob, and Armstrong, Scott. *The Brethren: Inside the Supreme Court*. New York: Simon & Schuster, 1979.

Woodward, W. E. *A New American History*. New York: Farrar & Rinehart, 1936.

_____. *George Washington: The Image and the Man*. New York: Boni & Liveright, 1926.

Wormser, Rene A. *The Story of the Law*. New York: Simon & Schuster, 1962.

Wu, John C. H. *Fountain of Justice*. Beaverton, Oreg.: International Scholarly Book Services, 1980.

Wysong, R. L. *The Creation-Evolution Controversy*. Midland, Mich.: Inquiry Press, 1976.

Zane, John M. *The Story of Law*. Garden City, N.Y.: Doubleday, 1927.

Index

THE MOVIE *THE SECOND AMERICAN REVOLUTION*

The Second American Revolution is a film project as well as a book. The film, produced by Franky Schaeffer V Productions, is an allegorical drama. In it, the Past brings suit against the Present for abandoning the Judeo-Christian ideals upon which the United States was founded.

Various witnesses are called from history and examined and cross-examined: John Witherspoon, signer of the United States Constitution, Thomas Paine, Joseph Stalin, and Supreme Court Justice Oliver Wendell Holmes. The testimony of two fictitious persons from our modern society—an activist lawyer and a Christian layman—is also heard. The forty-minute, color film, which is available in 35mm, 16mm, and video cassette, will inspire discussion and thinking on the issues raised in this book.

For information on how to use or obtain the film, write to: Franky Schaeffer V Productions, Inc., P.O. Box 909, Los Gatos, CA 95031.

About the Author:
JOHN WHITEHEAD is a practicing attorney in Manassas, Virginia, specializing in constitutional law. He was the lead counsel in *Walker* v. *First Orthodox Presbyterian Church* and *State* v. *Peter and Ruth Noble*. Mr. Whitehead is the author of two other books: *The Separation Illusion: A Lawyer Examines the First Amendment* and *Schools on Fire*, written with Jon Barton. John Whitehead received a juris doctor degree from the University of Arkansas School of Law.

About the Illustrator:
WAYNE STAYSKAL is an editorial cartoonist with the *Chicago Tribune*. His cartoons have been syndicated nationally since 1962. Three different collections of Wayne Stayskal's cartoons have been published: *Trim's Arena; Hey, How Come They Get Steak and We Get Chicken;* and *It Said Another Bad Word*. Max McCrohon, former editor and now *Chicago Tribune* executive, once called Stayskal "the epitome of all that is best in modern newspaper cartooning. . . . A reader feels Stayskal has a basic faith in his fellowman."